Redefining Academic Libraries in the Knowledge Society

Redefining Academic Libraries in the Knowledge Society

Festschrift Volume in Honour of M Ayub

Editors

M Bavakutty
Abdul Azeez T A

Ess Ess Publications
New Delhi

Redefining Academic Libraries in the Knowledge Society

ISBN: 978-81-7000-730-2

₹ 1475/-

First Published 2014

Published by:
Ess Ess Publications
4831/24, Ansari Road,
Darya Ganj,
New Delhi-110 002.
INDIA
Phones: 23260807, 41563444
Fax: 41563334
E-mail: info@essessreference.com
www.essessreference.com

Cover Design by *Patch Creative Unit*

Printed and bound in India at Salasar Imaging Systems.

Contents

Foreword

Mr. M. Ayub is well known throughout the library circles in Kerala. Having joined Farook College Library service in 1981, he had familiarized himself with the college library matters within a short time and endeared himself with one and all who came into contact with his charming manners and quiet dignity. When he joined Farook College service after a stint of six years at the Aligarh Muslim University where he had a sound residential post graduate education, I was one who used to frequent the Farook Library that was carefully built up under the able guidance of the late Professors Syed Mohideen Shah, N. V. Beeran Saheb, K. A. Jaleel Saheb and K. V. Abdurahiman Saheb. Mr. Ayub was fortunate in working under the traditions left behind in the library by these great book-lovers.

On joining the College, Mr. Ayub lost no time in coming into the grips with the affairs of library. The working hours were fitted so as to suit the library users, computerization introduced in suitable stages, initiative taken in shifting the library to a more suitable and spacious site and open access system introduced in all the library sections. He was also instrumental in introducing Digital Library, Digital Talking Book Library, Morning Views Corner for Editorials of Newspapers and Cartoon Corner. Yet another of his popular and timely venture was the starting of the Best User Award introduced for library users which created a user-friendly atmosphere in the campus. Equally valuable was Mr. Ayub's role as the Director of Publications. He published ten issues of Campus Vibes and four books during the tenure of his directorship. He also took initiative in bringing out four substantial volumes relating to the background, history and tradition of Farook College and sister-institutions in the campus. Mr. Ayub thus proved himself to be a truly reliable and useful asset to the library. No wonder, therefore, with his up-to-date knowledge of library and information science and spirit of team work he proved himself to be a people's librarian practically coping the visions of Dr. S. R. Ranganathan.

It was indeed remarkable that throughout his professional career as a librarian, he had remained really capable but not vociferous of his own abilities. I believe this Festschrift volume brought out in honour of Mr.Ayub is a most suitable acknowledgement of Mr. Ayub's meritorious achievements in life as a librarian. I wish him all that is best during the rest of his life.

Prof. U. Mohamed
Former Principal
Farook College, Calicut

Preface

It is our pleasure and privilege to publish this Festschrift volume on behalf of Farook College Library and Information Science Alumni Association (FLISA), in honour of Mr. M. Ayub, Chief Librarian, Farook College, Kozhikode, Kerala, on his superannuation from a long distinguished and remarkable career in LIS profession. Being a senior professional and practitioner for the last three decades, his name is synonymous with the massive Abussabah Library Complex, Farook College.

Mr. Ayub is instrumental in setting up an elegant library complex in Farook College with Kerala architecture named after Moulana Abussabah, the great visionary and founder of Farook College and its Sister Institutions. The new library complex is a hybrid library with a digital library developed along with traditional library collections and services. It also houses an ICT section called "INSIGHT" for visually challenged library users, besides many other innovative services and sections like "Cartoon Corner", "Scanner", "Morning Views" etc. explained elsewhere in this Festschrift volume. He also served as the Director of Publication Division of the College. Mr. Ayub thus proved to be a valuable and useful asset to the Farook College.

The primary objective of a library is to provide the right information at the right time in the right form to its users. To meet this objective libraries have to provide access to information irrespective of their form, format and location. Advances in ICT have drastically revolutionized the prospective of libraries and information centers to meet their objectives. The current digital revolution has radically changed the way in which information is acquired, stored, processed, organized, retrieved and disseminated.

The advances in ICT have revolutionized the concept of media for information storage and retrieval. There is a wide range of information sources in digital formats along with the traditional print sources. On the other hand, users' perception about library services also got changed drastically. Now, there are many institutions or centers that can disseminate information to the users. These centers pose challenges to the libraries. In this context, the present day libraries have to be redefined in order to meet the demands of the Knowledge Society. The Festschrift volume titled **"Redefining Academic Libraries in the Knowledge Society"** is focused on how the needs of technologically empowered academic community are met by technologically empowered libraries and library professionals. The papers in this volume are in the areas of E-resource management, Human resource management, Innovative library services, Open access and open content, Collaborative library services, Digital rights management, Continuing professional education and Workplace learning in academic libraries.

Out of the 60 papers received, after a rigorous process of refereeing, 28 were selected for inclusion in this volume. The papers selected were arranged under four sub themes, VIZ, E-Resource management, Human resource management, Collaborative library services and Innovative library services. The papers were contributed by friends, colleagues, and well wishers of Mr. Ayub in the field of Library and Information Science.

We would like to place on record our sincere gratitude to the Farook College Library and Information

Science Alumni Association (FLISA) for having bestowed on us the task of editing this prestigious volume. We also thank Prof. U. Mohamed, Former Principal, Farook College, for a befitting foreword to the volume. Our thanks are due to Prof. E.P. Imbichikoya, Principal, Farook College and Dr. T.P.O. Nasirudheen, Associate Professor and Head, DLIS, Farook College, for their valuable contributions. We thank all the contributors, felicitators, and all those who rendered their support, energy and time in bringing out this volume successfully. We also thank Mr. Sumit Sethi, Managing Director, Ess Ess Publications, New Delhi, who has taken lot of pain to bring out this volume so nicely. Finally, we would like to wish Mr. Ayub further success in all his endeavours and pray the Almighty for a long, peaceful and healthy life.

Dr. M. Bavakutty
Dr. Abdul Azeez T.A.

M. Ayub : The Epitome of Perfection and Dedication

Mr. Ayub, who had been in the service of Farook College as an ideal librarian for more than three decades, took his profession with greater passion and enthusiasm. It can not be gainsaid that he was the mastermind behind the modernization of our library complex. All who are closer to the campus will, gratefully, recall him as a devoted librarian, an efficient organizer and a great dreamer who could transform Farook College Library into one of the best libraries of the country through a wide variety of schemes and projects attached to it.

This great lover of books, during his tenure, has set up a 'Readers' Forum' to promote reading habits among the users and to make them aware of the socio-political issues of the period. It was under his patronage and guidance that the Publication Division of the college attained the present glory. 'Campus Vibes' a novel venture under the Division is a true mirror to reflect the activities of the campus. Exhibitions conducted by the librarian on special occasions and events have helped our students a lot to strengthen their bond with the past. True to the tradition of his Alma Mater, the Aligarh Muslim University, this man of inimitable style, did everything to cater to the pressing needs of student community including that of voiceless and the differentially abled classes. Installation of a 'Digital Talking Book Library' for the visually challenged is a unique step in this regard. Though at the helm of affairs, his modesty and unassuming nature prompted him to remain unnoticed.

Mr. Ayub has rendered his service and guidance to many other college libraries also and he was instrumental in their modernization. His selection to various governmental and non-governmental committees speaks a lot about his devotion and commitment. As the Principal of Farook College, I wholeheartedly, acknowledge his dedication and contribution and express my gratitude for all that he has done for the college. I hope that this Festschrift volume will be a great token of appreciation for the unrequited services of Mr. Ayub, the unsung hero.

15.04.2014

Prof. E.P. Imbichikoya
Principal
Farook College

M. AYUB
A Dedicated College Librarian

Mr. Mullath Ayub, a staunch believer in practicing profession with an illustrious career in college librarianship for more than three decades, has committed himself to the library profession. He was born on 12th December 1957 at Calicut as the youngest son of a leading advocate practicing in the city. His father Adv. M. V. Hydrose, a member of the Madras Legislative Council (MLC) was a great visionary of the times and one of the founders of the Rouzathul Uloom Association (RUA), the parent body of Farook College and its sister institutions, which took the lead in transforming the social fabric of the region through the expansion of the secular educational structure and in uplifting the backward Muslim community of the Malabar region by paving the road to higher education.

Mr. Ayub had his early childhood days at Shishu class of the Madrasathul Mohammedia Primary School where he had completed his primary education till VIIth Class. He was brought up in Farook College campus in 1971 for his secondary education at Farook High School which was running at the time under the patronage of the great teacher Mr. P. A. Latheef who was then the Headmaster. He was an inmate of the Raja Hostel located in the campus for three years during his high school days.

After completing the high school education, Mr. Ayub moved in 1975 for his higher education to the Aligarh Muslim University (A.M.U.) where he had completed Pre-University Course (PUC) and Bachelor of Arts in Economics (B.A. Eco.). He had also completed his Bachelor and Master Degrees in library science at A.M.U. His elder brothers Adv. M. Mohammed and Adv. M. Jamaludheen were the persons who persuaded him to go to Aligarh for his higher education.

Mr. Ayub got enrolled in the Dept. of Library Science for the Bachelor Degree (B.Lib.Sc.) course at Aligarh after completing his graduation in Economics in 1979. It was the ardent impression that he had with the well organized University Central Library housed in a splendid and elegant edifice opened by the first Prime Minister of India Pandit Jawaharlal Nehru in 1964 and named after Moulana Abul Kalam Azad, the first Cabinet Minister for Education in the Union Govt. of India, made his mind to take up the library science course for his career. He had truly experienced the services rendered by the Moulana Azad Library while undergoing the graduate course at Aligarh. It was also his conviction of library science course being a professional one that led him to join this course leaving behind the M. A. Economics course for which he was selected. The seniors in his department and hostel had their role in leading him to this decision. He recollects Dr. M. Abdul Azeez, a research scholar for Ph. D. degree in the Dept. of Economics who later became Professor of Economics in P. S. M. O. College at Tirurangadi, Kerala, among the seniors who encouraged him to join the library science course at Aligarh. After completing the Bachelor Degree course in Library Science he was selected for admission to the Master Degree course in Library Science (M.Lib.Sc.) by screening through a written test and an interview chaired by Prof. Irfan Habib, the great scholar and historian who was then the Dean of Social Science Faculty under which the Dept. of Library Science comes.

Prof. M. H. Rizvi was the University Librarian and Chairman of the Dept. of Library Science. Dr. Ishrath Ali Quereshi, Prof. Sirajudheen, Prof. Sabir Hussain and Mr. Hassan Zamrud were the faculty members of library science. Mr. Shamshad Ahamed who working as librarian in JN Medical College of AMU and Mr. Sunil Kesari who later became the librarian, Parliament Lbrary were among his batch mates in Master Degree Course. Mr. Musthafa Zaidi was the youngest faculty member who joined the Dept. fresh and he was teaching library classification theory and practice.

Mr. Ayub had entered the library profession even before completing his Master Degree course in Library Science. When the course was almost coming to an end and he was to write a dissertation for the Master Degree the University was closed indefinitely due to some internal problems erupted in the University Campus. The students were directed to vacate the hostels and to go home. Mr. Ayub returned to his home town Calicut along with other students from Kerala and got himself so engaged in completing the dissertation work that he could submit the dissertation and complete the course once the University is reopened. He was working for the dissertation under the supervision of Dr. Ishrath Ali Qureshi, University Deputy Librarian at Aligarh. When the dissertation work was in progress at his hometown he used to visit the libraries in Farook College and Calicut University for the dissertation work.

Meanwhile the post of librarian which was lying vacant for more than one year in Farook College was notified and it was for the third time the post was notified as no qualified person turned up to join the temporary vacant post due to the leave granted to the college librarian who had gone to take up a job of librarian abroad. The vacant post of librarian in Farook College came to his notice and Mr. Ayub applied in response to the notification for the post of librarian. He was persuaded to apply for the post of librarian by some of the teachers whom he got introduced to while working for dissertation in the Farook College Library. Prof. U. Mohamed in the Dept. of English who later became the Principal of the College and Prof. A. P. Abdurahiman in the Dept. of Islamic History were the two teachers worthwhile to be particularly mentioned in this regard. Some of the seniors with whom he was staying at Aligarh had by the time become the teachers in 'Farook College and they also encouraged him to take up the assignment of librarian at Farook College. Mr. Ayub was one of the two applicants for this temporary post and he was called for an interview. Mr. Ayub was selected for this post of librarian and he joined the college on 28th July 1981. He worked in the college for one month and then he had to leave for Aligarh to submit the dissertation and complete the M.Lib.Sc.course. Once he completed the course Mr. Ayub came back to Farook College to rejoin the post of librarian on 1st January 1982 and his service was regularized in this post of College Librarian in July 1983.

The skeleton staff put into the college library service was not technically qualified and they were not competent enough to discharge the house keeping jobs in such a reasonably large library with a collection of about forty thousand books and 240 periodicals. Mr. Ayub with his acumen managerial skills and gentle attitude coupled with his professional workmanship was able to bring back into order within reasonable time the library which was almost plunged into disorder and a shattered collection as the librarian was on leave. The first task before him as a librarian was the stock taking of the library collection which had dropped half way after the former librarian left for a job abroad. The next task that he accomplished was the reorganization of sections of library collection in the order of Colon Classification schedule which was adopted in the library for organizing its collection. Mr. Ayub could put the library collection in order and make the library functional with all the routine jobs in a college library like membership subscription and renewal, issue of user tickets, book bank loan etc. put in order within a reasonable time with the cooperation of library staff and teachers.

The postgraduate block of the library was extended during the early days of his tenure and more facilities were provided to postgraduate students, research scholars and teachers. The working hours of the library were extended from 8.30 a.m. to 6.30 p.m. Mr. Ayub took initiative for retro conversion of the library collection organized with Colon Classification scheme to Dewey Decimal Classification scheme as a precedent to the computerization of library services which he could complete with locally developed library software package 'Book Magic' installed in 1996.

Mr. Ayub also put several strides in library science education and library professional training. He took initiative for launching a Bachelor Degree Course in Library and Information Science (B.L.I.Sc.) in 1994 and later it became a full fledged postgraduate department offering graduate (B.L.I.Sc.) and postgraduate (M.L.I.Sc.) courses in library and information science. He was teaching cataloguing practice for B.L.I.Sc. Course in the Dept. since its inception. He also conducted a number of training programmes for college librarians under the auspices of many projects like College with Potential for Excellence (a UGC project), Campus Diversity Initiative etc.

Mr. Ayub served for a stint as the Director of Certificate Course in Library Science conducted by the Kerala Grandhsala Sangham and he was teaching for the certificate course. He was also an academic counselor of B.L.I.Sc. programme of IGNOU at Calicut Study Centr for four years. Mr. Ayub participated as part of improving his professional knowledge and skills in several orientation and refresher courses conducted by UGC

Academic Staff Colleges and attended many training programmes and workshops conducted by the Universities and Govt. Agencies throughout his career. Mr. Ayub served as a member in the Executive Committee of State Library Council for one term during the period 1994-99 and also an Expert Committee Member of the Council for two years during 2006-07. He was also a Member of Advisory Committee of the State Central Library at Trivandrum. Mr. Ayub was a member of the Expert Committee on College Libraries constituted by the Govt. of Kerala in 1994. He was a member in the Board of Studies in Library and Information Science of Calicut University for two years during 2012-13. He also served as a member or a functionary of many social and educational societies and institutions in and around Calicut.

A major landmark during his tenure was the shifting of the college library into an elegant building with Kerala architecture named after Moulana Abussabah, the great visionary and founder of Farook College and its sister institutions on the campus. The concept of a separate building for college library was first mooted by Prof. U. Mohamed when he was the Principal in 1986. The new library project was implemented during the tenure of Dr. P. M. Mubarak Pasha as the Principal. The Abussabah Library Complex was commissioned by A. P. J. Abdul Kalam, former President of India on 17th Nov. 2002. Besides the library and information system, the new complex houses the Department of Library and Information Science and an air-conditioned Audio-Visual Theatre with facilities for Internet access and digital presentation.

The retro conversion of library collection from Colon Classification to Dewey Decimal Classification and computerization of library services were completed after shifting the library into the new complex. Sections were again reorganized and open access was provided to the undergraduate students also in the new library. The entire library collection was reorganized in two parallel collections according to Dewey Decimal Classification Scheme – one for postgraduate students and another for undergraduate students.

Mr. Ayub envisaged the concept of a hybrid library with a digital library developed along with the traditional library collection and services in the Farook College Library and Information System. A digital library along with the application of ICT in the traditional library services would reinforce quality library and information services and provide user satisfaction. A proposal for a digital library project was submitted for a govt. grant under MPLAD scheme of Mr. P. V. Abdul Wahab, Member of Parliament and the digital library was launched in 2009. An institutional repository was developed with the digital version of college magazines, souvenirs and rare documents in the digital library. A project was undertaken for the digitization of rare documents under the CPE project. Farook College library has since beginning a good collection of Braille books. The ICT is also applied in library services for visually challenged students. A Digital Talking Book Library was developed with the help of software 'JAWS' in 2007. The digital library for visually challenged students has become significant in the Farook College campus as many such boys and girls are undergoing undergraduate and postgraduate courses in the college and many of them are staying in the college hostels.

Mr. Ayub took a good deal of interest and initiative in the application of ICT in all areas of library management and services. A library website was developed in 2007 and linked with the Farook College site. The bibliographical database developed in the college library was made accessible online through Web OPAC in 2009. Farook College is one of the first libraries in the country selected for the N-List online information service of a rich collection of e-books and e-journals made available through UGC Library and Information Network Programme (INFLIBNET).

Mr. Ayub introduced a monthly content service of the current issues of the subject journals subscribed in the library under the title 'Scanner' and circulated among the teachers, research scholars and postgraduate students of the departments and other wings of the college. A news corner was installed under the label 'Morning Views' at the entrance of the library for the Editorials of Newspapers in English and vernacular languages. A 'Cartoon Corner' was put in place to reflect the public opinions and social criticism of the contemporary political, social and cultural issues. He also introduced a Best User Award for library users which became popular among the students and created a user-friendly atmosphere in the campus. It was only during his tenure a Readers' Forum was formed with the aim of inculcating reading habit among the students and introducing to the students the newly published books authored by noted and contemporary writers in literature, culture and on emerging social issues.

Mr. Ayub serves as the Director of Publications Division of the college. Ten issues of the annual college news letter entitled 'Campus Vibes' and four books authored by the teachers of the Farook College were published during the tenure of his directorship. He also took initiative in bringing out four substantial souvenirs depicting the history, development and traditions of Farook College on the occasion of jubilee celebrations and other events.

Mr. Ayub puts on record his sincere gratitude for the whole-hearted support and encouragement rendered by all the former principals and members of College Managing Committee during his tenure as college librarian for achieving all these landmark developments in the college library services. He would like to recollect the late Mr. K. C. Hassan Kutty saheb, the Secretary of College Managing Committee for a long term, who was always kind enough to listen to the grievances, problems and requirements of the college library, for his seamless inspiration given throughout the career of Mr. Ayub.

Dr. T. P. O. Nasirudheen
Associate Professor & Head
Dept. of Library & Information Science
Farook College, Calicut - 673 632

List of Contributors

Abdul Azeez, T.A.
Deputy Librarian, C.H. Mohammed Koya Library,
University of Calicut

Abdul Majeed, K.C.
Associate Professor,
Dept. of Library and Information Science,
Farook College, Kozhikode.

Amudavalli, A.
Professor & Head, Dept. of Library &
Information Science, University of Madras,
Chennai 600 005.

Archana, N.S.
University Library, Cochin University of
Science & Technology, Cochin 682022.

Asadullah, B.
Librarian, Mazharul Uloom College,
Ambur – 635 802, Vellore District, Tamil Nadu

Aswathy S.
Sr. Scientific Assistant,
Library & Documentation Division,
Liquid Propulsion Systems Centre,
Indian Space Research Organisation,
Valiamala, Thiruvananthapuram

Bavakutty, M.
Visiting Professor, Dept. of Library and
Information Science, Kannur University.

Beena, C.
Deputy Librarian, University Library,
Cochin University of Science & Technology,
Cochin 682022

Dinesan, K.
Director, Dept. of Library and Information Science,
Kannur University

Gilsha. K.
Guest Lecturer, Dept. of LIS,
Kannur University Thalassery Campus

Humayoon Kabir, S.
Associate Professor,
Department of Library and Information Science,
University of Kerala, Trivandrum-695034.

Jalaja V,
Associate Professor (Retd) and Former Head,
Department of Library and Information Science,
University of Calicut

Jipsi Chacko
MLISc Student, Dept. of LIS,
Kannur University Thalassery Campus

Leena Khullar
Assistant Librarian, Punjab University,
Chandigarh

Mahjabeen Aydeed
Research Scholar,
Department of Library and Information Science,
University of Calicut.

Manzoor Babu.V
Librarian, TKM College of Engineering,
Kollam

Mehaboobullah K.
Technical Assistant, Kerala University Library,
Thiruvananthapuram

Mohamed Haneefa K.
Assistant Professor,
Department of Library and Information Science,
University of Calicut

Muhammed Najeeb V.
Librarian, King Saud bin Abdulaziz
University for Health Sciences, Riyadh, KSA.

Nasirudheen T.P.O.
Associate Professor, Dept. of Library &
Information Science, Farook College,
Kozhikode, Kerala, 673632.

Nikesh Narayanan
Discovery Service Engineer
EBSCO Information Services

Padmakumar, P.K.
University Library,
Cochin University of Science & Technology,
Cochin 682022.

Ramina Mukundan
PGT Librarian, Bal Bharati School
New Delhi

Sangeetha K. K.
Department of Library and Information Science,
Kannur University.

Sangita Purohit
Head, Library, Post Graduate Institute of Management,
Amrut Mody School of Management,
Ahmadabad University, Ahmadabad – 380009.

Sareef K.
Librarian, RUA College,
Farook College, Kozhikode.

Seena S.T.
Research Scholar,
Department of Library and Information Science,
University of Kerala,
Thiruvananthapuram-695 034

Shabir Ahmad Ganaie
Sr. Assistant Professor,
Department of Library and Information Science,
University of Kashmir

Shyni K.G.
Research Scholar, Department of Library and
Information Science, University of Calicut

Sreekumar, M.G.
UNESCO Coordinator,
Greenstone Support for South Asia,
Center for Development of Digital Libraries (CDDL)
Indian Institute of Management Kozhikode (IIMK)

Sreelatha K.
Guest Lecturer, Department of Library and Information Science, Kannur University.

Sudhier, K.G.
Librarian, Library & Knowledge Centre,
School of Distance Education,
University of Kerala,
Thiruvananthapuram - 695 034

Sumana K.P.
Guest Lecturer, Department of Library and Information Science, Kannur University.

Surendran Cherukodan
Junior Librarian, School of Engineering,
Cochin University of Science and Technology,
Kochi-682022

Suresh Kumar, P.K.
Assistant Librarian,
Kerala University Library, Palayam,
Thiruvananthapuram-34

Suthar, Ashokkumar A.
Librarian, Jawahar Navodaya Vidyalaya,
Dantiwada, Gujarat-385505

Vahida Beegam T.
Research Scholar, Department of Library and Information Science, University of Calicut.

Veerankutty Chelatayakkot
Assistant Librarian, Cochin University of Science and Technology, Kochi-682 022

Vijayakumar K. P.
Head, Dept. of Library and Information Science &
Hon. Director, Centre for Information Literacy
Studies, University of Kerala ,
Thiruvananthapuram - 695 034

PART I
E-RESOURCE MANAGEMENT

1

Choice of Discovery: Evaluating Web Scale Discovery Services

Nikesh Narayanan
Ramina Mukundan

ABSTRACT

Web scale Discovery services are becoming the most sought after solution for Libraries to connect its patrons with the relevant information they seek. Many studies show that these services are getting wide acceptance from users as well as Library staff and making revolution in Library Information retrieval arena. Given such broad implications, selecting a new discovery service for libraries is an important undertaking. Library professionals should carefully evaluate options to meet their goal of finding the best potential match for their library. This Paper attempts to provide a comprehensive overview of Library Web Scale Discovery solutions by depicting various facets of Web Scale Discovery, how it differs from federated searching and highlights the important parameters to be considered for taking an informed and confident decision on selecting discovery service.

Keywords : Resource Discovery Service, Web Scale Discovery Service, Federated Search

1. INTRODUCTION

Web scale Discovery services are becoming the most sought after solution for Libraries to connect its patrons with the relevant information they seek. This state of the art technology solution holds the potential to be the evolution that libraries have long sought for information discovery[1]. Web Scale Discovery solution is getting wide acceptance from library community which is evident from the fact that many libraries are replacing their Federated search Solutions of the past decade and adopting this state of the art technology.

In the interface level, Discovery system is simply a platform which facilitate Single Search box to search all resources of a Library and provides relevance based result sets. But there are multiple components and parameters which decides the quality and relevancy of search results. Competing Discovery products varies in Discovery content, Technology and features. An information profession is expected to be knowledgeable about "What & Why" of Discovery, how it differs from federated searching, and how can system parameters be evaluated for informed and confident decision on selecting discovery service.

2. WHAT IS WEB SCALE DISCOVERY?

Web scale discovery services are those integrated web based services with major potential to transform the nature of library systems. These services are offered as cloud computing model and have the capacity to more easily connect researchers with the library's vast information repository including remotely hosted resources and local content[2]. It provides a unified platform for library users to access and search from all the library resources to get single set of results by providing a Google like environment with the following basic features.

- Unified platform to search all the resources

including licensed, open and local collections including Library Catalog and Institutional Repository

- Pre-harvested central index of metadata
- Google like single search box
- Single results list for all collections
- Relevancy ranking across entire results
- Full featured user interface
- Facets and tools for narrowing results
- Connections to full text
- Infrastructure, processing and indexing provided and maintained remotely by the vendor.

3. WHY WEB SCALES DISCOVERY?

The impact of Internet and Google like search engines radically influenced the information behavior of Net Generation users. They expect same environment in library services such that all their required information make available in a single set of results through unified search across all the available resources. Today libraries subscribe lots of resources like electronic journals, electronic books, and databases and own digital repositories and OPACs. Here, in one sense, users are in a very advantageous position regarding the access of resources but often in the confusion, from where to start and which resource to be covered to get their information. This force users to depend on Google like search engines to get their information. Web Scale discovery solutions eliminate this confusion and provide Single search box environment to users to retrieve all the relevant information from multiple sources.

Web Scale Discovery solutions helps Libraries in getting back their users by providing simple and powerful search solutions and thus ensures justification for the huge investment on resources. For, publishes it gives greater visibility for their published resources and more chance to get used by the users which would surely enhance their market.

4. WEB SCALE DISCOVERY VS FEDERATED SEARCH

Federated search solutions are the technology utilized by Libraries for resources retrieval in the past decade. The inherent weaknesses of federated solutions are its slowness and associated problems as the searches are conducted on the fly against each and every databases. Federated system needs to have separate connectors for searching different databases. There are some distinctive features which delineate the reward of Discovery over Federation.

Discovery Service	Federated Search Engines
Search is very fast as retrieval is done in pre-harvested index	Slow (longer time for search completion) – Federated searching is performing the meta search on the fly from different resources
Standardized unified Index	Many indexes: Individual indexes and different database structures of various publishers makes it difficult for metadata retrieval.
Robust Relevancy Ranking as retrieval is from Unified index	Relevancy ranking is a major issue in retrieval of quality data.
Enhancement is possible on the harvested Metadata	Metadata enhancement is not possible
Comprehensive results	Shallow results in many cases-and eventually users will miss much relevant content.
Performance quality is very high	Many times important information from relevant resources are missed out due to connection error.
As employing harvesting method, Separate connectors are not needed for each and every publisher. Even small publishers data can be added in central index.	Many small publishes and societies with one or two journals normally, do not have federated search connectors and eventually out of the scope of federated searching.

5. WEB SCALE DISCOVERY ARCHITECTURE

Web Scale Discovery service constitutes two important components. Content or resources coverage is the prime factor and the second factor is appropriate technologies to make available the relevant information to the library users from available content. This include technologies that facilitate to harvest, index, relevance ranking, search and retrieve the content and user interface platform features to provide a user friendly environment to users.

5.1. Content

Normally, a Web Scale Discovery system covers all informative contents that scholarly users are interested. Web scale discovery services are able to index a variety of content, whether hosted locally or remotely. Such content can include library ILS records, digital collections, institutional repository content, and content from locally developed and hosted databases. In addition, Web scale discovery services pre-index remotely hosted content, whether purchased or licensed by the library. This latter set of contents - hundreds of millions of items - can include items such as e-books, publisher or aggregator content for tens of thousands of full text journals, content from abstracting and indexing databases, and materials housed in open access repositories. It may consist of free resources or of commercial publishers. Free content may include institutional archives of universities, research organizations etc and also from Open archives journals and publications. Harvesting of free content and creating its indexes can be made available with the appropriate technology but the distinction lies in the coverage of commercial contents. As content coverage is the most important parameter in deciding the quality of the discovery system, the comprehensiveness of commercial content is a decisive factor. Commercial Web scale discovery vendors have brokered agreements with content providers (publishers, aggregators), allowing them to pre-index item metadata and /or full text content (unlike the traditional federated search model). This approach lends itself to extremely rapid search and return of results ranked by relevancy, which can then be sorted in various ways according to the researcher's whims (publication date, item type, full text only, etc.)[2].

Different publishers are practicing different policies in providing full text content to Web Scale Discovery providers. In many cases, the publishers are providing the full text content for indexing purposes. Some publishers are providing their metadata only for indexing purpose. Vendors can develop multiple content streams for the same, finite content. For any given article, there are lots of potential sources for that exact same article, not just the original primary publisher. It depends on service provider's policy to identify the apt sources to be indexed in the system.

5.2. Technology

Web Scale Discovery systems make use of mash-ups of many technologies and tools to harvest, index, store, search, and retrieve the content in response to user queries through a unified web interface. The following are the core technology elements.

5.2.1. Harvester

Harvester is one of the most important tools to bring the content to the central index of the system. Each vendor has agreements with several content suppliers from whom they harvest materials. In addition, they harvest locally held material such as existing library catalogues and institutional repositories within the library using protocols such as OAI-PMH and FTP. Automated transfer routines, load tables, and indexing steps are in place to add newly published content and to keep the index up to date.

5.2.2. Metadata mapping

Metadata coverage and its mapping is a very important factor in deciding the quality of the system. Some providers cover only "thin metadata" with few record fields, perhaps a table of contents—and some other cover "thick metadata"—covering more fields, including additional abstracting and indexing by dedicated staff, or includes author-supplied subject headings and abstracts.

Metadata standards used in various resources may differ and thus make it necessary for Web scale discovery systems to normalize the harvested metadata in to a common Schema or record type. Also metadata for the same item may be received from multiple content providers such as the original publisher, aggregators etc, have to be joined through common match points and, through normalization and de-duplication processes to make it rich, and accurate, highly discoverable and relevant record.

5.2.3. Platform Blending of Subject Indexes

Platform blending is the technology to infuse results from important subject indexes into the discovery experience for users. This integration is really useful for users to get the benefit of thick quality metadata done by special subject experts of such indexing/abstracting databases.

5.2.4. Central Index

The normalized, de-duplicated metadata is aggregated in a huge central index database. The processed index is hosted in a cloud environment maintained by the service provider against which searches are performed in response to user queries. Web Scale Discovery systems utilize automated processes that allow new content to be added and indexed quickly. Different content providers provide new content on a variable basis, and content is indexed and included in the index on a schedule appropriate to the content, which, for example, may be daily for newspaper content and monthly for a monthly journal. The central index continues to grow when new items are getting published by existing content providers and agreement with news content providers.

5.2.5. Link Resolvers

Web Scale Discovery service makes use of OpenURL-compliant Link resolver software to work with the vast majority of information resources in the market today. It works in connecting the full text and objects associated with library's subscriptions and local repositories to provide direct access. Web Scale Discovery service providers make agreements with content providers to collaborate as targets to provide full text access to users based on their subscription.

5.2.6. Relevancy Algorithms

Relevance ranking in web scale discovery systems is an attempt to measure how closely a document or entry fits possible search terms. Search tools that display results in a relevance ranking order place their "best match," an entry with the highest relevance ranking on the top of the list, instead of using an alphabetical, date modified, or other more concrete sorting method. Each vendor has developed its own proprietary relevancy algorithms. However, no system will ever be perfect for all searches by all users. Some services allow the local library to influence the algorithm or otherwise promote or boost items within search results, and, depending on the service, this boost may be at the item level, collection level, or database level. Some vendors may place greater emphasis on currency, some on full text, and some on subject headings. Depends on the relevancy algorithms, search results may be different.

5.2.7. Interface

User interface is the front end of the Web scale Discovery service. Interface is often hosted by the vendor, but some systems allow for local hosting of the interface, but the content index is always remotely hosted in the cloud. Users can search the index and get results though the web interface. Vendors are providing various advanced features and functionalities and often include the following;

— A single search box (but with a link to advanced search modes)
— Faceted searching
— Each platform offers a modern interface with design elements expected by today's students.
— Faceted navigation (subject, content type, journal, publisher, date range, etc.) to help users drill down a large set of results
— Inclusion of enriched content such as book cover images
— Shopping carts to easily mark items and later export the materials (email, print, save)
— Social networking tools, etc.
— Web 2.0 features
— Ajax features to update data without re-loading the whole page, but only the relevant content.
— "Did you mean?" spell checkers
— User configurable RSS feeds to easily re-run searches later

5. MAJOR PLAYERS

Summon Web scale Discovery by Serial Solution[3]

Summon is one of the early entrants in to the library Web scale Discovery environment developed by serial solution and its first release was in July 2009. Summon is offered as a hosted software-as-a service solution.

EBSCO Discovery services by EBSCO[4]

Ebsco began development of Ebsco Discovery

Service (EDS) in 2008. Public announcement occurred in spring 2009, and after a beta period concluding later that year, public release occurred in early 2010.

Primo Central by Exlibris[5]

Ex Libris began development of its next-generation discovery layer, Primo, in 2005, with official public release occurring in 2007;. Primo Central, Ex Libris's Web scale discovery component, was officially released in mid-2010.

WorldCat Local by OCLC[6]

OCLC released the initial version of WorldCat Local in November 2007. In 2009 OCLC brought out their discovery platform, WorldCat local with centralized index with collaboration more content providers.

The comparative analysis shows that all the major service providers are extending competitive features and services, but varies in some features and the choice is depends on the concerned library's preferences and the cost involved.

7. Evaluation of Discovery Systems

Quality of Web scale discovery services depends on many factors with regard to the comprehensiveness of content and apt technology used for backend processing and delivering of requested data over web interface in response to user's request. The following are some of the evaluation parameters which may be considered while selecting a discovery service.

7.1. Content Coverage

Content Coverage or central index is the knowledge base of a Discovery service. As Searches are made against this knowledge index, comprehensiveness and quality of information retrieval is primarily depends on the coverage. Therefore, it is always advisable to ask the following information from the Discovery vendor to make it sure that comprehensive coverage is included in the central index.

- Content partners list to whom Discovery providers have agreement to get the metadata.
- Content analysis report of customer's subscribed resources to make it sure that all the resources are covered in Discovery index. Content Analysis reports are of two types. First level analysis which clearly lists the resources which are covered and not covered in Discovery. Second level analysis provides individual journal wise report. If some Databases are not covered in Discovery service, customers can ask to integrate it through federated search solution along with the discovery and Display of combined results sets in one platform. It is always better to select the vendors who provide federated searching option to complement Discovery for non covered resources.

7.2. Interoperability with Institution-specific services

Most of the Libraries prefer to integrate their Catalog, IR and Learning Management System (LMS) with Discovery solution and in such case, libraries should make it sure the capability of Discovery solution to Integrate these system. Some Discovery providers explore working with integrated library system (ILS) vendors for mutual cooperation. Collaboration discussions revolve around whether the ILS should serve as the front end (bringing in the discovery results) or whether the discovery service should be the front end (interacting with traditional ILS functionalities, like holds lists) which provides flexible options for libraries. Integration of LMS with Discovery system would really be advantageous to students, Research Scholars and faculties so that they can add the desired search results directly into the reading list of LMS system.

7.3. Interoperability with Library's Single Sign on Systems

It is very important to make it sure that Discovery

Service is compatible with the Authentication or remote access system of the library. Some of the most common remote access mechanisms are Eduserv Athens, Ezproxy, Shibboleth etc. In case the institution is using LDAP kind of system for Authentication, check it with Discovery vendor regarding its integration possibility.

6.4. Relevance ranking algorithm

Relevance Ranking is really the Intelligence of the Discovery system. It is important for a user to get the most relevant articles in the first page of the result list. Different Vendors are using their own ranking algorithms. Library should clarify with Discovery service providers regarding the ranking methods used and relative emphasis given for Subject, Title, and Author supplied keyword etc. Subject is the most important factor and better if relevancy algorithm gives first priority to Subjects rather than title or author supplied keywords.

6.5. Quality of Metadata

Metadata Quality has great influence in the discoverability of documents. There is high chance that documents with enhanced metadata would get retrieved compared to items with skeleton metadata. It is most ideal if subject index blending is possible through Discovery for Mutually Licensed Content. That is the subject index Content licensed by both the library and the WSD vendor. The Integrated Abstracting & Indexing databases are fully searchable in their original unmodified form including all A & I metadata. This helps in retrieving richest sources of metadata based on subject based relevance and controlled vocabularies. PsycInfo, INSPEC etc are some of the examples of A/I content that can be shown in a WSD system if the library subscribes to PsycInfo and INSPEC.

6.6. Quality of Linking Technology

Linking is critical to the success of discovery services. The discovery service offers to limit search results to material held by the library; in that case, the patron is entitled to expect that any search results within that limit will successfully link to the item.

Web Scale Discovery products make use of different linking methods and technologies. Some of them are

- Openurl link resolvers
- Direct custom linking to each publishers site
- Smart linking – if customers' licensed full text is already available in WSD provider database.

Leading Discovery service providers have their own proprietary link resolvers but if library is already having another link resolver, the ability of that link resolver to work with the discovery service is important.

Alternatives to Link resolver is also very important as some studies shows Link resolvers fail nearly a third of the time. Custom linking is one of the alternatives where Discovery service providers maintains separate local collection of each the publishers subscribed resources and provide custom link to connect directly to that publishers site.

Some Discovery vendors provide another linking facility which they call as "Smart linking" where users can easily follow an article citation in one database to the full text of that same article in another database. For example, EBSCO SmartLinks provide linking between EBSCOhost databases where publications overlap.

6.7. Refinement of Search results

Often, Discovery Service search provides millions of result. So there should be refinement options to narrow down to more specific results. Some of the important refinement options are;

Source Type : Academic journals, e-books, books, trade publications, newspapers etc

Subjects : Related subject group where the search term is associated with. For example, if we are searching for " Indian Economy", the subject segmentation may be like Economic forecasting, Gross domestic products, Investment, Economic Policy etc.

Publisher : This filter is very important, as users might be interested to know from which source all the results are coming from. Also users can filter the results from a particular publisher such as Elsevier, Springer, Wiley, Taylor and Francis, Emerald etc.

Publication : This filter facilitates the user to limit to one particular journal only among the top hit journals.

Language : Users can restrict the resources for selected languages.

Geography : Users can restrict documents based on country of affiliation of authors.

Content provider : Through this filter users can identify and limit various aggregators such as EBSCO, JSTOR etc. and Indexing and Abstracting database such as Scopus, Medline, Web of science etc.

6.8. Widgets option

Widget is a software application with limited functionality that can be installed and executed within a web page by an end user. It just occupies a portion of a webpage and does something useful with information fetched from other websites and displayed in place. In the Discovery context, Widgets can be utilized well to fetch information from useful resources which are not part of Discovery. For example, information can be retrieved from Google Scholar, Ted talk, NTLTD Theses and Dissertation, Open Access Repositories etc. This option facilitates the freedom to Libraries to add useful resources or applications as widgets.

6.9. Other Enhancements options and features

Discovery solutions adopt variety of ways that to enhance the quality of results. Some of the enhancement options that may be considered for deciding the quality of Discovery system are given below.

- Catalogue Enhancement such as including book jackets, table of contents, books by the same author, related books, Google Books Proview, users review etc.
- Journal ranking such as scimago journal rank with H-Index details (free), Igenfactor(free), journal citation report (for mutual customers)etc. Some Discovery Service providers make available these options through widgets.
- E-mail , print and save retrieved records
- Setting up search alerts through e-mail, RSS etc.
- Export to Reference Management tool (Endnote , Zotero, Procite, Reference Manager etc.)
- Option for citation style formats
- Personalization options like making notes while reading and share with others
- Bookmark to social networking tools
- Sending or sharing the permanent links of retrieved documents.

7. EVALUATION STUDIES

There are some good studies on evaluation parameters and case studies of Discovery implementations in Libraries which would really helpful in understanding various stakeholders experience and opinion about different Discovery solutions.

American Library Association's technical report "Web Scale Discovery Services" [7] by Jason Vaughan is the first comprehensive work on web scale discovery services which includes chapters starting from "web Scale Discovery – what and why?" to implementation and evaluation methods.

In his another work "Evaluating and Selecting a Library Web-Scale Discovery Service" [8] Vaughan provides a frame of evaluation, based in part on the evaluation process used at the University of Nevada, Las Vegas Libraries. It highlights the important internal and external steps library staff may wish to consider as they evaluate these discovery services for their local environment.

David Bietila and Tod Olson[9] consider a three-tiered approach to the application, considering technical, functional, and usability layers. As the current generation of discovery tools is very flexible, the process discussed uses an initial pass of evaluation to gain insight into the abilities of the tool and how users approach it.

The Results of some interesting usability case studies have also been published which depicts the results of evaluation studies of web scale discovery services implemented in different universities.

At Grand Valley State University, Doug Way[10] conducted an analysis of usage statistics after implementing the discovery tool Summon in 2009; the usage statistics revealed an increased use of full-text downloads and link resolver software but a decrease in the use of core subject databases.

North Carolina State University Libraries released a final report about their usability study of Summon.[11] Study reveals users were satisfied with the ability to search the library catalog and article databases with a single search, but users had mixed results with known-item searching and confusion about narrowing facets and results ranking.

Boock, Chadwell, and Reese conducted a usability study of WorldCat Local at Oregon State University.[12] They summarized that users found known-title searching to be easier in the library catalog but found topical searches to be more effective in WorldCat Local. The participants preferred WorldCat Local for the ability to find articles and search for materials in other institutions.

Kemp reports in his study that, after the first year following Summon implementation at the University of

Texas at San Antonio Libraries[13], the statistics on the use of collections showed significant increases in the use of electronic resources: link resolver use increased 84%, and full-text article downloads increased 23%. During the same period, use of the online catalog decreased 13.7%, and use of traditional indexing and abstracting database searches decreased by 5%. The author concludes that the increases in collections use are related to adoption of a Web-scale discovery service.

Anita in her case study of EBSCO Discovery Service[14] at Illinois State University's Milner Library states that EBSCO Discovery Services has resulted in a significant increase in Milner's database usage.

Andrew, Lynda and Suzanne[15] in their article reports the research conducted at Bucknell University and Illinois Wesleyan University in 2011 to compare the search efficacy of Serial Solutions Summon, EBSCO Discovery Service, Google Scholar and conventional library databases. They used a mixed-methods approach by gathering qualitative and quantitative data on students' usage of these tools. They found regardless of the search system, students exhibited a marked inability to effectively evaluate sources and a heavy reliance on default search settings. On the quantitative benchmarks measured by this study, the EBSCO Discovery Service tool outperformed the other search systems in almost every category.

8. CONCLUSION

Web Scale services are fairly new entrant in Library and Information Retrieval arena and still in its initial stages of development with regard to its features, functionality, level of integration with other systems, interoperability, scope of content, soundness of metadata, flexibility of the interface etc. Different Discovery Services vary in its offerings. The best way to evaluate and experience WSD system is to request fully customized trial including Catalogue and Institutional repository integration from the Discovery Vendors. Above mentioned evaluation parameters would help in preparing the evaluation matrices for the selection process. Customer Success stories and available evaluation studies of early adopters would also throw lights in exploring the competency of different Discovery Systems. Library should also make sure the proficiency of the vendor in providing local support and necessary training sessions. The final choice is always depends on the concerned library's preferences.

REFERENCES

1. Vaughan, J. (2011). Web scale Discovery Services. Library Technology Reports, 47(1), 5–11.
2. Vaughan, J., & University of Nevada, L. V. (2011). Investigations into library web scale discovery services. Retrieved from *http://digitalscholarship.unlv.edu/cgi/viewcontent.cgi?article=1043&context=lib_articles*
3. The Summon Service | Serials Solutions. (2012). Retrieved from *http://www.serialssolutions.com/en/services/summon/*
4. EBSCO discovery services. (2012). Retrived from: *http://www.ebscohost.com/discovery*
5. Ex Libris the bridge to knowledge, Primo Central Index. (2012). Retrieved from *http://www.exlibrisgroup.com/category/PrimoCentral*
6. WorldCat Local. (2012) Retrieved from *http://www.oclc.org/WorldCatlocal/*
7. Vaughan, J. (2011). Web scale Discovery Services. Library Technology Reports, 47(1), 5–11.
8. Vaughan, J. (2012). Evaluating and Selecting a Library Web-Scale Discovery Service. In D. Dallis (Ed.), Planning and Implementing Resource Discovery Tools in Academic Libraries. IGI Global. Retrieved from *http://www.igi-global.com/chapter/evaluating-selecting-library-web-scale/67814*
9. David, B., & Popp, M. P. (Eds.). (2012). Designing an Evaluation Process for Resource Discovery Tools. Planning

and Implementing Resource Discovery Tools in Academic Libraries. IGI Global. Retrieved from *http://www.igi-global.com/chapter/designing-evaluation-process-resource-discovery/67818*

10. Way, D. (2010). The Impact of Web-scale Discovery on the Use of a Library Collection. Serials Review, 36(4), 214–220.

11. Summon Usability Testing (2010) | User Studies. (n.d.). Retrieved August 19, 2012, from *http://www.lib.ncsu.edu/userstudies/studies/2010summon*

12. Michael Boock, Faye Chadwell, and Terry Reese, WorldCat Local Task Force Report to LAMP, retrieved August 19,2012 from *http://hdl.handle.net/1957/11167.*

13. Kemp, J. (2012). Does Web-Scale Discovery Make a Difference?: Changes in Collections Use after Implementing Summon. Planning and Implementing Resource Discovery Tools in Academic Libraries. IGI Global. Retrieved from *http://www.igi global.com/chapter/does-web-scale-discovery-make/67836*

14. Anita K, F., & Popp, M. P. (Eds.). (2012). Early Adoption: EBSCO Discovery Service at Illinois State University. Planning and Implementing Resource Discovery Tools in Academic Libraries. IGI Global. Retrieved from *http://www.igi-global.com/chapter/early-adoption-ebsco-discovery-service/67838*

15. Asher, A. D., Duke, L. M., & Wilson, S. (2012). Paths of Discovery: Comparing the Search effectiveness of EBSCO Discovery Service, Summon, Google Scholar, and Conventional Library Resources. College & Research Libraries. Retrieved from *http://crl.acrl.org/content/early/2012/05/07/crl-374.short*

16. Williams, S. C., & Foster, A. K. (2011). Promise Fulfilled? An EBSCO Discovery Service Usability Study. Journal of Web Librarianship, 5(3), 179–198.

17. Freund, L., Poehlmann, C., & Seale, C. (2012). From Metasearching to Discovery: The University of Florida Experience. *http://services.igi-global.com/resolvedoi/resolve.aspx?doi=10.4018/978-1-4666-1821-3.ch002.* Retrieved from *http://www.igi-global.com/chapter/content/67812*

18. Axford, M. A. (2012). Ultimate Debate Program on Web-Scale Discovery Services. A Report of the LITA Internet Resources

and Services Interest Group Meeting, American Library Association Annual Conference, New Orleans, June 2011. *http://dx.doi.org/10.1080/07317131.2012.650937.*

19. Comeaux, D. J. (2012). Usability Testing of a Web-Scale Discovery System at an Academic Library. *http://dx.doi.org/10.1080/10691316.2012.695671*

20. FEATURE: The Ins and Outs of Evaluating Web-Scale Discovery Services. (2012). Retrieved from *http://www.infotoday.com/cilmag/apr12/Hoeppner-Web-Scale-Discovery-Services.shtml*

21. Graves, T., & Dresselhaus, A. (n.d.). One Academic Library—One Year of Web-scale Discovery. *Serials Librarian (SERIALS LIBR), 2012 Jan-Jun.*

22. Hoy, M. B. (n.d.). An Introduction to Web Scale Discovery Systems. *Medical Reference Services Quarterly (MED REF SERV Q), 2012 Jul-Sep.* Retrieved from *http://www.tandfonline.com/doi/abs/10.1080/02763869.2012.698186*

23. Kornblau, A. I., Strudwick, J., & Miller, W. (2012c). How Web-Scale Discovery Changes the Conversation: The Questions Librarians Should Ask Themselves. *http://dx.doi.org/10.1080/10691316.2012.693443.*

24. Leebaw, D., College, C., Conlan, B., College, S. O., Sinkler-Miller, C., College, C., Wilson, N., et al. (2012). Improving Library Resource Discovery: Exploring the Possibilities of VuFind and Web Scale Discovery in a Consortial Environment. *Library Technology Conference.* Retrieved from *http://digitalcommons.macalester.edu/cgi/viewcontent.cgi?article=1263&context=libtech_conf*

25. Pitts, J., & University, K. S. (2012). The Advent of Web Scale Discovery Tools: What it Means for Undergraduate Research. *SIDLIT Conference.* Retrieved from *http://scholarspace.jccc.edu/c2c_sidlit/2012/Thursday/6*

26. Thompson, J. L., Obrig, K. S., Abate, L., Thompson, J. L., Obrig, K. S., & Abate, L. (2012). Web-Scale Discovery in an Academic Medical Library: Our Experience with EBSCO's Discovery Service. Retrieved from *http://hdl.handle.net/1961/10413*

2

Institutional Repositories : An effective vehicle for Scientific Data Curation

C.Beena
P.K Padmakumar
N.S Archana

ABSTRACT

The technological revolution has provided the means for researchers to make the results of their research available to anyone, anywhere, at any time. Large volumes of scholarly literature are coming out from different R&D laboratories and Academic Institutions like Universities and colleges. Faculty and scientific community create research materials and scholarly publications in increasing complex digital formats. It is a real challenge to provide the right content to the right person at right place. Institutional repositories are an effective vehicle for Scientific Data Curation, Management and Dissemination of Knowledge. This paper explores how the institutional repository of Science and Technology is recycling the intellectual outputs of Faculty and scientific community in Cochin University of Science & Technology (CUSAT).

Keywords : Institutional Repository, Data Curation

1. INTRODUCTION

Globalization is revolutionizing the development of a knowledge society. Use of ICT in education and scientific research is transforming access to knowledge, learning process and information delivery in a big way. This does not necessarily mean that traditional practices should be abolished but, rather, that conventional teaching, learning and research approaches are merging with new ones that facilitate education and research at any time, in any location as required, while also addressing individual and institutional and local needs.

Due to changing scenario of higher education and research, huge volume of learning resources and scientific literature are born in digital format. And the research data are valuable and ubiquitous. The permanent access to research data is a challenge for all stakeholders in the scientific community. The long term preservation of and principle of open access to research data provides opportunities for the scientific community. Vitally important, however, is to guarantee that research data sets can be found and cited. More and more universities and research centers are starting to build research data repositories allowing permanent access to data sets in a trustworthy environment. Due to disciplinary requirements, the landscape of data repositories is very heterogeneous. Thus it is difficult for researchers, funding bodies, publishers and scholarly institutions to select appropriate repositories for storage and search of research data.

Many scholarly outputs are in different types and formats. The contents of an IR covers scholarly literatures, conference proceedings, Theses, teaching and learning materials, audio, video contents, reports, white papers, gray literature , chapters of books, Pre-prints, working papers, technical reports, progress/ status reports, committee reports, etc. Data sets, models, simulations models etc.

1.1. Background of the study

CUSAT is one of the premier institutions promoting research in Science & Technology in India. Research work spreads in various disciplines such as Nano materials & Technology, Electronics, Polymer Science & Rubber Technology, Physics, Chemistry, Photonics, Biotechnology, Marine science, Earth Science, Marine Sciences and Fisheries Technology, Ship Technology, Atmospheric & Environment Science, Communications etc.

Departments conducting research in different areas produces huge volume of analytical and scientific data. After analysis by respective researchers, the observed data is interpreted as a finding which is published as a research paper.

The data recorded and analyzed by a researcher in a particular discipline if made available to another researcher in a related field may be interpreted in a different perspective which may result into a totally different finding. For encouraging this type of research, the data has to be preserved in some specific form in a repository. Due to the advancement of ICT, the output from research is data produced chiefly in electronic form especially remarkable for its exponential rate of increase in size and speed.

Research data are valuable and ubiquitous and is currently hot topic. Scientific research data, based on a typical approach to scientific experimentation is to pose a hypothesis and then determine a methodology for testing it. Data are often generated from observation in raw forms, which are analyzed and interpreted to confirm the validity of the hypothesis. The result of this analysis and interpretation results in a journal or conference article.

2. WHAT IS INSTITUTIONAL REPOSITORY?

An institutional repository is a digital archive of the intellectual product created by the faculty, research staff, and students of an institution and accessible to end users both within and outside of the institution, with few if any barriers to access.

University-based institutional repository is a set of services that a university offers to the members of its community for the management and dissemination of digital materials created by the institution and its community members. (Lynch C.A 2003)

2.1. Why Institutional Repository?

Institutional repositories (IR) are a new breed of services and software, still in their infancy. IR is defined as a set of services that an Institution offers to the members of its community for the management and dissemination of digital materials. The open source movements adopting the idea of institutional repositories are Eprints, Green Stone and DSpace. Government is promoting the development of Institutional repositories, Digital repositories, digital archives etc in the institutional, national and Global level. Institutional repositories are created to manage, preserve, and maintain the digital assets, intellectual output, and histories of institutions. These repositories provide services to faculty, researchers and administrators who want to archive historic and creative materials. The open access and open archives movement are trying hard for the changes in scholarly communication pattern, removing barriers to access, increasing awareness that universities and research institutions are losing their valuable digital and print materials, thus motivating establishment of institutional repositories.

3. DATA CURATION

Managing data to ensure they are fit for

contemporary use and available for discovery and reuse. Archiving and preservation are subsets of the larger curation process, which is a much broader, planned, and interactive process.

Archiving : Ensuring that data are properly selected, appraised, stored, and made accessible. The logical and physical integrity—including security and authenticity—of the data are maintained.

Preservation : Ensuring that items or collections remain accessible and viable in subsequent technology environments.

Data curation is the management of data throughout its lifecycle, from creation and initial storage to the time when it is archived for posterity or becomes obsolete and is deleted. The main purpose of data curation is to ensure that data is reliably retrievable for future research purposes or reuse. (David Minor 2012)

3.1. Why Data curation?

Data curation is critically important for a research institution because it provides two vital services: (1) data are not merely stored, but are preserved in order to overcome technical obsolescence inherent in any storage system; and (2) data are documented in such a way that they can be referenced in, and linked from, scientific publications and meet the requirements of funding agencies.

Academia of Cochin University of Science & Technology are regularly producing large amount of data that need to be stored, analyzed, and preserved. These data sets and their derivatives (publications, visualizations, etc.) represent the intellectual assets of the University. They have inherent and enduring value and must be preserved and made accessible for reuse by future researchers.

Today's interdisciplinary research challenges cannot be addressed without the ability to combine data from disparate disciplines. Researchers need to know what relevant data exist, as well as how to retrieve, combine, mine, and analyze data using the latest tools.

4. HOW IR SUPPORTS DATA CURATION

Institutional repository is collecting verifiable research informatics within the institution. It must be curated or preserved in a proper way for providing search and retrieval. It provides the curatorial oversight and bibliographic control and integration services. It curate the metadata and citations and relationships and collaborations within the campus.

- It provides the certification of the trustworthiness and integrity of the collective content.
- It collecting raw data, structured data for analysis, analytical out put such as figures, graphs , tables etc.
- It supports data sharing and reuse across different communities.
- Preserving more digital data products.
- It also supports the ontological continuity and comparability of the collection.
- IR supports the open standards and formats for preservation and future proofing by migration of data
- It curates the metadata
- Curate the raw data derivatives (publications, citations etc.)
- It curate the collaborations and dependency of the context of a research
- It provides the opportunities for future research

Collaboration, Publication and Curation of CUSAT Scientific outcomes

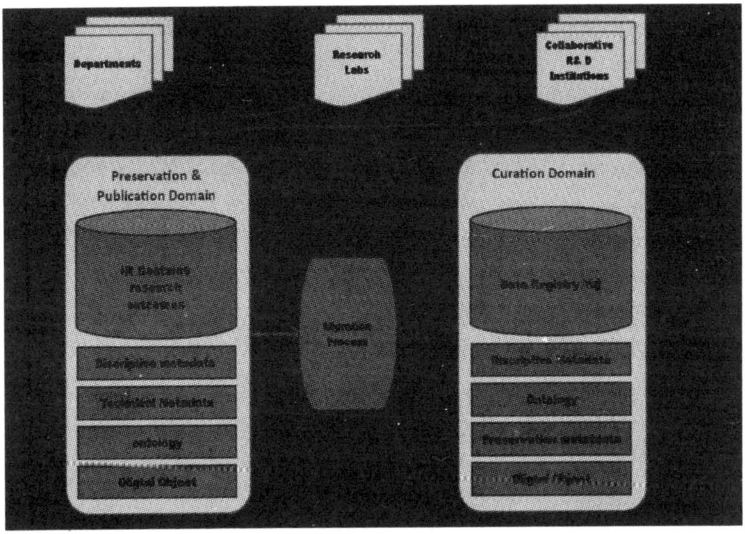

Fig. 1. Scientific Data curation at CUSAT through IR

5. BENEFITS OF RESEARCH DATA PRESERVATION

The costs of securing the long-term persistence of research data must be balanced against the anticipated benefits. It is a fact that the discoveries of the future rely on the work of the past and thus the maintenance of scholarly record is essential for continued progress in research and learning. But this requires a significant commitment of funds, equipment, and expertise.

The rising tide of digital research data (Hey and Trefethen 2003) raises issues relating to access, curation and preservation in respect of how an institution might improve its international profile and support its primary purposes of research, learning and teaching by pursuing an effective digital preservation strategy for research data. In parallel with this there are often legal requirements and grant terms and conditions relating to the storage of and access to research data

6. CONCLUSION

The need to share and reuse data is an important topic in almost high-level report or discussion concerning contemporary science. Data curation is the activity of managing data from their point of creation to ensure they are available for discovery and reuse in the future. The role of Institutional Repository (IR) is multifaceted. The roles are not only in archiving, managing and disseminating knowledge, but also contribute to a great extent in promoting interdisciplinary research. It supports the institution to improve its profile in National as well as international. This is small initiatives by Cochin University Library, but we have to go long way in this regard.

REFERENCES

1. Lynch, Clifford. "Institutional Repositories: Essential Infrastructure for Scholarship in the Digital Age." *ARL Bimonthly Report*, No. 226, February 2003. *<http://www.arl.org/newsltr/226/ir.html>*.
2. Hey, T., Trefethen, A. (2003). The data deluge: An e-science perspective. In F. Berman, G.C. Fox, & T. Hey, (Eds.), *Grid computing: Making the global infrastructure a reality.* New York: Wiley.
3. Karen S. Baker, Lynn Yarmey, (2009) Data Stewardship: Environmental Data Curation and a Web-of-Repositories the International Journal of Digital Curation Vol.9 No.2
4. David Minor (2012) *http://rci.ucsd.edu/data-curation/definition.html* Retrieved on 11-11-2013
5. re3data.org Vocabulary Version 2.0 / December 2012 Retrieved on 3-11-2013

3

UGC – INFLIBNET for Bridging the Digital Divide in Academia

Dr. Abdul Azeez T. A

ABSTRACT

Information and Library Network (INFLIBNET) Centre is an autonomous Inter-University Centre (IUC) of UGC established in 1996. The Centre is involved in creating infrastructure for sharing of library and information resources and services among Academic and Research Institutions. INFLIBNET works collaboratively with Indian university and college libraries to shape the future of the academic libraries in the country. The paper discusses the activities and services of INFLIBNET Centre like Infonet Digital Library Consortium, NLIST Programme, Shodhganga, Union Databases etc. The paper also discusses the activities that help in bridging the digital divide among academic community of the country.

Keywords : INFLIBNET, Infonet, NLIST, Library Consortia, Shodhganga

1. INTRODUCTION

The Information and Library Network (INFLIBNET) Centre is an autonomous Inter-University Centre (IUC) of the University Grants Commission (UGC) established in 1996. The Centre is involved in creating infrastructure for sharing of library and information resources and services among academic and research institutions. Major activities and services of the Centre are geared towards modernization of academic libraries and information centers, to promote information transfer and access, to support scholarship, learning and academic pursuits. The Centre acts as a nodal agency for networking of libraries and information centers in universities, institutions of higher learning, R & D institutions and colleges in India. INFLIBNET works collaboratively with Indian university libraries and college libraries to shape the future of academic libraries in the country and has become a major player for promoting scholarly communication among academicians and researchers across the country.

2. OBJECTIVES OF INFLIBNET

INFLIBNET Centre, leveraging on the latest technology, creates a virtual network of people and resources in academic institutions with an aim to provide effective and efficient access to knowledge through perseverance, innovation and collaboration. The other specific objectives as per the Memorandum of Association (MOA) are as follows:

- To promote and establish communication facilitates to improve capability in information transfer and access that provide support to scholarship, learning, research and academic pursuits through cooperation and involvement of concerned agencies;
- To establish information and library network-a computer communication network for linking libraries and information centres in universities, deemed to be universities, colleges, UGC information centres, institutions of national importance and R&D institutions, etc. avoiding duplication of efforts;

- To facilitate academic communication amongst scientists, engineers, social scientists, academicians, faculty, researchers and student through electronic mail, file transfer, computer/ audio/video conferencing, etc;
- To undertake system design and studies in the field of communications, computer networking, information handling and data management;
- To establish appropriate control and monitoring system for the communication network and organize maintenance;
- To collaborate with institutions, libraries, information centres and other organizations in India and abroad in the field relevant to the objectives of the Centre;
- To promote R&D and develop necessary facilities to create technical positions for realizing the objectives of the Centre;
- To generate revenue by providing consultancies and information services; and
- To do all other such things as may be necessary, incidental or conducive to the attainment of all or any of the above mentioned objectives.

3. MAJOR INITIATIVES AND SERVICES

As the technology, especially Information and Communication Technology (ICT), being a driving force in the contemporary education system, the UGC has taken-up a number of major initiatives for academic community in universities and colleges under its purview, like UGC-Infonet Digital Library Consortium, National Library and Information Services Infrastructure for Scholarly Content (N-LIST), Union Databases, Shodhganga etc. The INFLIBNET Centre is responsible for execution and monitoring of these initiatives.

3.1. UGC-Infonet Digital Library Consortium

The UGC-Infonet Digital Library Consortium was launched by Dr. A.P.J. Abdul Kalam, the then President of India during December 2003. The UGC-Infonet Digital Library Consortium provides current as well as archival access to more than 8,000 core and peer-reviewed journals and nine bibliographic databases from 26 publishers and aggregators in different disciplines. The programme has been implemented in a phased manner. In the first phase that began in 2004, access to e-resources was provided to 50 universities who had Internet connectivity under the UGC-Infonet Connectivity Programme of the UGC. In the second phase, 50 more universities were added to the programme in the year 2005. So far 182 universities that come under the purview of UGC have been provided differential access to subscribed e-resources. In addition, another 25 universities are getting access to e-journals from selected publishers on complementary basis. These e-resources cover almost all subject disciplines including arts, humanities, social sciences, physical sciences, chemical sciences, life sciences, computer sciences, mathematics and statistics, etc. The Centre has also initiated

Inter-Library Loan (ILL) through JCCC (Journal Custom Content for Consortium). The JCCC provides article-level access to all the journals subscribed by the UGC-Infonet Digital Library Consortium and journals subscribed by 22 university libraries designated as ILL Centres of the INFLIBNET Centre.

The website especially designed for the UGC-Infonet Digital Library Consortium provides an interface to search e-journals subscribed under the consortium as well as to search member institutions and corresponding e-resources subscribed for them. The list of major resources available under Infonet is given below.

Full-Text E-Resources

American Chemical Society	http://pubs.acs.org/
American Institute of Physics	http://journals.aip.org/
American Institute of Physics Archive	http://journals.aip.org/digital_archive.html
American Physical Society	http://publish.aps.org/browse.html
Annual Reviews	http://arjournals.annualreviews.org
Cambridge University Press	http://journals.cambridge.org/
Economic & Political Weekly	http://epw.in/
Emerald	http://www.emeraldinsight.com/
Institute of Physics	http://iopscience.iop.org/journals
JSTOR	http://www.jstor.org/
Nature	http://www.nature.com/
Oxford University Press	http://www.oxfordjournals.org
Portland Press	http://www.portlandpress.com/pp/default.htm
Project Euclid	http://projecteuclid.org
Project Muse	http://muse.jhu.edu/
Royal Society of Chemistry	http://www.rsc.org/
ScienceDirect (10 Subject Collection)	http://www.sciencedirect.com/
SIAM	http://epubs.siam.org/
Springer Link	http://link.springer.com/
Taylor and Francis	http://www.tandfonline.com/
Westlaw India	http://www.westlawindia.com/
Wiley Blackwell Publishing	http://onlinelibrary.wiley.com/

Bibliographic Databases

ISID	http://isid.org.in/
JCCC	http://jgateplus.com/search
MathSciNet	http://www.ams.org/mathscinet
SciFinder Scholar	http://www.cas.org/products/scifinder
Web of Science	http://apps.isiknowledge.com/

3.2. N-LIST

The National Library and Information Services Infrastructure for Scholarly Content (N-LIST) is being jointly executed by the UGC-INFONET Digital Library

Consortium, INFLIBNET Centre and the INDEST-AICTE Consortium, IIT Delhi. N-LIST provides for i) cross-subscription to e-resources subscribed by the two Consortia, i.e. subscription to INDEST-AICTE resources for universities and UGC-INFONET resources for technical institutions; and ii) access to selected e-resources to colleges. The N-LIST provides access to e-resources to students, researchers and faculty from colleges and other beneficiary institutions through Servers installed at the INFLIBNET Centre.

This programme is open to all colleges in India except Agriculture, Engineering, Management, Medical, Pharmacy, Dentistry and Nursing colleges. For member institution, N-LIST provides current as well as archival access to more than 6000 core and peer-reviewed journals in different disciplines. It also provides access to more than 97000 digital books from various publishers and aggregators. The major electronic resources provided through N-LIST programme are;

E- Journals

American Institute of Physics (18 titles)	http://journals.aip.org/
American Physical Society (10 titles)	http://publish.aps.org/browse.html
Annual Reviews (33 titles)	http://arjournals.annualreviews.org/
Cambridge University Press (224 titles)	http://journals.cambridge.org/
Economic and Political Weekly (EPW) (1 titles)	http://www.epw.in/
Indian Journals (150 titles)	http://www.indianjournals.com/
Institute of Physics (46 titles)	http://www.iop.org/EJ/
JSTOR (2000 titles)	http://www.jstor.org/
Oxford University Press (206 titles)	http://www.oxfordjournals.org
Royal Society of Chemistry (29 titles)	http://www.rsc.org/Publishing/Journals/
H. W. Wilson (1420 titles)	http://vnweb.hwwilsonweb.com/hww/jumpstart.jhtml

E-books

Cambridge Books Online (1800 titles)	http://ebooks.cambridge.org
E-brary (83000+ titles)	http://site.ebrary.com/lib/inflibnet
EBSCoHost-Net Library (936 titles)	http://www.netlibrary.com/
Hindustan Book Agency (65+ titles)	http://hindustan.igpublish.com
Institute of South East Asian Studies (ISEAS) Books (382+titles)	http://iseas.igpublish.com
Oxford Scholarship (1402+ titles)	http://www.oxfordscholarship.com/
Springer eBooks (2300 titles)	http://www.springerlink.com.
Sage Publication eBooks (1000 titles)	http://knowledge.segepub.com.
Taylor Francis eBooks (1800 titles)	http://www.tandfebooks.com.
Myilibrary-McGraw Hill (1124 titles)	http://lib.myilibrary.com/
Bibliographic Database	
MathSciNet	http://www.ams.org/mathscinet/

The faculty members and students can make use of these resources from anywhere and any time through User name and password provided by the Inflibnet centre. The most remarkable feature of this project is the provision of access to more than 97000 digital books under various disciplines.

3.3. Union Databases

Union Database is called IndCat: Online Union Catalogue of Indian Universities. It is a unified Online Library Catalogues of books, theses and journals available in major university libraries in India. The union database contains bibliographic description, location and holdings information for books, journals and theses in all subject areas available in more than 157 university libraries across the country. A Web-based interface is designed to provide easy access to the merged catalogues. The IndCat is a major source of bibliographic information that can be used for inter-library loan, collections development as well as for copy cataloguing and retro-conversion of bibliographic records. The IndCat consists of the following three components available in open access to users and librarians;

Books Database : It contains over twelve million bibliographic records of books from 157 university libraries.

Theses Database : It contains the bibliographic details of more than 2, 50,000 Doctoral theses submitted to 287 universities in India.

Serials Databases : This database contains information on currently subscribed journals by the universities and holdings information on serials available in various university libraries. There are more than 33,000 records in this database.

3.4. Research Project Database

Research Project Database provides the details of the accomplished and ongoing funded projects, carried out by various faculty members, working at various universities in India. Currently, it contains more than 13600 research project's information funded by various funding agencies viz. *UGC, ICAR, ICMR, DST* and *DBT* etc. The details of the project information have been collected from the project directors, and funding agencies. The database can be accessed at *www.inflibnet.ac.in/researchproject/*

3.5. Vidwan: Expert Database

VIDWAN is the premier database of profiles of scientists / researchers and other faculty members working at leading R & D Organisation and other Academic Institutions involved in teaching and research in India. It provides important information about expert's background, contact address, skills and accomplishments.

The database offers experts of various subjects from Nation's leading institutions. Attempt has been made to provide access to relevant and accurate information collected from various sources. Web enabled interface has been incorporated to facilitate the search and update names listed in the database. On Expert Database, experts are not limited to publishing a static Profile(s). Members can take advantage of many "value – added" offerings such as having Books and Articles published on the personal website and linked to their Profile(s).

Further, every expert whose profile is available in the database, has been provided login ID and password with the persistent URL for future updating of their profiles. The databases can be searched on parameters such as name, designation, institution, specialization, state, etc. Expert database is committed to excellence and value. The details can be seen at *http://vidwan.inflibnet.ac.in*

3.6. Shodhganga: a reservoir of Indian Theses

The UGC Notificatio (Minimum Standards & Procedure for Award of M.Phil. / Ph.D Degree, Regulation, 2009), dated 1st June 2009, mandates submission of electronic version of theses and dissertations by the researchers in universities with an aim to facilitate open access to Indian theses and dissertations to the academic community world-wide. This would overcome serious problem of duplication of research and poor quality resulting from the "poor visibility" and the "unseen" factor in research output. As per the Regulation, the responsibility of hosting, maintaining and making the digital repository of Indian ETD is assigned to the Inflibnet Centre.

"Shodhganga" is the name coined to denote digital repository of Indian Electronic Theses and Dissertations set-up by the INFLIBNET Centre. The word "Shodh" originates from Sanskrit and stands for research and discovery. The "Ganga" is the holiest, largest and longest of all rivers in Indian subcontinent. The Ganga is the symbol of India's age-long culture and civilisation, everchanging, ever-flowing, ever-loved and revered by its people, and has held India's heart captive and drawn uncounted millions to her banks since the dawn of history. Shodhganga stands for the reservoir of Indian intellectual output stored in a repository hosted and maintained by the INFLIBNET Centre. The Shodhganga project was started in 2010. As on 1st March 2014, there are 13,955 full text theses uploaded to Shodhganga repository from 159 universities. The details are available at *http://shodhganga.inflibnet.ac.in*

3.7. ShodhGangotri: Repository of Indian Research in Progress

Shodhgangothri is a repository of Indian research in progress which contains details of synopsis or research proposals for Ph.D programme. The word "Shodh" originates from Sanskrit and stands for "research and discovery". "Gangotri" is one of the largest glacier in the Himalayas and source of origination of Ganges, the holiest, longest and largest of rivers in India. The Ganges is the symbol of age-long culture, civilization, ever-aging, ever-flowing, ever-loving and loved by its people.

Under the initiative called "ShodhGangotri", research scholars / research supervisors in universities are requested to deposit electronic version of approved synopsis submitted by research scholars to the universities for registering themselves for the Ph.D programme. The repository on one hand, would reveal the trends and directions of research being conducted in Indian universities, on the other hand it would avoid duplication of research. Synopsis in "ShodhGangotri" would later be mapped to full-text theses in *"ShodhGanga"*. As such, once the full-text thesis is submitted for a synopsis, a link to the full-text theses would be provided from ShodhGangotri. to *"ShodhGanga"* At present, it contains 1713 synopses which can be accessed at *http://shodhgangotri.inflibnet.ac.in*

3.8. e-Pathsala

e-Pathsala is an MHRD project under its National Mission on Education through ICT (NME-ICT). It acts as a gateway to all postgraduate course contents. Under this project, MHRD has assigned work to the UGC for development of e-content in *77 subjects* at postgraduate level. The content and its quality is the key component of education system. High quality, curriculum-based, interactive content in different subjects across all disciplines of social sciences, arts, fine arts & humanities, natural & mathematical sciences, linguistics and languages is being developed under this initiative named e-PG Pathshala. UGC has assigned the task of uploading the content of e-Pathshala to INFLIBNET Centre. Now, it contains more than 500 modules of course contents in different subjects. The details can be accessed at *http://epgp.inflibnet.ac.in*

3.9. e-EDUCATION

e-EDUCATION is a collaborative endeavour between Consortium for Educational Communication (CEC) and INFLIBNET Centre to reach out to the unreached for disseminating its information and e-resources through the use and application of ICT. CEC and the INFLIBNET Centre of UGC provide information support for education and research in colleges and universities through their services and facilities. Under this project CEC develops video programmes, e-contents, and Learning Object Repository (LOR) based on the model curriculum of UG programmes . In this repository, more than 14,000 items are available which can be accessed at *http://www.inflibnet.ac.in/edu/*

3.10. Open Journal Access System

The Open Journal Access System (OJAS) at INFLIBNET Centre uses Open Journal System (OJS), an open source solution developed by the Public Knowledge Project through its federally funded efforts to expand and improve access to research. The OJAS is designed for managing and publishing scholarly journals online.

The INFLIBNET Centre has installed and configured

Open Journal System on servers at Inflibnet to facilitate hosting of electronic version of journals into open access mode with all processes of submission, peer-reviewing, editing, layout designing and publishing built into it. OJAS encourages universities and institutions that are publishing journals in print format to use the OJAS at Inflibnet Centre for hosting electronic version of their journals free-of-cost on servers at Inflibnet Centre. The initiative also encourages faculty in universities to start their own open access journals using this platform. Currently OJAS at Inflibnet Centre hosts fourteen journals published by various universities and institutions of higher learning. The details can be seen at *www.inflibnet.ac.in/ojs/*

3.11. Institutional Repository @ INFLIBNET

The Inflibnet Centre has established an institutional repository using D-Space, an open source software. The papers published in CALIBER and PLANNER proceedings are being uploaded into the repository in PDF format. The repository also includes Course Materials, Newspaper Clippings, Inflibnet Publications etc. The resources available under this repository can be accessed at *http://dspace.inflibnet.ac.in*

4. CONCLUSION

The INFLIBNET Centre is involved in creating infrastructure for sharing of library and information resources and services among academic and research institutions. INFLIBNET Centre works collaboratively with Indian university libraries and college libraries to shape the future of academic libraries in the country and has become a major player for promoting scholarly communication among academicians and researchers across the country. The paper so far discussed the major activities and services of INFLIBNET Centre that help in bridging the digital divide among academic community of the country. Apart from the above, INFLIBNET Centre provides a number of services like Human Resource Development, Open Source Software R&D, Access Management R&D, Special Drive for North-Eastern Region etc. for the benefit of academic community of the country. In a nutshell, INFLIBNET Centre can be conceived as a largest educational system of the country connecting more than 600 universities, 17,500 colleges, 6-8 lakhs teachers and 110 lakhs students, thereby making a revolution in higher education scenario of the country.

REFERENCES

1. Prem Chand and Jagdish Arora (2008) *Access to scholarly communication in higher education in India: Trends in usage statistics via INFLIBNET*. Program: electronic library and information systems, Vol. 42 Iss:4 pp. 382- 390.
2. Suresh K Chauhan and Prem Chand (2007) *UGC-Infonet: E-Journals Consortium and Indian Academics: the Right Initiative at the Right Time*. Library Philosophy and Practice, February.
3. *http://www.inflibnet.ac.in* (Accessed on March 1, 2014)

4

Use of INDEST-AICTE Consortium by Researchers in Indian Institute of Technology Delhi

Dr. P.M Naushad Ali
Dr. Tabassum Ara

ABSTRACT

With the advent and application of IT in libraries, the concept of Resource Sharing has gained popularity and eased the sharing resources from one library to another library. The more accepted system of resource sharing is library consortia. The present study aims to find out the awareness and opinion of users regarding INDEST-AICTE Consortium in IIT Delhi and to identify to what extent the research publications of research scholars and faculty members have increased by using e-journals subscribed under INDEST-AICTE Consortium in IIT Delhi. It also examines the usage of e-journals subscribed under consortia through usage statistics maintained by IIT Delhi under study.

Keywords : Library Consortia, INDEST-AICTE Consortium, Resource Sharing

1. INTRODUCTION

In the present scenario, academic libraries are facing some major problems such as rapid expansion of knowledge, proliferation of literature, escalation of price, growing demand of users, recoil of budget etc. To overcome all these problems, libraries should come forward and share their resources among themselves. With the advent and application of IT in libraries, the concept of Resource Sharing has gained popularity and eased the sharing resources from one library to another library. The more accepted system of resource sharing is library consortia. Consortia approach is one of the many ways to maintain cooperation and coordination amongst the libraries and in fact it has emerged as the 'state of the art' programme in the area of library cooperation in recent years. Library consortia is a group of two or more libraries that have agreed to cooperate with each other in order to fulfil certain similar needs, usually resource sharing.

2. INDEST-AICTE CONSORTIUM

The "Indian National Digital Library in Engineering Sciences and Technology (INDEST) Consortium" was set-up by the Ministry of Human Resource Development (MHRD) in the year 2003 on the recommendation of an Expert Group appointed by the Ministry. The name of INDEST consortium has been changed as INDEST-AICTE Consortium in 2005, with the collaboration of All India Council of Technical Education (AICTE). The IIT Delhi has been executing all the activities as the Consortium Headquarter. The INDEST-AICTE Consortium is the most ambitious initiative and biggest consortium in terms of number of member institutions in India as well as in Asia. The consortium attracts the best possible price and terms of agreement from the publishers on the basis of strength of its present and prospective member institutions. The consortium subscribes to over 12,000 electronic journals from a number of publishers and aggregators (INDEST-AICTE Consortium, Annual Report, 2012).

3. INDIAN INSTITUTE OF TECHNOLOGY DELHI

IIT Delhi established in 1963 is one among the seven institutes of technology in India established as centres of excellence for higher training, research and development in science, engineering and technology. The IIT Delhi Library System consists of a Central Library and 18 Department Libraries which collectively support the teaching, research and extension programs. Central library of IITD provide access to full text and bibliographic databases under consortium to their academic user community through their advanced and well developed library web page. Users can access these e-resources from their library web page where all the e-resources are hyperlinked with publishers' websites (Central Library, IITD, 2012).

4. REVIEW OF THE LITERATURE

As far the use and impact of e-journals under consortia is concerned; it has gradually increased in acceptance amongst faculty members and users in more recent years. As cleared from the review, at the Ohio State University, an increase in faculty use of e-journals i.e. from 36.2 percent to 53.9 percent was found from the year 1998 to 2000 (Rogers, 2001). Siebenberg, Galbraith, & Brady (2004) indicated that both faculty and students heavily used e-journals simultaneously however, their use of paper journals also increased. Lack of training is a major de-motivating factor in the usage of e-journals, so that needs to be improved (Borrego, Anglada, Barrios & Comellas, 2007).

5. OBJECTIVES OF THE STUDY

i. To find out the awareness and opinion of users

regarding INDEST-AICTE Consortium in IIT Delhi under study.

ii. Identify to what extent the research publications of research scholars and faculty members have increased by using e-journals subscribed under INDEST-AICTE Consortium in IIT Delhi under study.

iii. To examine usage of e-journals subscribed under consortia through usage statistics maintained by IIT Delhi under study.

6. METHODOLOGY

Questionnaire and personal interview were used as major tools for collection of data. A well define questionnaire was prepared to collect the related data. The questions were formulated keeping in view the objectives of the study and personally administered to the research scholars and faculty members of IIT Delhi.

7. DATA ANALYSIS AND INTERPRETATION

The collected data is analyzed, tabulated and presented as follows.

7.1. Awareness of INDEST-AICTE Consortium

The apex body had initiated a programme to provide electronic access over the internet to scholarly literature to the institutes of higher education in India. The investigator asked to the respondents about their awareness of INDEST-AICTE Consortium at IIT Delhi. It is clear from the Table-1, 65.74% of the research scholars and 70.00% of the faculty members are aware of INDEST-AICTE Consortium, whereas 22.22% research scholars and 16.66% faculty members are not aware of it. About 12.31% research scholars and faculty members did not respond on this issue.

It can be deduced from the analysis that 21.01% of

the respondents are not aware of INDEST-AICTE Consortium.

Table 1. Awareness of INDEST-AICTE Consortium

Awareness	Number of Respondents IIT Delhi		
	Research scholar N=216	Faculty N = 60	Total N=276
Yes	142(65.74)	42(70.00)	184(66.66)
No	48(22.22)	10(16.66)	58(21.01)
No response	26(12.03)	8(13.33)	34(12.31)

(Figures in parenthesis are percentages)

7.2. Increase in number of Publications by using e-journals

An interesting question was raised to the respondents of IIT Delhi library that during the span of their research work whether the e-journals comes under INDEST-AICTE consortium has help them in improving their research as well as in increasing their number of research publications.

Table-2 reveals that about 10% of the research scholars and faculty members *Strongly agree* that their research publications have increased by using e-journals under consortia, however majority i.e.76.19% research scholars and 60.00% faculty members are *Agree* with this statement. Moderate percentages (15.38% research scholars and 12.30% of the faculty members) said that, they are *Uncertain* about it. Few of them i.e. 4.07% of the users *Disagree* that research publications have increased by using e-journal under consortia.

It is observed from the analysis that majority (72.59%) *Agree* with this account that research publications have increased after using e-journal under consortia and negligible percentage are *Disagree* with this statement.

Table 2: Increase in number of publications by using e-journals

Category	Number of Respondents IIT Delhi Research scholar N=210	 Faculty N=60	 Total N=270
Strongly agree	25(11.90)	2(4.16)	27(10.00)
Agree	160(76.19)	36(60.00)	196(72.59)
Uncertain	20(15.38)	16(12.30)	36(20.22)
Disagree	5(2.38)	6(4.61)	11(4.07)
Strongly disagree	–	–	–

(Figures in parenthesis are percentages)

7.3. Usage trend of e-journals under consortia in IITD (2007-2011)

The usage of INDEST-AICTE consortium's e-journals in IITD is presented in Table-3. The total downloads recorded in the year 2007 in IITD is 4046527. In 2008 downloads went up to 4158883 but from 2009 to 2011 analysis shows that it has decreased year by year with 3603482, 3069698 and 2773582 down loads in 2009, 2010 and 2011 respectively.

Over all analysis e-journals come through INDEST-AICTE consortium from 2007 to 2011 shows that *CAPITALINE* (70.67%) database is the leading publisher covers more than 70% i.e. greater part of the total usage of it. But it is surprising to note that usage of *CAPITALINE* is also decreased with 77.76% in 2007, 75.92% in 2008, 66.56% in 2009, 65.84% in 2010 and 63.14% in 2011.

8. FINDINGS

1. It was observed that 66.66% of the users are aware of INDEST-AICTE Consortium whereas 21.01% of them are not aware of it.
2. It was noted that large percentage of respondents in IITD (72.59%) *agree* that their research publications have increased by using e-journals

Table 3 : Usage trend of e-journals under consortia in IITD (2007-2011)

Publishers' Name	Down Loads					
	2007	2008	2009	2010	2011	Total
ABI/Inform Complete	4711(0.11)	8901(0.21)	14790(0.41)	12608(0.41)	16020(0.57)	57030(0.32)
ACM	5260(0.12)	10789(025)	9761(027)	9624(0.31)	8825(031)	44259(0.25)
AIP/APS	32394(0.80)	39550(0.95)	68352(1.89)	38479(1.25)	45641(1.64)	224416(1.27)
ASCE	6654(0.16)	24486(058)	8092(0.22)	4673(0.15)	6482(0.23)	50387(0.28)
ASME	3961(0.09)	10562(025)	8753(0.24)	2976(0.09)	4130(0.14)	30382(0.17)
ASTM	-	-	1377(0.03)	1939(0.06)	2987(0.10)	6303(0.03)
CAPITALINE	3146955 (77.76)	3157725 (75.92)	2398900 (66.56)	2021194 (65.84)	1751363 (63.14)	12476137 (70.67)
EBCSO	2386(0.05)	3180(0.07)	5083(0.14)	6019(0.19)	6318(0.22)	22986(0.13)
Elsevier' Science Direct	449831(11.11)	506852(12.18)	620711(6.30)	521356(16.98)	519450(18.72)	2618200(14.83)
Emerald	23051(0.56)	18676(0.44)	17320(0.48)	17005(0.55)	14274(0.51)	90326(0.51)
EROMONIOTOR	608(0.01)	1233(7.73)	2413(0.06)	3746(0.12)	6318(0.22)	14318(0.08)
IEEE/IEE	127911(3.16)	154300(3.71)	119523(3.31)	138059(4.49)	171858(6.19)	711651(4.03)
Nature	6493(0.16)	6994(0.16)	9191(0.25)	27925(0.90)	33218(1.19)	83821(0.47)
Optical Society of America	-	-	14082(0.39)	17997(0.58)	16749(7.73)	48828(0.27)
SCOPUS database	-	-	-	-	-	-
Springer Link	41407(1.02)	39908(0.95)	48107(1.33)	6113(0.19)	78696(2.83)	214231(1.21)

Publishers' Name	Down Loads					
	2007	2008	2009	2010	2011	Total
COMPENDEX/ INSPEC	37435(0.92)	14923(035)	356(0.009)	5377(0.17)	NS	58091(0.32)
JCCC	398(0.009)	1006(0.02)	21413(0.59)	16719(0.54)	NS	39536(0.22)
SciFinder	63829(1.57)	127872(3.07)	58904(1.63)	46785(1.52)	40686(1.46)	338076(1.91)
MathSciNet	18258(0.45)	14920(0.35)	20579(0.57)	15347(0.49)	17522(0.63)	86626(0.49)
WOS	22244(0.54)	17006(0.40)	155757(4.32)	155757(5.07)	33045(1.19)	282809(1.60)
Total	4046527 (22.92)	4158883 (23.55)	3603782 (20.41)	3069698 (17.38)	2773582 (15.71)	17652472 (100)

(Figures in parenthesis are percentages)

subscribed under consortia and none of the respondents *strongly disagree* with this statement.

3. Study reveals that usage of INDEST-AICTE consortium has decreased from 2007 (4046527 - 22.92%) to 2011 (2773582 -15.71%). In spite of that among all the full text and bibliographic databases comes under INDEST-AICTE Consortium, *CAPITALINE* is highly used database but its usage is also decreases from 3146955 (77.76%) in 2007 to 1751363 (63.14%) in 2011.

9. SUGGESTIONS

1. IITD library should promote their e-journals available through consortia by raising awareness amongst their user community as the usage of INDEST-AICTE Consortium base e-journals has decreased year by year.
2. Library staff should receive training courses for providing the proper accessibility of e-journals under consortia IIT Delhi.
3. IITD library users are required cooperation from staff for the better use of e-journals.
4. INDEST-AICTE Consortium regularly organizes user convention in various member institutions. Number of this user convention should be increased to accommodate maximum number of e-journal users to maximize utilization of e-journals under consortia.
5. The National Negotiation Committee (which is responsible for subscriptions to e-resources) should put more effort into covering information from all fields and disciplines.
6. There is a need to recruit more qualified young staff specially for handling e-resources with better exposure to modern technological devices.

REFERENCES

1. Borrego, A., Anglada, L., Barrios, M., & Comellas, N. (2007). Use and users of electronic journals at Catalan Universities: The results of a survey. *Journal of Academic Librarianship*, 33, 67-75.Retrieved December 22, 2011, from http:// www.sciencedirect.com/science/journal/00991333.

2. Central Library, Indian Institute of Technology Delhi. (2012). *Library services and facilities*. Retrieved September 16, 2013, from http://library.iitd.ernet.in/library/ brochures/erl.pdf.

3. INDEST-AICTE Consortium. (2012). *Annual Report*. Retrieved December 28, 2012, from http://indest.iitd.ac.in

4. Rogers, S.M. (2001). Electronic journal usage at Ohio State University, *College and Research Libraries*, 62, 25-34.

5. Siebenberg, T.R., Galbraith, B. and Brady, E.E. (2004). Print versus electronic journal use in three sci/tech disciplines: what's going on here? *College & Research Libraries*, 65 (5), 427-38.

5

Information and Communication Technology tools for Knowledge Management

Dr. Mehaboobullah K

ABSTRACT

Knowledge Management is integral to the success of any organizations. The central idea of Knowledge Management is to create, codify and share knowledge valuable to the organization. This paper precisely surveys the available software systems that support different knowledge management activities. In addition, the paper gives an overview of KM concepts, need of Knowledge Management; various steps involved in the KM process and explore a variety of potential application areas. The organizations who want to survive in unpredictable and complex competitive markets should quickly adapt to the new dynamics of business and must endeavor to effectively link KM initiatives and processes with their ICT infrastructure to advance their goals.

Keywords: Knowledge Management, Information and Communication Technology (ICT), KM tools, Knowledge Management software

1. INTRODUCTION

Knowledge is information or data, organized in a systematic way that is useful to the organizations and institutions. Every organizations and institutions that wants to be competitive must identify, manage, protect, organize and share their valuable explicit knowledge and tacit knowledge. The imperative for achieving efficiency in an organization is in transfer of relevant information for decision-making across all levels of organization structure. It can be done with well-disposed knowledge management system, which is responsible for implementing and evaluating strategies of knowledge, aimed at improving of internal and external knowledge in the organization, and overall corporate performances. Nowadays for many companies by the very nature of their business consider knowledge as their most important, valuable and critical asset. Managing this valuable knowledge is an art of creating value from organizations intangible assets. Hence knowledge management concerned with the exploitation and developments of the knowledge assets of an organization with a view to furthering the knowledge objectives.

The development in the field of ICT for organization has produced many successful tools for knowledge management and mange its well defined process. KM practitioners use a wide range of ICT tools to create, organize, codify and share knowledge. Modern ICT tools are widely used for authoring, indexing, abstracting, classifying, storing, contextualizing and retrieving information, as well as for collaboration and application of knowledge. Development in the field of online web technology, in coming years, will present a set of new tools for managing knowledge by providing an extremely rich common language for representing knowledge (Ghani, 2009).

2. KNOWLEDGE MANAGEMENT: THEORETICAL BACK GROUND

There is no concrete definition for the concept of knowledge management (KM). Karl Sveiby (2003) defined KM as the art of creating value from organizations intangible assets. According to Davenport and Prusak (2005), KM is concerned with the exploitation and development of the knowledge assets of an organization with a view to furthering the knowledge objectives. Despres and Chauvel (2001) defined knowledge management as a mechanism for enhancing organizational performance by explicitly designing and implementing tools, processes, systems, structures, and cultures to improve the creation, sharing, and use of different types of knowledge that are critical for decision-making. According to Agresti (2000) Knowledge management is the practice of transforming the intellectual assets of an organization into business value.

Nomaka and Takeuchi, (1995), classified knowledge in an organization as tacit or explicit. Tacit knowledge is knowledge that rests with the employees and explicit knowledge is the knowledge that resides in the knowledge base. Conversion of knowledge from one form to another could lead to the creation of new knowledge. The definitions of tacit and explicit knowledge, as given are:

- "Tacit knowledge is internalized, context-specific. Tacit knowledge is the knowledge of the employees."
- "Explicit knowledge refers to that type of knowledge which is transmittable in formal, systematic language. Explicit knowledge is easily distributable."

The schematic representation of tacit-explicit model of knowledge management put forwarded by Nomaka and Takeuchi is given in figure.1.

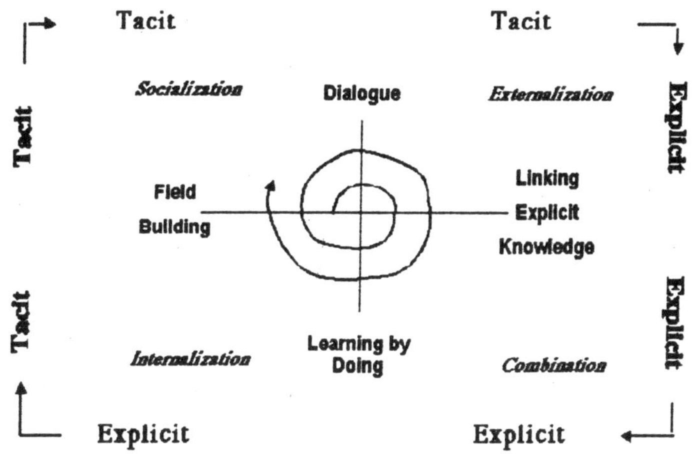

Figure 1: The Tacit-Explicit Model (Nonaka, I. and Takeuchi, H., 1995)

3. NEED OF KNOWLEDGE MANAGEMENT

It is a fact that a large amount of organizational knowledge is undocumented and organizations in contemporary society have realized that they lose knowledge when employees leave the company. When an employee leaves, the organization also loses the knowledge the employee gained. The frequent mobility of employees from organization to organization has created a growing need to retain employees and, more importantly preserves their knowledge especially the tacit knowledge which has led to a growing call for knowledge management. Another aspect of knowledge management is that of lessons learned. When people in the organization commit similar mistakes, the organization ends up wasting time and money to rectify them .Avoiding repeating mistakes could save money for most organizations; hence, they need to gather and maintain lessons learned from the various projects undertaken. Organizations also strive to repeat successes, making it important to manage knowledge about strategies that led to previous successes. Organizations might have a lot of knowledge regarding the products, processes, practices, policies, customers, vendors, and partners already captured, but spread in different locations and using different applications. This makes the staff access to this information very difficult, if not impossible. The company ends up having tons of information stored but not used. KM can help information be organized and stored such that every employee can retrieve it easily. In a typical knowledge management system, a knowledge base is maintained which documents and organizes the knowledge of the organization. It keeps track of the individuals of the organization and the collective knowledge, too. Such a system also maintains FAQ lists and expert lists which aid in running the organization more smoothly and profitably (Lindwall et al, 2001).

4. STEPS IN KNOWLEDGE MANAGEMENT

Asian Productivity Organization (APO) explained the KM activities in well defined five-steps process. These five-step KM processes are:

1. Identifying the knowledge
2. Creating knowledge
3. Storing knowledge
4. Sharing knowledge
5. Applying knowledge

This five-step process is a key part of the overall APO KM framework illustrated in figure.2. *(www.apo-tokyo.org)*

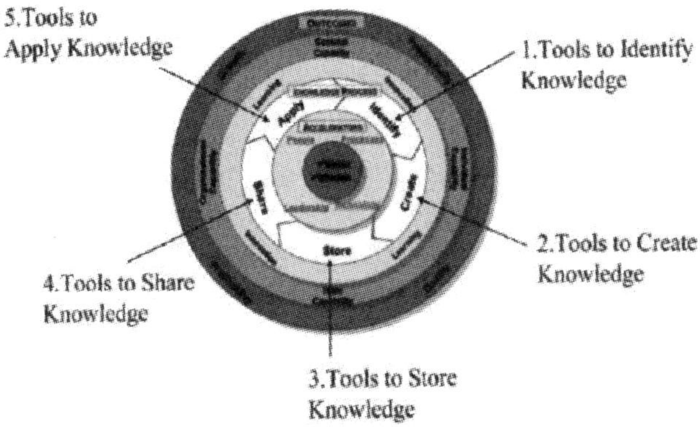

Fig. 2. Mapping K.M tool and techniques to APO K.M frame work

5. KNOWLEDGE MANAGEMENT AND ICT

The application of Information and Communication Technology is an integral part in the implementation of knowledge management. ICT enables and provides the entire infrastructure and tools to support KM processes within an enterprise. To succeed in KM, it is important that assessment and defining of ICT capabilities are done properly as it supports and facilitates KM processes such as knowledge capture, storage, retrieval, sharing and collaboration, dissemination and updates of knowledge of organizations. KM practitioners use a wide range of IT tools to create, codify and share knowledge. The trend in the development of IT for organizations is towards more communication and collaboration tools.

Omona et. al (2010) conducted a detailed study on ICT and knowledge management and identified various general ICT tools and their roles in knowledge management (Table.1).

Table 1. K.M Enabling ICT Tools and Networks

Sl. No.	ICT Tools/Networks	Description of Roles	Examples
1	Knowledge portals	Search and access to web based Knowledge	Google, Yahoo
2	E-Document Management System	Knowledge repositories created by individual academic institutions	Digital Library
3	Academic Publishing	Propitiatory digital libraries for electronic access to academic publishing	Emerald, Elsevier
4	Academic Contents and Exchanges	Electronic collections of course materials and learning objects	MIT Open Courseware
5	Database Management System(DBMS)	Set of computer programmes that control the creations, maintenance and the use of a database	Students records
6	Data Warehouse	A depository that facilitates reporting and analysis of data	Financing data, budgeting data
7	Data Mining	The process of extracting patterns from data	Academic profiling
8	Groupware	Is designed to help people involved in a common task achieve their goals	Knowledge Forum, Synergeia, Wikis
9	Communities of Practices (CoP)	Groups of practitioners networking in a particular fields of endeavor to define a practice and knowledge domain	Consortia, Educational research services
10	Social Communities of Interests	Social networks drawn together to share knowledge and build relationships	FaceBook, MySpace, Flickr
11	Individual communities of Interests	Tools for individuals to mange personal knowledge and networks	Blogs, Twitter

6. ICT BASED TOOLS FOR KNOWLEDGE MANAGEMENT

Different ICT based tools are available for the purpose of Knowledge Management. It can be divided broadly in to two: Information technologies tools and Web-based (IT) tools. Web, in coming years, will present a set of new tools for managing knowledge by providing an extremely rich common language for representing knowledge.

6.1. Domino.doc

It is an IT based tool for document and records management. Domino.Doc delivers scalability, flexibility and low cost of ownership required to support both enterprise-wide documents and records management, while serving as a foundation for knowledge management. Domino.Doc offers complete Document Life Cycle Management, from authoring through review, approval, distribution and archiving.*(http://www.lotus.com/home.nsf/welcome/km).*

6.2. Skillscape

Competence Manager Skillscape is an example of a system that helps an organization manage its competence. The system supports assessment and ranking of individual skills and competencies and builds snapshots of the organization's overall knowledge capital. The tool helps utilize this information to perform individual and organizational analysis, reduce educational costs, and improve hiring practices and human resources performance. It also facilitates developmental planning processes and effective deployment of human capital, and helps management make strategic decisions regarding readiness to take one or more projects. The Competence Manager of Skillscape automatically recommends training to professional based on their skill gaps, and can automatically launch technology-based training. *(http://web.skillscape.com).*

6.3. AskMe and AskIt

AskMe and AskIt are very similar systems. AskMe Enterprise creates employee knowledge networks within the organization and thus delivers employee expertise to other employees. It enables employees to discover the best expertise within the organization for their problem at hand, facilitates the exchange of that expertise, captures the outcome for re-use, dispatches best practices to employees, and provides the tools to analyze the results. Employees can submit problems and receive solutions, insights, advice, and answers from subject-matter experts throughout the company. The results are automatically captured in a searchable knowledge base so that other employees can later benefit from this exchange of knowledge.

AskIt (for customers) and AskMe (for employees) enable external customers and employees respectively to learn from the expertise of coworkers and other customers by reviewing FAQs and by asking new qu)estions. In both systems, the resulting solutions are catalogued and stored in a searchable knowledge base for future sharing. (http://www.askit.com) (http://www.askmecorp.com)

6.4. Email Ferret

E-mail Ferret is a small utility for finding electronic mail address of people on the web. Unlike most e-mail directories, it runs as a client as your desktop rather than in a browser. Email Ferret seeks out e-mail addr small esses by simultaneously querying multiple web based e-mail directories. Addresses can then be added to an electronic address book, copied or mailed to, using a standard electronic mail client (*www.ferretsoft.com*).

6.5. G2 webMiner

G2 webMiner enables applications created with G2 to access and reason about data available over the internet to provide intelligent internet website or Intranet, perform rule-based analysis and then make intelligent decisions.(*www.gensym.com*).

6.6. Profiler

Profiler is an intelligent employee-screening package that enables employers to select job applicants who are like their company's proven performers. If enough data is collected, information on current employees can help to determine which applicants for the same job would or would not, meet the criteria for that job. Evaluating these complex patterns within large amount of data is a very difficult job for a person, but quite easy for the computer when given the task. (Dhiman & Sharma, 2006).

6.7. Firstdoor Enterprise Solution

Firstdoor Enterprise Solution integrates human resource (HR) knowledge management with corporate learning to provide the background knowledge necessary to make informed decisions in the organization. Various tools in this suite are ASK Firstdoor, RESEARCH Firstdoor, and TRAIN with Firstdoor. *(http://www.firstdoor.com)*

6.8. Knowledge-Mail

Knowledge-Mail automatically creates employees' profiles by mining various sources of information. The profiling mechanism works by extracting terms and phrases from e-mail communications and more than 30 types of documents produced or shared by individual users. Each user profile provides a detailed index of an individual's knowledge, experience, and work focus. A set of profiles, therefore, represents a composite 'snapshot' of all the expertise within an organization. The same technology is used to create profiles of any entity in the organization, such as projects, customers, partners, and vendors. The information about projects can be used for marketing purposes, while a customer profile can be used to better serve the customer.*(http://www.tacit.com/solutions/km.html)*

6.9. Spotfire

It is an example of a general visualization tool. DecisionSite, an e-analytic application of Spotfire, incorporates an intuitive dynamic visualization environment. DecisionSite also provides a platform environment for simplifying data access through its Information Library and configuration of end-user guides that automate common decision-making tasks.*(http://www.spotfire.com)*

6.10. ThoughtFlow

ThoughtFlow is a goal oriented collaboration frame work. It can assist in task such as goal setting, strategic planning, problem solving, decision making and performance management. It provides a method of organizing information and sharing knowledge during such tasks. ThoughtFlow has a goal oriented language definition frame work that gives users a shared verbal and visual language about the domain under decision. Key issues and the connection between them are shown visually and knowledge elements are made explicit and indexed, allowing context specific retrieval. (*www.vidyainc.com*).

6.11. DigiMine Analytic Services

DigiMine analyzes customers' interaction with a website to help the institution to organize content and act as a business intelligence solution that delivers insight and decision support. DigiMine software has the ability to pull web server logs and gather data from any kind of database. Once data is transferred to digiMine's data center, it is parsed, cleaned and loaded into a data warehouse. Based on this warehouse, DigiMine can produce analytics that can be delivered on demand. DigiMine shows how customers interact with a website, and in what combination they consume content or purchase merchandise, so the company can organize content and merchandise to provide a more targeted and profitable customer experience. (*http://www.digimine.com)*

6.12. Abuzz

Abuzz supports an interactive knowledge-sharing community provided by the New York Times for its readers. It is very similar to AskMe, but it is in the form of a Web Portal. It is open for everybody who wants to ask or answer questions. Abuzz is a system that receives e-mail containing requests for information and routes it to experts, based on profiles. It updates profiles based on who answers the question. The system comes in intranet, extranet, and Internet versions and provides different categories such as art, education, cities, careers, health, travel, sports, etc. It has a central repository that stores the top-ranked question-answer e-mail series. (*http://www.abuzz.com*).

6.13. eRoom

eRoom enables collaboration among knowledge workers. It provides integration with the documentum enterprise content management (ECM) platform. The key features include customizable database and global roll-ups, Real Time Services (RTS), and Microsoft Office integration, as well as the capture of metadata within the eRoom workplace. (*http://www.documentum.com/products/glossary/eroom_ecm.htm*)

6.14. Solution Series

Solution Series is problem resolution software for capturing, diagnosing, solving and distributing resolutions to problems. Users describe problems in natural language. Knowledge is external documents and third party knowledge bases can also be used. All solution is a collection of statements that describe a problem in terms of its cause and symptoms. Its search method is described as associative problem solving technology and a customizable dictionary is used to recognize synonyms.*(www.primus.com).*

6.15. Axielle Portal tool

Axielle provides a Warehouse-to-web solution that delivers information with a single entry point to the enterprise, providing users with access to a company's information assets through the use of metadata integration. Axielle contains the most flexible platform in the industry for building, managing and delivering information across the Web. (*http://www.ascentialsoftware.com/products/axielle*)

7. CONCLUSION

Knowledge Management is the deliberate and systematic coordination of an organization's people, technology, process and organizational structure in order to add value through reuse and innovation. Knowledge management implementation requires wide range of quite diverse tools that came in to play throughout the KM cycle. Technology is used to facilitate primary communication, collaboration and content management for better knowledge capture, sharing, dissemination and application. A number of the tools presented here help to discover existing valuable knowledge , experts, communities of practice and other valuable intellectual assets that exists within an organization. Once this is done, the intellectual assets can be better accessed, leveraged and employed. The KM tools and techniques have an important role in ensuring the KM applications. It is therefore important to understand what is out there already and some of the emerging tools in order to adapt and make use of them for KM purposes.

REFERENCES

1. Abuzz. (2013). Retrieved November, 8, 2013 from *http://www.abuzz.com.*
2. Agresti, W. (2000). Knowledge management. *Advances in Computers*, 53(2), 171-283.
3. APO KM framework. (2013). Retrieved November, 3, 2013 from *www.apo-tokyo.org.*

4. Askit. (2013). Retrieved November, 3, 2013 from *http://www.askit.com*
5. Askme. (2013). Retrieved November, 5, 2013 from *http://www.askmecorp.com*
6. AxiellePortaltool. (2013). Retrieved November, 9, 2013 from *http://www.ascentialsoftware.com/products/axielle*
7. Davenport, Thomas H. & Prusak, Larry. (2005). Knowledge management: Executive brief. *In* Baets, Walter (Ed.), Knowledge management and management learning: Extending the horizons of knowledge-based management (2nd ed., pp 69-70). USA: Springer.
8. Despres, Charles & Chauvel, Daniele. (2001). *In* Knowledge horizons: The present and the promise of knowledge management, 2nd Ed., Butterworth-Heinemann, Boston, pp. 106-07.
9. Dhiman, Anil Kumar and Sharma, Hemant. (2006). *Knowledge Management for Librarians*(p.618). New Delhi : Ess Ess Publication
10. digiMine Analytic Services. (2013). Retrieved November, 3, 2013 from http://www.digimine.com
11. Domino.doc. (2013). Retrieved November, 3, 2013 from *http://www.lotus.com/home.nsf/welcome/km.*
12. eRoom. (2013).Retrieved November, 3, 2013 from http://www.documentum.com/products/glossary/eroom_ecm.htm
13. Email Ferret. (2013). Retrieved November, 3, 2013 from *www.ferretsoft.com.*
14. Firstdoor Enterprise Solution.(2013). Retrieved November, 6, 2013 from *http://www.firstdoor.com*
15. G2webMiner. (2013). Retrieved November, 3, 2013 from *www.gensym.com.*
16. Ghani, Syed Raiyan. (2009). Knowledge management: Tools and techniques. *DESIDOC Journal of Library & Information Technology,* 29(6), 33-38.
17. Knowledge Management: Facilitators. (2013). *Guide Retrieved 14 November 2013 from www.apo-tokyo.org*
18. Knowledge-Mail. (2013). Retrieved November, 4, 2013 from http://www.tacit.com/solutions/km.html
19. Lindwall, Mikael, Rus, Loana, Rajaskhar, J & Rikin, Thakker. (2001). A State of art report: Software tools for Knowledge

Management. Defence Technical Information centre, Rome. Retrieved November, 10, 2013 from *http://citeseerx.ist.psu.edu/viewdoc/download?doi=10.1.1.116.3021 &rep=rep1 &type=pdf.*

20. Nomaka, I. & Takeuchi, H. (1995). The Knowledge creating company. Oxford: Oxford University Press.
21. Omona, W & Van Der Werde,T & Lubega, J. (2010). Using ICT to enhance knowledge management in higher education: A Conceptual frame work and research agenda. *International Journal of Education and Development using Information and Communication Technology (IJEDICT)*, 6(4), 83-101.
22. Skillscape. (2013). Retrieved November, 5, 2013 from *http://web.skillscape.com*
23. Spotfire. (2013). Retrieved November, 6, 2013 from http://www.spotfire.com
24. SolutionSeries.(2013). Retrieved November, 8, 2013 from *www.primus.com*
25. ThoughtFlow. (2013). Retrieved November, 4, 2013 from *www.vidyainc.com.*
26. Sveiby, Karl. (2003). The Facts about knowledge. *In Knowledge management: Cultivating knowledge professionals* (Al-Hawamdeh, Suliman (Ed.) pp 32-33). Oxford : Chandos Publishing.

6

Building Digital Libraries Using Greenstone

M.G. Sreekumar

ABSTRACT

Digital Libraries (DL) are structured storage environments of digital data with a consistent format for index and content abstraction. DLs do enable the seamless integration of the scholarly electronic information, help in creating and maintaining local digital content, and strengthen the mechanisms and the capacity of the library's information systems and services. Considering the fact that currently the penetration of electronic content into our libraries and information centers is an unprecedented 70-80 percentage, it unequivocally prompts us to leverage on the latest digital technologies towards building practical digital libraries and in setting up dynamic electronic information systems. . This paper therefore aims at portraying the unlimited potential of digital libraries in real world perspective by trying out open source solutions. It attempts to unleash and demystify the plethora of features and functionalities of the open source software 'Greenstone'. It is a top of the line and internationally renowned software system for developing digital libraries, promoted by the New Zealand Digital Library project research group at the University of Waikato. It is developed and distributed in cooperation with UNESCO and the Human Info NGO. The aim of the software is to empower users, particularly in universities, libraries, and other public service institutions, to build their own digital libraries. One of the key features of Greenstone is that it is quite easy to install, configure, customize and administer, even by the novice. It also facilitates seamless aggregation and integration of the digital content possessed by the library.

Keywords: Digital Library, Institutional Repository, Greenstone Digital Library

1. INTRODUCTION

Libraries all over the world are in the constant business of providing their clientele nascent as well as legacy information and in the process they buy, subscribe, license and accumulate information in an unprecedented array of content categories or publication types, and in a rapidly proliferating mix of formats (digital as well as print). There is a great deal of cultural divide and philosophical deviation between the traditional information resources being handled by libraries for centuries now and the new genre of electronic and digital information being sourced and accessed. In the traditional paradigm, the books and journals bought and subscribed to by the libraries were naturally owned by them, allowing them to make the best use of the resources within the 'fair use' clause or principle. Whereas in the electronic publishing scenario all the traditional belief, approach and understanding about the digital documents that the library purchase / subscribe to, have a world of difference. Libraries get only a license to use the electronic information (books, journals, databases, softwares etc.) while purchasing, and even this license is issued only for a prescribed period of time. Librarians at same time, have the professional responsibility to assure uninterrupted as well as perpetual access to the information subscribed to by the library. Issues of copyright, intellectual property, and fair use are very much important to libraries [Orsdel, 2002].

In the current practical library setting there is an amazing penetration of digital information through a variety of publication forms such as books (published as such or issued as accompaniment), journals, portals, vortals, reports, CBTs, WBTs, cases, databases etc. The penetration level of electronic information in the special libraries and libraries belonging to centers of higher learning are supposed to be 70% as against their print counterparts. To make matters more complex the vast array of different formats, standards and platforms in which documents are published, pose a multiplicity of threats to the librarian who is supposed to be the custodian and service provider of these information products once it has found its way into the library. As librarians, we are sometimes the stewards of unique collections too.

2. DIGITAL LIBRARIES

Digital Libraries (DL) are now emerging as a crucial component of global information infrastructure, adopting the latest information and communication technology. Digital Libraries are networked collections of digital texts, documents, images, sounds, data, software, and many more that are the core of today's Internet and tomorrow's universally accessible digital repositories of all human knowledge. According to the Digital Library Federation (DLF, USA - http://www.dlf.org), "Digital libraries are organizations that provide the resources, including the specialized staff, to select, structure, offer intellectual access to, interpret, distribute, preserve the integrity of, and ensure the persistence over time of collections of digital works so that they are readily and economically available for use by a defined community or set of communities".

Currently in vast majority of instances, the concept 'Digital Library' is being practiced by and large loosely or even confused by many information systems. It is therefore imperative that the concept is properly understood so that there is no ambiguity while we progress with the work of designing or developing a digital library which is fully justified in the technical sense of the word. It is important that embarking on a digital library project is something which will take away substantial amount of time, energy, manpower and of course the hard earned money being pumped into it – be it for system development or towards development and maintenance of the collection, in a meaningful way. There is consensus all over that there exists a very large quantum of digital information, scholarly as well as trade, which are scattered and distributed throughout the Net and also being stored in numerous other databases and repositories spread across the world. Also there is an unprecedented technology support and availability of infrastructure for digital libraries.

3. DL SOFTWARE

Undoubtedly it is essential to have a robust and flexible digital collections management and presentation software for creating and delivering digital collections. The preservation of digital objects is currently intimately tied to software that presents those objects. Complete preservation of complex digital objects, especially, is likely to require preservation of the software needed to use those objects. [Borgman, 1996]. The complexity of the situation is that digital library technologies and contents are not static. Continual evolution and investment are required to maintain the digital library. Commercial digital library products are comprehensive and extensible enough to support this evolution, but in many cases they are beyond the reach of most of the libraries in India. Some of the popular commercial DL software in the Indian libraries are VTLS (http://www.vtls.com) from the international market and ACADO (*http://www.transversalnet.com/acado/index.htm*) as an Indian initiative. The latter is definitely less costlier when compared but still striving its best to get a critical mass of users. The whole lot of associated issues include initial purchase fee, licensing fee, upgrade fee, annual maintenance contacts (AMCs) and so on. The best available choice for the librarian now is to turn to an Open Source Software (OSS). OSS has grown tremendously in scope and popularity over the last several years, and is now in widespread use. The growth of OSS has gained the attention of research librarians and created new opportunities for libraries [Frumkin, 2002]. OSS is close to our hearts primarily for their free (or almost free) availability and the broad rights it awards to the consumer. According to Stallman and others at OSS, 'Free Software' uses the 'free' from 'freedom', not the one from 'free beer' [*http://www.opensource.org/docs/definition_plain.html*].

"OSS is software for which the source code is available to the end-user. The source code can be modified by the end-user. The licensing conditions are intended to facilitate continued re-use and wide availability of the software in both commercial and non- commercial contexts. The cost of acquisition to the end-user is often minimal. According to the proponents of OSS, 'Open source is a development methodology; free software is a social movement'. There are number of other notable features to OSS. Firstly, it has no secrets and the innards are available for anyone to inspect. It is not privately controlled and hence likely to promote open rather than proprietary formats. It is typically maintained by communities rather than corporations and hence bug fixes and enhancement are often frequent and free. It is usually distributed free of charge (developers make their money from support, training, and specialist add-ons; not marketing). It is also essential to clear up some of the misunderstandings about OSS. Open source software may or may not cost money. The cost of ownership often bears little relation to the cost of acquiring a piece of software. 'Public domain' is something different. Open source software has a copyright holder and conditions of legal use. Open source software does not mandate exclusivity. One can use open source programs under Windows. Also one should not choose software solely on the basis of open source. Interoperability and open standards for data are equally important" [OSS Watch, 2005].

According to Altman, for the library fraternity there are other set of reasons too for preferring OSS over commercial software. Long term preservation, assurance of privacy, provision for auditing, facilitating community resources, and conformity to open standards are hallmarks of OSS. Since commercial software is usually distributed only as a binary that will run only on a single hardware platform (and often only under a single version of a particular operating system) commercial software is very difficult to preserve over the long run without developing hardware emulation (and possibly OS 'emulation', as well). OSS, in contrast, can often be recompiled, or at least ported, to new hardware and operating systems [Altman, 2001]. In order to get a picture about the availability of OSS for digital library applications, it is encouraged to visit the directories of OSS projects, such as GNU [*http://www.gnu.org/*] and Sourceforge [*http://www.sourceforge.net/*] open source directory which lists over fifty-thousand projects, and the numbers continue to grow.

4. SELECTION OF THE DL SOFTWARE

The software selection based on set parameters is an uphill task, as the technology itself was still emerging only. In general, what is desirable is a system that is flexible enough to fit the current digital information system as above and to accommodate future migration. It should be robust in technical architecture as well as the content architecture. The system should address all major digital library related issues such as 'design criteria', 'collection building', 'content organisation', 'access', 'evaluation', 'policy and legal issues' including 'intellectual property rights'. That the system should be in a position to embrace almost all predominant and emerging digital object formats and capable of supporting the standard library technology platforms, should be the major focus. It should provide two important user interfaces: a public user interface for presentation and a metadata creation interface for administration. The system should also provide a powerful search engine and the interface should be easy to navigate and there should be provision for customisation.

There are many digital library softwares available, proprietary as well as open source, and most of them conform to international standards. As mentioned earlier, VTLS and ACADO are the commercial ones available and popular in the Indian market. Some of the popular Open Source Softwares for digital libraries, which are in use internationally, are 'DSpace', 'Dienst', 'Eprints', 'Fedora', 'Greenstone' etc. In line with the subject thrust of this paper, the Greenstone features are discussed in this paper.

5. DEVELOPING DIGITAL LIBRARIES USING OPEN SOURCE SOFTWARE

Digital libraries do enable the creation of local content, strengthen the mechanisms and capacity of the library's information systems and services. They increase the portability, efficiency of access, flexibility, availability and preservation of content. A state-of-art Digital Library shall give a real boost to the library's modernization activities and its endeavours to launch innovative digital information services to the user community. Once the information is made digital, it could be stored, retrieved, shared, copied and transmitted across distances without having to invest any additional expenditure. Value added and pinpointed information at the click of the mouse will become a reality if there is a Library Portal to provide access to the invaluable collection hosted by the Digital Library.

World over there is increasing appreciation of the Open Access movement and the Open Source Software philosophies and for may a libraries it is a chosen decision, be it technical or financial reasons, not to go for a proprietary digital library software. One needs to evaluate some of the popular Open Source Software for digital libraries, which are in use internationally. 'Dienst', 'Eprints', 'Fedora', 'Greenstone' etc. are among the candidates for the preferred software. Obviously **Greenstone** outscores the group as a general purpose digital library software from the point of view of a multi-publication type, multi-format, multi-media and a multi-lingual practical digital library [Greenstone]. And once finalized, it could be formally adopted as the software for creating the digital library.

The **Greenstone Digital Library Software (GSDL)** is a top of the line and internationally renowned Open Source Software system for developing digital libraries, promoted by the New Zealand Digital Library project research group at the University of Waikato, led by Dr. Ian H. Witten, and is sponsored by the UNESCO. Greenstone software uses three more additional associated softwares namely, Java Run Time Environment (JRE), ImageMagick and Ghostscript. The software suite is available at the open source directory 'Sourceforge.Net'.

6. GREENSTONE FACT SHEET (WWW.GREENSTONE.ORG)

Greenstone is a suite of software for building and distributing digital library collections. It is not a digital library but a tool for building digital libraries. It provides a new way of organizing information and publishing it on the Internet in the form of a fully-searchable, metadata-driven digital library. It has been developed and distributed in cooperation with UNESCO and the Human Info NGO in Belgium. It is open-source, multilingual software, issued under the terms of the GNU General Public License. Its developers received the 2004 IFIP Namur award for "contributions to the awareness of social implications of information technology, and the need for an holistic approach in the use of information technology that takes account of social implications."

There are presently two versions of Greenstone going around, Version 2 and 3, and they are generally represented as Greenstone2 and Greenstone3. The latest in Greenstone2 as on December 2013 is V.2.86 and that of Greenstone3 is V.3.05. Greenstone2 will be there for some more years, but ultimately Waikato/Greenstone see that Geenstone3 will replace it.

7. TECHNICAL FEATURES

7.1. Platforms

Greenstone runs on all versions of Windows, and Unix, and Mac OS-X. It is very easy to install. For the default Windows installation absolutely no configuration is necessary, and end users routinely install Greenstone on their personal laptops or workstations. Institutional users run it on their main web server, where it interoperates with standard web server software (e.g. Apache).

7.2. Interoperability

Greenstone is highly interoperable using contemporary standards, It incorporates a server that can serve any collection over the Open Archives Protocol for Metadata Harvesting (OAI-PMH), and Greenstone can harvest documents over OAI-PMH and include them in a collection. Any collection can be exported to METS (in the Greenstone METS Profile, approved by the METS Editorial Board and published at *http://www.loc.gov/standards/mets/mets-profiles.html*), and Greenstone can ingest documents in METS form. Any collection can be exported to DSpace ready for DSpace's batch import program, and any DSpace collection can be imported into Greenstone.

7.3. Interfaces

Greenstone has two separate interactive interfaces, the Reader interface and the Librarian interface. End users access the digital library through the Reader interface, which operates within a web browser. The Librarian interface is a Java- based graphical user interface (also available as an applet) that makes it easy to gather material for a collection (downloading it from the web where necessary), enrich it by adding metadata, design the searching and browsing facilities that the collection will offer the user, and build and serve the collection.

7.4. Metadata formats

Users define metadata interactively within the Librarian interface. These metadata sets are predefined: Dublin Core (qualified and unqualified) , RFC 1807, NZGLS (New Zealand Government Locator Service), AGLS (Australian Government Locator Service). New metadata sets can be defined using Greenstone's Metadata Set Editor. "Plug-ins" are used to ingest externally-prepared metadata in different forms, and plug-ins exist for XML, MARC, CDS/ISIS, ProCite, BibTex, Refer, OAI, DSpace, METS.

7.5. Document formats

Greenstone basically supports all popular file formats and media. Plug-ins are also used to ingest documents. For textual documents, there are plug- ins for PDF, PostScript, Word, RTF, HTML, Plain text, Latex, ZIP archives, Excel, PPT, Email (various formats), source code. For multimedia documents, there are plug-ins for Images (any format, including GIF, JIF, JPEG, TIFF), MP3 audio, Ogg Vorbis audio, and a generic plug-in that can be configured for audio formats, MPEG, MIDI, etc.

8. USER BASE

8.1. Distribution

As with all open source projects, the user base for Greenstone is unknown. Tens of thousands of installations of Greenstone are estimated across world as is evidenced by the increasing volume of messages being exchanged in the various fora, especially the Greenstone E-lists. It is distributed on SourceForge, a leading distribution centre for open source software.

8.2. Greenstone Example Collections

Examples of public Greenstone collections (see *http://www.greenstone.org* for URLs) can be found at:

- Association of Indian Labour Historians, Delhi
- Auburn University, Alabama
- California University at Riverside
- Chicago University Library
- Detroit Public Library
- Gresham College, London
- Hawaiian Electronic Library
- Illinois Wesleyan University
- Indian Institute of Management Kozhikode (IIMK)
- Kyrgyz Republic National Library
- LeHigh University, Pennsylvania
- Mari El Republic, Russia
- National Centre for Science Information, Bangalore, India
- Netherlands Institute for Scientific Information Services
- New York Botanical Garden

- Peking University Digital Library
- Philippine Research Education and Government Information Network
- Secretary of Human Rights of Argentina
- Slavonski Brod Public Library, Slovenia
- State Library of Tasmania
- Stuttgart University of Applied Sciences
- Texas A&M University Center for the Study of Digital Libraries
- University of Illinois
- University of North Carolina Bibiblio project
- Vietnam National University
- Vimercate Public Library, Milan, Italy
- Washington Research Library Consortium
- Welsh Books Council

9. LANGUAGES

One of Greenstone's unique strengths is its multilingual nature. The reader's interface is available in the following languages: Arabic, Armenian, Bengali, Catalan, Croatian, Czech, Chinese (both simplified and traditional), Dutch, English, Farsi, Finnish, French, Galician, Georgian, German, Greek, Hebrew, Hindi, Indonesian, Italian, Japanese, Kannada, Kazakh, Kyrgyz, Latvian, Maori, Mongolian, Portuguese (BR and PT versions), Russian, Serbian, Spanish, Thai, Turkish, Ukrainian, Vietnamese.The Librarian interface and the full Greenstone documentation (which is extensive) is in: English, French, Spanish, and Russian.

10. TRAINING

Training is a bottleneck for widespread adoption of any digital library software. Greenstone's Waikato site *http://www.greenstone.org*; the Greenstone Wiki *http://*

greenstone.sourceforge.net/wiki/index.php/GreenstoneWiki, and the Greenstone Support for South Asia *http://greenstonesupport.iimk.ac.in* give many training materials and guidance on the software. It is observed that Greenstone training and workshops are quite common in digital library conferences and seminar all over the world and this itself speaks volumes the importance of Greenstone.

11. E-MAIL SUPPORT

There are many E-Lists and E-Groups available for Greenstone support. For subscribing to the main Greenstone lists, visit *https://list.scms.waikato.ac.nz/mailman/listinfo/greenstone-users* for User's List (*greenstone-users-request@list.scms.waikato.ac.nz*) and *https://list.scms.waikato.ac.nz/mailman/listinfo/greenstone-devel* for Developer's list. There is also an E-List for supporting the South Asian Greenstone users *greenstonesupport@iimk.ac.in.* You can join the South Asia Support E-List by filling the form at *http://eprints.iimk.ac.in/mailman/listinfo/greenstonesupport.*

12. GREENSTONE : FEATURES

The salient features of Greenstone are basically taken from two of the official publications of the software development team appeared in D-Lib Magazine during the year 2001 [Witten, 2001] and 2003 [Witten, 2003]. Greenstone builds collections using almost popular and standard digital formats such as HTML, XML, Word, Post Script, PDF, RTF, JPG, GIF, JPEG, MPEG etc. and many other formats which include audio as well as video. It is provided with effective full-text searching and metadata-based browsing facilities that are attractive and easy to use. Moreover, they are easily maintained and can be augmented and rebuilt entirely automatically. The system is extensible: software "plug-ins" accommodate different document and metadata types. Greenstone incorporates an interface that makes it easy for people to create their own library collections. Collections may be built and served locally from the user's own web server, or (given appropriate permissions) remotely on a shared digital library host. End users can easily build new collections styled after existing ones from material on the Web or from their local files (or both), and collections can be updated and new ones brought on-line at any time. The Greenstone Librarian Interface (GLI) is a Java based GUI interface for easy collection building. Greenstone software runs on a wide variety of platforms such as Windows, Unix / Linux, Apple Mac etc. and provides full-text mirroring, indexing, searching, browsing and metadata extraction. It incorporates an interface that makes it easy for institutions to create their own library collections. Collections could be built and served locally from the user's own web server, or (given appropriate permissions) remotely on a shared digital library host. The other set of features include OAI plug-in (introduced since the 2.40 version) and DCMI compliance, UNICODE based multi-lingual capabilities and a user-friendly multimedia interfacing [Unicode]. Further more, it has a powerful search engine 'Managing Gigabyte' Plus-Plus ('MG' PP) and metadata-based browsing facilities. A very interesting feature of Greenstone is its exhaustive set of well documented and articulated manuals (*http://www.greenstone.org/cgi-bin/library?e=p-en-docs-utfZz-8&a=p&p=docs)* such as 'Installer's Guide', 'User's Guide', 'Developer's Guide', and 'From Paper to Collection' a document describing the entire process of creating a digital library collection from paper documents. This includes the scanning and OCR process and the use of the "Organizer". There is one more interesting documentation 'Inside Greenstone Collections' which clarifies most of the trickier parts of using Greenstone, especially dealing with configuration file for the collection in question.The primary objective of any digital library will be to enhance the digital collection in a substantial way, by strategically sourcing digital materials, conforming to copyright permissions, in all possible standards / formats so that scalability and flexibility is guaranteed for the future and advanced information services and are assured to the user community right from beginning. The digital library has to be planned in such a way that it will integrate and aggregate the existing collections and services with an outstanding user interface. Accordingly, necessary strategies are to be adopted towards working out the digital library system. This implies that the digital library system should have a strong collection interface capable of embracing almost all the popular digital standards, digital formats and software platforms, in line with the underlying digital library technologies in vogue. This is crucial in the case of multimedia integration, which is again important as it is planned to host digital audio and video library as part of the core library collection.

13. GREENSTONE INSTALLATION

The GNU Public License version Greenstone can be downloaded from *'http://www.greenstone.org'* or *'http://sourceforge.net/index.php'*. You can download the binaries for Linux or Windows. The associated softwares such as Java Runtime Environment (JRE) and the Imagemagick also to be downloaded. A graphical tool is used for collection building and configurations and customization. This is called the Greenstone Librarian Interface (GLI) and it requires the Java Runtime Environment (JRE). The latest version pertaining to Volume 2 release of Greenstone as on December 2013 is V.2.86.

14. COLLECTION BUILDING AND CONFIGURATION

Greenstone used to have three modes for collection building, viz., Command Line, Web Interface and the

Greenstone Librarian Interface (GLI). Among these GLI is the one getting more prominence as far as the librarian / information professionals are concerned.

15. GREENSTONE LIBRARIAN INTERFACE (GLI)

The GLI (Greenstone Librarian Interface) was introduced recently, progressing with the version 2.4x. Soon the GLI got strengthened as well as popularized, and the Web Interface mode has been withdrawn temporarily, while it could also be reinforced if one wishes so. The GLI based collection building is quite easy and simple a method. Collection developers can activate the GLI software and use the '**Gather**', '**Enrich**', '**Design**', '**Create**', and the '**Format**' panels for making, configuring, customizing and managing collections.

16. HIERARCHY STRUCTURE

To create indexes for section and sub-section, the pre-requisite is that the document should be in HTML format. Therefore your collection files in other formats like PDF, Word, etc. are first to be converted into HTML format. Also in the Collection Configuration file (for GLI, in the Design Panel, in the Document Plugin section, while configuring the Arguments in the HTML Plugin, click and enable the 'description_tags'), the HTML plugin has to be modified to 'plugin HTMLPlug –description_tags'. Corresponding changes have to be made in the 'indexes' and the 'collectionmeta' lines. Obviously now the Source File has to be edited as a HTML file structure. For the section and sub sections, you need to edit the source file as follows, giving XML tags as comments in the body of the HTML file.

16.1. Customization of User Interface (MyLibrary)

In order to change the look and feel of the Greenstone user interface, you need to work on the Collection Configuration (Collect.cfg) files. Customising the User Interface requires a certain degree of knowledge on HTML and some level of Web Designing skills are pre-requisites for this.

17. GSDL : HELPLINE, ARCHIVES

Greenstone's E-Mail list is a very useful and active listserv which shares and clarifies user experiences and stories dealing with real life situations. To subscribe or unsubscribe to the list via the World Wide Web, visit "https://list.scms.waikato.ac.nz/ mailman/listinfo/ greenstone-users" or, via email, send a message with subject or body 'help' to *"greenstone-users-request@list.scms.waikato.ac.nz"*. Greenstone has started one more List recently, for the Greenstone 3 Version (the latest Beta version) user group, and the details are available at "https://list.scms.waikato.ac.nz/mailman/ listinfo/greenstone3".UNESCO has initiated a Greenstone support organization for South Asia in 2006, supported by a group of experts in the region, and it is coordinated by IIM Kozhikode *http://greenstonesupport.iimk.ac.in.* The site is rich with many of the Greenstone support materials. In addition, an E-list *greenstonesupport@iimk.ac.in* offers online support to professionals on Greenstone.For those looking for quick solutions for their real-time or on-the-job trouble shooting while using the software, 'Greenstone Archives' is a treasure house. It is a database of the email messages circulated in the List, and is searchable. The mails generated from the List and its threads are archived and made available for the user community. The archive is available at *"http://www.sadl.uleth.ca/nz/cgi-bin/ library?a=p&p=about&c=gsarch-e"*. This is the major list used worldwide for Greenstone and the content of the messages is usually global in nature. Developers and Greenstone users can avoid a great deal of unwanted labour by carefully going through the archive before they start working on problem solving, or before shooting a mail to the List.

18. CONCLUSION

The ever changing landscape of the information paradigm poses a host of new IT and information challenges not only to the library and information professionals, but to the users, patrons and scholars and the publishing community as well. Indeed the new environment throws up a host of unprecedented features and avenues, and interestingly enough, if we know how to tap them well, we find there is a plethora of opportunities, and most of them even for free. The 'free things', so belovedly called world wide the 'Open Source Softwares', many of them could even be compared against their commercial counterparts in terms of their strength, efficiency, power and the ever increasing user base. Among the major challenges include the information professionals' emergent need to acquire the necessary skill sets and working knowledge on the cutting- edge information science and information technology areas and in leveraging them in a contextually relevant manner.

Working on a Digital Library project in general, especially working with the Greenstone Digital Library Software in particular, has been highly exhilarating, enriching as well as rewarding. The treasure of knowledge, skills, experience, expertise, and exposure we have achieved and accomplished during the past four years have been extremely enjoying and simply terrific. It is also important sharing the real life experience of a particular software as a an application user, as there exist a great deal of difference in view points when it comes from the software developers themselves. Frankly, we also have grown with the software from strength to strength. We have every appreciation to Greenstone as far as its usability, extensibility and flexibility are concerned. We are also indeed pleased with its consistent technology catch-up strategies and their untiring extension activities. One should appreciate the dynamic Greenstone team for their selfless open source philosophy, and their relentless work in this regard just for the cause of science. We have been closely watching the world scenario in the area of digital library research and we are quite convinced that Greenstone is a fast growing community coupled with deep commitments from the developers in taking this software to further heights and making this an outstanding open source model for digital library development. The Wiki and the OAI features of Greenstone and the ambitious 'Greenstone 3', released already and running in its version 3.04, which draws its strength from the open source family of 'Web Services' technologies facilitating configurable, extensible and dynamic digital libraries are all testimony to their commitment to excellence in digital library softwaredevelopment. In the meanwhile UNESCO came forward to support them unconditionally and it is a proud privilege to announce that we have the Greenstone Support for South Asia already launched with their support, to take care of the DL needs of this region.

REFERENCES

1. Orsdel, Lee Van; Born, Kathleen. 2002 Doing the Digital Flip.*Library Journal,* 127 (7): 51-55.
2. OCLC Report on Five-Year information format trends. 2003 <*http://www.oclc.org/reports/2003format.htm*>
3. Marchionini, G. 1998 Research and development in digital libraries. Allen Kent (Ed.) *Encyclopedia of Library and Information Science,* 63: 259-279.
4. ICDL 2004. <*www.teriin.org/events/icdl/background.htm*>
5. Sreekumar M.G. and Sunitha T. 2005 Essential Strategies and Skill Sets Towards Creating Digital Libraries Using Open Source Software. [Proceedings of NACLIN 2005, DELNET, Bangalore, India].
6. Borgman, Christine L. 1996 Social Aspects of Digital Libraries,pp170[Proceedings of the first ACM international conference on Digital libraries Bethesda, Maryland, United State, March 20-23, Organised by Association of Computing Machinery]

7. Frumkin, Jeremy (ED). 2002 Special Issue: Open Source Software *Information Technology and Libraries* 21*(1)*
8. Stallman, Richard <*http://www.opensource.org/docs/* definition_plain.html>
9. OSS Watch <*http://www.oss-watch.ac.uk/talks/2003-09-24-* csg/index.xml.ID=body.1_div.37>
10. Altman, M. 2001 Open Source Software for Libraries: from Greenstone to the Virtual Data Center and Beyond. IASSIST Quarterly. Winter : 1-7.
11. GNU (GNU's Not Unix!) <*http://www.gnu.org/* (13 June, 2005)>
12. SourceForge.Net (world's largest Open Source software development website)<*http://www.sourceforge.net/*>
13. RDF (Resource Description Framework) <*http://www.w3c.org/RDF*>
14. DCMI (Dublin Core Metadata Initiative) <*http://dublincore.org*>
15. Greenstone Digital Library Software <htttp*://www.greenstone.org*>
16. Witten, Ian H. et al. 2001 Greenstone : Open-Source Digital Library Software*D-Lib Magazine,* 7 (10): 1-16.
17. Witten, Ian H. 2003 Examples of Practical Digital Libraries : Collections Built Internationally Using Greenstone *D-Lib Magazine* 9 (3): 1-15.
18. Unicode Consortium <htttp://unicode.org>
19. IIMK Digital Library <*http://iimk.ac.in/gsdl/cgi-bin/library*>
20. Greenstone Support for South Asia <*http://greenstonesupport.iimk.ac.in*

7

Content Management Systems and Library Portal

Dr. Sangita Purohit

ABSTRACT

Library website is considered as a communication tool, which help to create and publish the information regarding its activities and services. Development of websites using traditional technologies involve big amount of coding and great efforts in small tasks. Academic libraries, and their parent institutions, are increasingly using Content Management Systems (CMS) for website portal managements. Today librarians are using various kind of Open Source Software for various purposes like Library Automation , Digitization , Institutional Repository etc. CMS has excellent indexing and retrieval features with integrated meta-search and content management system to manage online, offline digital as well as physical resources. Librarians can create their library website without knowledge of HTML programming.

Keywords: Content Management System, Library Portal

1. INTRODUCTION

Library websites have evolved over the years, so has their role and complexity. In the beginning, the purpose of most library websites was to convey basic information, such as hours and policies to library users.

As time passed, more and more library products and services became available online, increasing the size and complexity of library websites In this age of Information & Communication Technology (ICT), website has become one of the most powerful tools to accelerate the awareness of users about the activities and services of libraries and information centers. Developing a library website and making it up-to-date at regular interval is one of the most creative and challenging work, all of which require sound knowledge and professionalism of library personnel on web designing along with performing their day to day library activities

Library portals are important vehicles by which to support the information needs and uses of library patrons. These systems provide users with convenient, personalized Web-based access to a comprehensive collection of information resources of relevance and authority. Moreover, library portals support a broad range of information seeking activity from browsing to search, provide mechanisms for communication and collaboration, and facilitate knowledge creation and sharing – all through a usable, intuitive interface

A library Web portal has the potential of changing how libraries are used and how librarians will do their work. These portals have the potential of bringing about real change to our professional and organizational culture. These changes will enable libraries to be customer centered. Systems and processes will be based on dynamically linked and scalable databases that will enable library staff to concentrate on content delivery and teaching. These trends will inevitably enhance the academic library's ability to deliver positive learning outcomes to customers and stakeholders.

However, library portals are slightly different than enterprise portals. Though both provide a path to all-encompassing content and services from one access point, library portals serve patrons who may or may not be members of a single organization and, as a result, have a wider range of information needs and a larger distribution of people in terms of their familiarity and comfort with computers. For example, in an academic setting, library portals would serve students, faculty, alumni, community members, as well as the general public. Here, the library portal serves as a gateway by which students and faculty can locate and access information resources in a convenient and efficient manner, as well as a place where teaching and learning can occur

Earlier websites were developed using Hyper Text Markup Language (HTML), and with further developments in technology website designers started using XHTML, CSS, JavaScript, VBScript, AJAX and XML. Development of websites using such technologies involve much amount of coding and big efforts in small tasks such as alignment of its contents. Many academic library web designers found that their web authoring tools were no longer adequate for their needs and turned to content management systems to help them manage and maintain their websites / web portal. For other web designers, the choice was not theirs to make. Their institution transitioned to a CMS and required the academic library to follow suit, regardless of whether the library staff had a say in the selection of the CMS or its suitability for the library environment

2. WHAT IS CONTENT MANAGEMENT?

A content management system (CMS) is a computer application used to create, edit, manage, and publish in a consistently organized fashion. CMSs are frequently used for storing, controlling, versioning, and publishing documentation. The content managed info may include computer files, image media, audio files, video files, electronic documents, and Web content. CMS and Wikis are great tools for libraries. It can also be defined as "A content management system is software that is used to support the creating, updating, publishing, translating, archiving, and retiring of digital information. Standard features, such as tracking the changes made to digital information are often included". CMS is a generic term that can be applied to many different types of software. Subcategories of CMS include web content management and digital asset management software.

A content management system provides an interface for content providers to add their contributions to the Web site without requiring knowledge of HTML; it separates the layout and design of the Web pages from the content, and provides the opportunity for reuse of both content and the code running the site. These features of a CMS permit a library to professionalize its Web site by enforcing a consistency of design across all pages, while at the same time increasing efficiency by making the maintenance of the content itself less technically challenging

- Librarians need not to know the Content Management technology, but they need to understand it. They will still need a committed technical assistance to help in deciding and implementing the appropriate solution, in terms of interoperability and scalability suitable to the library requirements. In order to meet this recommendation, the librarians should be made aware of the potential strengths of CM, and should play a proactive role in exploiting these systems.
- Libraries must strive to adopt and adhere to open frameworks - open source, open access, and open standards which when put together will offer significant benefits of free flow of information to libraries using CMS.
- Efforts of CM implementation within libraries are much more in India, and libraries are emitting signals of its impending need. The effects of CM in

these libraries would be long-term but not necessarily immediate. The organization and deliveries of information are far more too complex for legacy systems to handle, yet not so complex to demand a high-end CM solution. CM implementations can be effective only if they are 'integrated' with present legacy systems

3. HOW DOES IT WORK?

CMS consists of a set of core modules and a further, more larger set of optional modules. The core modules must be installed and decisions made about what, if any, optional ones to use. A basic website can be constructed using only the core modules. The extra modules act as extensions to the software, similar to the plug-ins and add-ons used by web browsers. These enable administrators to add more functionality to their websites. All this CMS software is free and developed by a community of programmers, who either see a need and create a module to fit, or create one to fit their own need and then make it available..

Once set up, it is a simple matter to login to the software and create content, work on particular pages, customizing, adding content, creating views, drawing in content from other sources to display on your site and much more. Once installed, it is a very easy interface to work with, even for a novice web content creator. The following types of material records can be managed with CMS;

- Language material
- Notated music
- Cartographic material
- Manuscript cart material
- Projected medium
- Nonmusical sound recording

- Musical sound recording
- Two-dimensional, non-projected graphics
- Computer file
- Kit
- Mixed materials
- Three-dimensional objects
- Manuscript language material

4. CONTENT MANAGEMENT SYSTEMS: TRENDS IN LIBRARIES

When attending conferences and hearing the stories of other libraries, it became apparent that a typical relationship between librarians and a campus IT staff is often much less communicative and much less positive .. Because of the relatively smooth collaborative spirit, a librarian was invited to participate in the selection of a CMS system.

It was emphasized the advantageous relationships that can develop when a positive approach is used, "Rather than simply complaining that staff from other departments do not understand library needs, librarians should respectfully acknowledge that campus Web developers want to create a site that attracts users and consider how an attractive site that reflects the university's brand can be beneficial in promoting library resources and services

Content management systems uses different programming and technology such as PHP, ASP, PERL, Python and Java. Databases supporting are MySQL, Postgre and Oracle with Windows or Linux. Today most popular content management systems developed on PHP-MySQL-Windows/Linux platform. PHP is a popular open-source programming language used for developing server-side applications and dynamic web content. Configuration and installation of PHP based content management systems requires only minimum technical knowledge. Popular PHP-MySQL based content management systems are,

1. Adobe CQ
2. Alterian
3. Amaxus (Box UK)
4. Blaze (Byte9)
5. concrete5
6. Cookie Jar (Solid State Group)
7. Drupal (Acquia)
8. Ektron
9. EPiServer
10. GOSS Interactive
11. IBM Web Content Manager
12. Joomla (Open Source Matters)
13. LavaSuite Content (DesignUK)
14. Limelight Networks Dynamic Site Platform
15. OpenText Web Experience Management
16. SDL Tridion (SDL)
17. SilverStripe
18. Sitecore
19. Squiz Matrix (Squiz)
20. TERMINALFOUR

All these open source content management systems are powerful, multifunctional and can be used to develop websites, intranet and portals.

5. CONTENT MANAGEMENT SYSTEM REQUIREMENTS

The requirements were gathered into few categories: Content Creation and Ownership, Content Management, Publishing, Presentation, and Administration and Technical. These categories were modeled after those used for the library portal. The full list is detailed below...

Content Management

A. Link maintenance

- Does not allow internal pages to be deleted if linked to by another CMS page
- Can regularly check the viability of externals links
- Periodic reminders to content owners to check their content

B. Way to repurpose content elements to multiple pages for content such as:

- Descriptions of article and research databases
- Highlight or feature content elements

C. Access controls

- That allows content owners to only edit their content
- That allows web liaisons to provide first line support for their departments.

Content Creation and Ownership Requirements

A. Content owners can create tables and/or databases for display of tabular in the web GUI interface

B. Multi-user authoring without overwriting

C. Option for faculty and professional staff to have pages featuring their work and their profiles

- All staff must have some control over the personal information available about them on the public Web site

D. Metadata created and maintained for each Web page or equivalent content level that contains:

- Owner
- Subject terms or tags describing the content

E. Handle a large number of content providers

F. Web-based GUI content-editing environment that

is intuitive and easy to learn without knowledge of HTML

G. Integrate RSS and other dynamic content from other sources handle different content types, including:
   - Text
   - Images
   - Videos
   - Camtasia/Captivate tutorials
   - Flash files

H. Separation of content and presentation: the content can add and edit content without impact on the presentation

Presentation

A. Searching
   - Search engine for Web site
   - Can pass searches on to other library web servers

B. Meets established usability standards

C. Delivery presentable in the browsers used most heavily by OSU Libraries Web sites visitors

D. Easy search engine optimization

E. Page load time is acceptable

F. Dynamic navigation generated for main and sub-sections of Web site that includes breadcrumbs and menus

G. Meets ADA and W3C Accessibility requirements

H. Code validates to current HTML specifications

I. Mobile device friendly version (optional)

6. CONCLUSION

After the arrival of web 2.0 technologies many tools are there in the market , which are more flexible and easier than the traditional tools. The new technologies include content management systems (CMS), Blogs, wikis, and RSS etc. A CMS is a computer application that enables users to manage content in an orderly fashion. The benefit of using a CMS, especially for website creation, is that it does not require an extensive knowledge of coding. The adoption of CMSs to manage academic libraries' websites is increasing, but not all CMSs are created equal. When given input into switching website management tools, library staff have many factors to take into consideration. These include, but are not limited to, in -house technical expertise, desirability of open source solutions, satisfaction of peer libraries with considered systems, and library specific needs, such as workflow management and customization requirements.

REFERENCES

1. Egbert De Smet. *ABCD: A New FOSS Library Automation Solution Based on ISIS.* Information Development. (2009). 25; 61-67
2. Library Website Design and Management (April 2012): no. 2 91–100. *Journal of Electronic Resources Librarianship*
3. Holly Yu, ed., *Content and Workflow Management for Library Web Sites :Case Studies* (2005) Hersey, PA: Information Science Publishing
4. Michael Seadle, "Content Management Systems," *Library Hi Tech* (2006) 24, no. 1, 5-7
5. Terry L. Huttenlock, Jeff W. Beaird, and Ronald W. *Fordham,* "Untangling a Tangled Web: a Case Study in Choosing and Implementing a CMS," *Library Hi Tech* (2006) 24, no. 1 , 61-68
6. Doug Goans, Guy Leach and Teri M. Vogel,"Beyond HTML: Developing and Re-imagining Library Web Guides in a Content Management System," *Library Hi* Tech (2006) 24, no. 1,29-53
7. Yan Han, "Digital Content Management: the Search for a Content Management System," *Library Hi Tech* (2004) 22, no. 4, 355-365
8. David Kane and Nora Hegarty, "New Web Site, New

Opportunities: Enforcing Standards Compliance within a Content Management System," *Library Hi Tech* (2007) 25, no. 2 , 276-287

9. Ed Sal CMS Matrix, "The Content Management Comparison Tool," *http://cmsmatrix.org/* (accessed August 16, 2010).

10. De Smet, Egbert; & Dhamdhere, Sangeeta N. (2010). ABCD: An open source automation tool for libraries. *Pearl: A Journal of Library and Information Science,* 4(4), 215-219. Also available online at: *http://www.scribd.com/doc/49086810/ABCD-as-a-Digital-Library-Tool*

8

Indian Copyright (Amendment) Act 2012 and Libraries

Dr.Veerankutty Chelatayakkot

ABSTRACT

In the age of digitization and digital library, it is very important to librarians to understand to what extend they can digitize a copyrighted work. The author examines the 'fair dealing' exception in Indian Copyright (Amendment) Act 2012. According to author, in the light of Section 52(1) (o) and 52(1) (n) of Copyright Act, a public library can digitize any document which are available in the library in non-digital format for preservation purpose only and can make three (hard) copies of a book for library use (circulation also) if that book is not available for sale in India.

Keywords : Indian Copyright Act, fair dealing

1. INTRODUCTION

There was no copyright law till 17th century. The invention of printing press necessitated some regulations to printing and publishing. Till that time, people had limited access to manuscripts and can make handwritten copies or memorise them. In 1709, the British Parliament enacted first Copyright statute known as Statue of Anne[1] This law granted some right to authors to control over the printing of their work and sue for infringement. By the law, authors got some monitory benefit and that encouraged the community to write more.

2. INDIAN COPYRIGHT ACT, 1957

After the independence, Government of India enacted Copyright Act in 1957. Similar to other countries, Indian Copyright Act 1957 also provides some 'fair dealing' exception along with privileges to authors. Section 52 of Copyright Act carries an extensive narration of uses by various actors - both individual and institutional - that would not amount to infringement of copyright.

Section 52(1) (o) of Indian copyright Act 1957 declare that "the making of not more than three copies of a book (including Pamphlet, sheet of music, map, chart or plan) by or under the direction of the person in charge of a public library for the use of library, if such book is not available for the sale in India."

As per this clause, public libraries can make three copies of a book if that book is not available for sale in India. This clause is very clear, but the terms 'book', 'public library' and 'use of library' have not been explained well. A library may have the collection of books and non-book materials. Whether this exception is applicable to non-book materials? Similarly, in the absence of a definition to 'public library' we have to adopt definition of public library from other enactment done by State legislature in Public library Acts. Similar concern may arise in the wording 'not available for sale in India'. Suppose, if a particular edition of a book is not available for sale, whether the library can make three copies of that particular book? Even though some vacuum opens in wordings, the law permits public library to make three copies of a book for the use of library.

After the enactment of the Indian Copyright Act in 1957, the World witnessed drastic technological changes especially in Information Communication Technology during last two decades. Due to the technological development, the word 'copies' is become unqualified, and could quite naturally include the freedom to make 'electronic copies' so long as other requirements of the clause especially that the copy being required for the "use of the library " are fulfilled [2]. The emergence of new technologies in reproduction and dissemination necessitated some amendments in Indian Copyright Act, 1957.

3. THE COPYRIGHT (AMENDMENT) ACT 2012

In June 8, 2012, Copyright (Amendment) Act 2012 came into force. This act introduced a number of amendments in Copyright Act 1957. The Section deals with fair use by the library are also amended. Section 52(1) (o) amended by substituting the word 'public library' with 'non-commercial public library'. However, there is no well explanation to the word 'non-commercial public library'. On the same time, in Section 2 (fa) of amendment, an explanation is given to 'non-profit library' or 'non-profit educational institution' as follows.

"Non profit library or no-profit educational institution means a library or educational institution which receives grant from the Government or exception from payment of Income Tax under the Income Tax Act 1961." If a similar definition is given to 'non-commercial public library', it will reduce unambiguous.

Another remarkable amendment which relates to library is the permission to digitization of non-digital work for preservation purposes. The Section 52(1) (n) read as follows.

"The storing of a work in any medium by electronic means by non-commercial public library, for preservation if the library already possesses a non-digital copy of the work"

As per this clause, a library can digitize any document for preservation if the library already possesses a non-digital copy of the work.

4. DISCUSSION

In the age of digitization and digital library, it is very important for librarian to understand to what extend they can digitize a copyrighted work. Section 52(1) (o) permits library to make three copies of a book for *the use of library* if the book is not available for sale in India. But there is no explanation to word 'copies' in the amendment in the light of digitalization. At the same time, as per Section 52(1) (n), libraries have permission to digitalize any work which is available in the library in non-digital format *for preservation* purpose.

When we analyse these two clauses together, the following interpretations are possible. Firstly digitization is permitted for preservation purpose only and such materials *cannot be circulated.* Secondly, a library can make and use i.e. *circulate* three (*hard)* copies of book which is not available for sale in India. Here, the word 'hard'(supplemented by the author) is very important in the light of digitalization. The limit of three (in quantity) indicates the *physical form* of the book not in *digital form.* There is no meaning to limit the quantity of copies *(digital or soft)* while we digitize a book.

Thirdly, the clause 52(1) (o) used the word 'book' and clause 52(1) (n) used the word 'work'. Here, the 'work' is a broader term and 'book' is a narrow term. Libraries are a store house of documents which consists of book and non-book materials. So a library can digitalize any materials (work) for preservation and can make three copies of a 'book'.

5. CONCLUSION

In the light of Copyright (Amendment) Act 2012, we may conclude that a library can make digital copy of a work for preservation purpose only i.e. *not for circulation.* Similarly, *a* Library can make up to three (*hard copy)* of *a book* for the *use* of library i.e. *library can circulate.* These two activities will be considered as 'fair dealing' and will not come under infringement of Copyright.

REFERENCE

1. Narayanan P. *Copyright Law,* Culcutta: Eastern Law House, 1986 p.5
2. Prashant Iyengar "The Library Exception under the Indian Copyright Act 1957" in *Digital Content Copyright: Challenges to Libraries,* Inter University Centre for Intellectual Property Right, Cochin University of Science and Technology, 2011 p.70-101.

PART II
HUMAN RESOURCE MANAGEMENT

9

Soft Skills and Proficient Library and Information Professionals Personality

Prof. A. Amudavalli

ABSTRACT

A literature review of competencies needed in Library & Information Science (LIS) industry clearly indicates that expectations of recruitment forces are more than that of the formal & traditional technical skills. What does that imply??? In the New Age a LIS personality with new skills is the desired and expected features to be a proficient professional. The set of new skills widely range from personality to business skills. The significant issue is its inclusion in formal education stream and as well subsequently in-house training for those employed to update and brush themselves periodically to meet the changing information environment. The need for the soft skills amongst the LIS professionals and training, formal and informal, are emphasized in this paper.

Keywords : Soft skills, Skill Training, Proficient LIS Professional, Professional Development

1. INTRODUCTION

Personality Development is gaining more and more importance because it enables people to create a good impression about themselves on others. It helps them to build and develop relationships, helps in your career growth and also helps to improve your financial needs. After all, Personality Development is nothing but a tool that helps you realize your capabilities and your strengths making you **a stronger, a happier and a cheerful person.** An individual's personality is an aggregate conglomeration of the decisions they have made throughout their life and the memory of the experiences to which these decisions led. There are inherent natural, genetic, and environmental factors that contribute to the development of our personality. Amongst the environmental factors, the major is one's profession and the workplace related issues. Everyone wants to be successful in one's career. One needs to rediscover one's strength & weaknesses to move forward. Change and challenges are inevitable. Skills – personal and professional are two eyes of a professional. Technical and job-related skills are a must, but they are NOT sufficient when it comes to progressing up the ladder. With the traditional paternalistic style of leadership becoming passé, professionals are expected to be proactive and communicate openly. Soft skills are personal attributes that enhance an individual's interactions, job performance and career prospects. Unlike hard skills, which are about a person's skill set and ability to perform a certain type of task or activity, soft skills are interpersonal and broadly applicable.

2. SOFT SKILLS

Soft skills is a sociological term relating to a person's, the cluster of personality traits, social graces, communication, *language*, personal habits, friendliness, and optimism that characterize relationships with other people. Soft skills are often described by using terms often associated with personality traits, such as:

- optimism
- common sense *"EQ" (Emotional Intelligence Quotient)*

- responsibility
- a sense of humor
- integrity

and abilities that can be practiced such as:

- empathy
- teamwork
- leadership
- communication
- good manners
- negotiation
- sociability
- teaching & training.

It is often said that hard skills will get you an interview but you need soft skills to get (and keep) the job.

Soft skills refer to the cluster of personality traits, social graces, facility with language, personal habits, friendliness, and optimism that mark people to varying degrees. Soft skills complement hard skills, which are the technical requirements of a job. They include both "personal skills" and "inter personal skills". It is essential to be technically sound, but one should also have the ability to convey the idea to the masses in the simplest possible manner. Their approachability and people skills are what ultimately sustain the contract their employers have bagged. Planning is necessary but execution is also equally important. And it takes soft skills to execute any idea because it involves dealing with people directly.

Behavioural training experts say that several soft skills are required in these circumstances. Some of them include:

- Communication
- Interpersonal skills

- Team spirit
- Social graces
- Business etiquette
- Negotiation skills
- Behavioural traits such as attitude, motivation and time management

3. NEED FOR SOFT SKILLS

Our education system has a greater focus on learning analytical skills, logic, etc. This is important for technical education which is more structured. Soft skills training is no longer considered just a matter of self-development; companies are finally beginning to understand its value in doing business. The transformation that occurs in demeanor, language and conduct following even a two-day workshop justifies the time, effort and resource deployment in soft skills training. Soft skills are very important as they help :

- To take appropriate decisions
- To communicate effectively
- To have good impression and impact to gain professional development

There is a lot of argument in the industry as to whether it is possible to enhance soft skills in a few hours of training, especially when one considers the fact that a person has lived with those traits all his life. To this, the answer is harsh but real — a professional who wants to do well in his/ her career does not really have a choice.

Training on soft skills becomes all the more relevant in a countries like India and China where the education system does not delve sufficiently into personality development.

- In the initial years of one's career, technical abilities are important to get good assignments. However, when it comes to growing in an organisation, it is one's personality that matters.

- This is more so in large organisations where several people with similar technical expertise will compete for a promotion.
- Soft skills training are essential because we do not have it in our academic curricula.
- Therefore, corporate houses have felt it necessary to take up the task of grooming employees who are the link between the company and the external world, so that they are able to present themselves better

4. TYPES OF SOFT SKILLS

Based on more than three decades of professional and corporate experience, it is felt that at least 60 specific skills can be identified which are essential for entry into and subsequent performance in industry. These can be categorised into two basic categories:

4.1. Individual related skills

- Personal appearance
- Personal values
- Personal Behaviour
- Knowledge and Analytical skills
- Communication skills

Each of the above can be further subdivided into specific and definable attributes

4.2. Work related Skills

- Performance
- Social skills and etiquette
- Supervisory skills
- Corporate Understanding
- Work Life Balance

Each of the above can also be further subdivided

into several specific and definable attributes. Some examples:

Communication skills : Reading skills - Writing skills - Listening skills - Non verbal skills - Understanding and comprehension - Interviews - Business writing - Group discussions - Business meetings - Presentations - Business communications - e mail etiquette – conference calling - Negotiations .

Performance : Reliability – Flexibility - Team skills – Cooperation – Adaptability - Reporting to work on time - Wanting to do a good job – Following rules and regulations - being a good worker and going beyond the traditional eight-hour day – Dependability - Good attendance - Work experience - Good references.

To quote literature, the popular soft skill courses include:

- Advanced Interpersonal Communication
- Building Strategic Partnerships
- Business Ethics
- Business Problem Solving
- Business Writing
- Change Management
- Cross Cultural Business Communication
- Effective Presentations
- Effective Presentations
- E-mail Etiquette
- Financial Control
- Fund Raising
- Fundamentals of Customer Service
- Fundamentals of Customer Service
- Grammar Skills
- Interviewing Skills

- Language Proficiency
- Managerial Leadership
- Marketing
- Negotiation
- Personality Development
- Psychology
- Team Development
- Time Management

5. SOFT SKILLS TRAINER

Acquiring Soft Skills is not a one time activity but a continuous learning process. It needs to be viewed at three levels:

Employability skills: These have to be mastered by employable graduates and freshers and include communication, team working, leadership, initiative, problem solving, flexibility and enthusiasm.

Corporate skills: These are generally CEO level skills, and help in steering an organisation towards success i.e working together for a common goal as a team.

Life skills: These skills are related to the head, heart, hands and health i.e highly personal and behavioural skills which reflects our personality and naturally helps in personality development over a life time.

Many of us believe that there is nothing great in being a "trainer" for "Soft Skills". Haven't we all undergone training in some form or the other at some stage of our lives? And haven't we all trained others – children, subordinates, students.............. So why is Soft skills training different?

- The challenge for the Soft skills trainer is to exceed the expectations of the participants by providing them with information at the appropriate measure, way and time.

- The trainer should create a lot of learning as well as unlearning for the participants
- The learning experience must be delightful
- At the end of the day, the participant must be inspired to greater action
- At the end of the programme there must be at least one take home message for the participant
- And last but not least, the trainer must bring in "corporate" flavour to the training programme
- Soft skills training has been seen to be too important to be designed without a specialist, given the fact that IT companies run thin on resources in HR and training
- Hence a majority of IT companies are now outsourcing their requirements to training houses
- Outsourced companies perform objective analysis and proper Training Need Analysis (TNA) before they commence training.
- Customised solutions are offered for different batches and groups.

Academic institutions, particularly in India have their own constraints in imparting Soft Skills training as part of their regular programme. These include:

- Paucity of time
- Regular feedback from industry on the felt needs
- Consequently, the non availability of a structured syllabus to satisfy these needs
- Lack of trained faculty backed up by adequate corporate experience who could deliver the syllabus

The above obviously does not apply to institutions, like the University of Madras, which are already including Soft skills training as part of their structured curriculum or offering it as extracurricular options. In such cases, outsourcing is the order of the day. The fact is training human resources in new and soft skills is mandatory to raise as proficient professionals in any sphere of activity in this new age.

5.1. Attributes of a Soft skills trainer

- Deep understanding of human nature and behaviour
- Professional knowledge and experience
- Good Communication skills
- Pleasing personality
- Positive attitude
- Perseverance
- Result orientation
- Commitment
- Understand that each participant in a training programme is different
- Establish rapport with the group as a whole
- Encourage participation, particularly of the weaker participants
- Radiate good humour
- Remember the over all objectives
- Be flexible
- Lead by personal example
- Demonstrate empathy
- Highlight "Key learning"
- Relate them to the work spot
- Always have a "re-cap" of the programme

6. SOFT SKILLS TRAINEES - LIS PROFESSIONALS

A professional degree in the subject - Library and Information Science - is only the eligibility to enter the profession. Unlike the past, today the need of the hour is for those LIS professionals with multidimensional aptitude in the areas of technical work, administrative work and also in providing user oriented services along with soft skills. Like any other profession, the soft skills are required in day-to-day working for carrying out routine jobs more effectively. The librarians working in large organizations like corporate offices are already practicing these skills through by experience or training. One may learn these soft skills easily provided they are aware what these are!!

Other than the domain knowledge, the range of transferable and soft skills expected of LIS professionals include: generic and cut across disciplines, especially skills in communication (listening, speaking, writing, presentation), public relations, inter personal relation, customer services, motivation negotiation, marketing skills, management, leadership, language proficiency, teaching and training, and teamwork, as well as the ability to empathize with users and understand their information needs, IT skills, value-adding skills and appropriate attitudes, values and personal traits, especially those of user orientation and service orientation, flexibility and willingness to handle a wide range of tasks, adaptability and ability to handle change, continual learning, and an entrepreneurial attitude.

7. DISCUSSION

Skill building in the country is the need of the hour, especially when China, North America and Western Europe are behind India in terms of "demographic dividend. The education system needs to focus on communication and soft skills. For young professionals, there is a tremendous competition; soft skills would be added advantage to impress the prospective employers. Developing soft skills ensures graduate employability. Workforce gain access to employment and ensure India's competitiveness in the dynamic global market. Recruitment drives are directed towards communication and soft skills and they opine loud and clear that getting standard expected workforce with Library & Information professionals is a challenging factor.

The LIS schools have consciously included communication & soft skills as part of their syllabus. A sustainable solution is training of LIS professionals in site as the case may be. Training of trainers must be promoted to meet the demand and supply gap in the field of skill development. A series of workshops are organised all through the year by LIS Schools, Library Associations, Corporate Sectors, and Government Departments.

8. SUMMARY

Learning new skills is one of the best ways to make oneself both marketable and happy, but actually doing so isn't as easy as it sounds. The science behind how one learns is the foundation for teaching oneself new skills. Here's what we know about learning a new skill. Our brains are still a bit of a mystery. We'll likely be learning about how our brain works for years to come, but we are starting to get a better idea of how we learn new things. To that end, let's start by talking about what happens in your brain as you take on a new skill set before moving onto some of the scientifically effective ways to learn. Every time you learn something new, your brain changes in a pretty substantial way. In turn, this makes other parts of your life easier because the benefits of learning stretch further than just being good at something. Learning a new skill has all kinds of unexpected benefits, including improving working memory, better verbal intelligence, and increased language skills.

Lead researcher, Denise Park from the University's School of Behavioral and Brain Sciences, says: "*We need, as a society, to learn how to maintain a healthy mind, just like we know how to maintain vascular health with diet and exercise.*" We are constantly reminded to "use it or lose it. Park so poetically says: "*When you are inside your comfort zone you may be outside of the enhancement zone.*"

10

Workplace Learning in Academic Libraries

Dr. Mohamed Haneefa K.
Shyni K.G.

ABSTRACT

Workplace learning in academic libraries offers immense potentialities for library professionals to compete with latest developments in technology to deliver quality information resources and services. Scope of workplace learning in academic libraries has been enhanced by the invasion of Information and Communication Technologies. New tasks, roles, organisational structure, user expectations, services and learning environments are being established in academic libraries. These trends demand a rethinking and redesign in workplace learning in academic libraries. This paper discusses workplace learning in academic libraries in the changing electronic environment.

Keywords : Workplace learning, Academic libraries, Formal learning, Informal learning, Continuing Professional Development.

1. INTRODUCTION

Academic library services are getting transformed to new dimensions by adopting Information Communication Technologies (ICT). This transformation is triggered by increased user expectations and competition from IT professionals. The situation demands a new outlook on workplace learning in academic libraries. Workplace learning includes all the interventions in the workplace that assist the learning process and the internal and external factors contributing to it. This paper discusses the transformation in the workplace and the scope for workplace learning in academic libraries.

Changes in workplace are evident in the products, services and interfaces of academic libraries. Academic libraries are in the fore front with consortia of all types and at all levels with an objective to take advantage of current global network to promote better, faster and more cost-effective ways of providing electronic information resources to the information seekers. UGC-INFONET and INDEST are the two major e-journal and e-book consortia in academic libraries in India.

Open Source Software (OSS) have been implemented in libraries mainly for automated management, development of digital libraries, institutional repositories, and designing of library websites (Dora, Maharana & Jena, 2008). Government support towards this direction is encouraging. A move towards open access is observed in academic libraries in order to overcome the huge expense of buying e-resources, site licensing, purchasing and maintenance of software and hardware.

Libraries represent academic excellence of their parent organisations through institutional repositories which can be developed using open source software like DSpace and E-prints. Sawant (2011) reported that apart from institutional repositories, subject specific repositories like Librarians Digital Library (LDL) of the Documentation Research and Training Centre (DRTC), Bangalore, *OpenMed@NIC*, maintained by the National Informatics Centre, New Delhi and repository of document type specific collections such as Vidyanidhi of the

University of Mysore are remarkable contributions of libraries.

It is possible to create an interactive digital learning environment in academic libraries with effective utilisation of the latest developments in ICT. The major task before the professionals is to face the challenges and equip themselves with the digital learning environment. There is an increasing demand for transformation at the individual level regarding the work. The library professional as a learner in the workplace is to be recognised by the individuals as well as the management. Traditional role of librarian have been changed and the professional competencies have been redefined. So library professionals need to think deeply about what engagement in virtual world means for libraries and not assume that one can simply take what libraries are doing now into a new technological regime. Understand what this new environment can bring in the way of opportunities (Brantly, 2008). Workplace in academic libraries have some unique features such as its resources, services, in built learning environment, close association with education and research community, user interaction and opportunities for career development.

2. WORKPLACE LEARNING IN ACADEMIC LIBRARIES

Workplace learning is defined as a process whereby people, as a function of completing their organisational tasks and roles, acquire knowledge, skills, and attitudes that enhance individual and organisational performance (Hicks et al. 2007). Holliday and Retallick (1995) stated that workplace learning refers to the processes and outcomes of learning that individual employees and groups of employees undertake under the auspices of a particular workplace. A workplace is understood to include the physical location, shared meanings, ideas, behaviours and attitudes which determine the working environment and relationships. Workplace learning involves the process of reasoned learning towards desirable outcomes for the individual and the organisation. These outcomes should foster the sustained development of both the individual and the organisation, within the present and future context for achieving organisational goals and individual career development (Matthews, 1999).

Learning is an ongoing process in the life time of an individual. Learning is necessary to adapt with change, for professional growth, for personal growth, to understand people and to manage in the workplace (Sachanand, 2000). For a library professional, the workplace has a significant role to play in the process of learning. Learning occurs in the workplace by formal, informal and incidental means. Here the discussion is confined to those aspects of workplace learning associated with Human Resource Management (HRM) and Human Resource Development (HRD) in libraries. Workplace learning has gained attention in recent years as it is realised that there exists a positive correlation between organisational performance and workplace learning.

3. WORKPLACE LEARNING FACILITATORS

Individual learning situations in the workplace are formal or informal, can stimulate learning process. Workers achieve learning experiences from real work situations they are confronting with (Hicks et al. 2007). Workplace learning facilitators, specific to professionals or occupational groups (Eraut et al., 2003; Hicks et al, 2007) has been identified in previous studies. Facilitators of workplace learning are those factors that motivate, sustain and/or enhance learning. A broad classification can be made on the factors contributing to workplace learning as organisational factors, factors of informal learning and factors of formal learning in libraries.

3.1. Organisational Factors of Workplace Learning

Organisational factors affecting workplace learning include organisational climate of libraries and the managerial support from the authorities. Organisational and managerial support has been identified as a strong facilitator of workplace learning (Paula, 2011).

3.1.1. Organisational Climate

Cultural, structural, and managerial support in the organisation can create a work environment that is conducive to learning. Organisational climate factors like staff empowerment, shared leadership and mutual respect among staff, communication pattern, and clear decision-making structure matters in shaping a good organisational climate in academic libraries. The characteristics of climate also include motivational forces, goal-setting process, etc. These organisational factors reflect the personality of the organisation and affect employees' performance and attitude (Manorama Srinath, 1993). The workplace climate, if healthy, will attract and retain talented workers, which will, in turn, help the organisation to adapt to changes, navigate challenges, and plan succession more effectively (Li and Brayan, 2010). Organisational culture plays a crucial role regarding workplace learning as it has to create favourable conditions, stimulate and support employees, to acquire knowledge, search for their own solutions, and develop their own professional behaviour and expertise (Harrison & Kessels, 2004).

3.1.2. Managerial Support

As a manager the librarian can provide an adequate match between work and personal needs, and thus assist individual commitment and performance at work. These will in turn increases job satisfaction thereby improve individual commitment and performance at work. According to Ellinger (2005) organisational contextual factors are critical to determine informal learning in the workplace. As a manager, librarian can influence the employers to a great extent throughout the informal learning process. Ellinger identified those managers and leaders who create informal learning opportunities; serve as developers (coaches or mentors); visibly support and make space for learning; encourage risk taking; instil the importance of sharing knowledge and developing others; give positive feedback and recognition; and serve as role models positively influence informal learning in the workplace. The leadership style adopted by librarian may also play a role in shaping the workplace learning culture of libraries.

3.2. Informal Learning in Academic Libraries

Informal learning is a major form of learning in the workplace of academic libraries. It can be supported, encouraged and developed within organisational setting. According to Ellinger (2005) organisational contextual factors of leadership, internal culture, work tools and resources, human relations are significant contributors of informal learning in workplace.

Informal learning in the workplace occurs in different workplace environments in academic libraries. It is oriented to the self improvement to render quality service to the users. Informal learning is mediated through user interactions, queries at reference desk, and passive observation. Informal learning facilitators in libraries are the following.

3.2.1. The Job Itself

As a learning organisation libraries provide maximum opportunities for learning at work as the work itself is oriented to collection, organisation and dissemination of information. The services are designed so as to meet the information requirements of the user community extending from the institution to worldwide. Acquisition of workplace learning is associated with the entire process of knowledge organisation in libraries.

3.2.2. Exposure to Change

A library is an open system which holds the mission of service. Social responsibility of such a system is important. So the workers need to realise their roles to provide quality service to the society. Experience sharpens their attention towards providing a desirable outcome of their services. Attempts to keep pace with the latest developments in the field will give a competitive advantage to revamp the services.

3.2.3. Autonomy in Work

Job autonomy refers to the degree to which a job provides an employee with the direction and independence to schedule their work and determine how it is to be done. Studies have revealed that job autonomy is limited in librarianship. Job autonomy allows experimenting with the work. This may give opportunities to learn from the errors.

3.2.4. E-resources and E-learning Facilities

The nature of e-resources and services in academic libraries demand new skills and techniques for e-learning. So recognition of learning facilities in the workplace is essential for development. The learning environment in libraries are characterised by availability of information resources in different formats.

E-learning is evolving so quickly that those who are involved in training, teaching, and learning can remain in a perpetual state of learning, which can be turned to the advantage as trainer-teacher-learners. Fontanin (2010) observed that the e-learning platform created in the University library of Trieste, Italy, was a successful attempt were library professionals explored the possibilities of Moodle, a Learning Management System (LMS), to assist them for workplace learning.

Participating in Personal Learning Networks (PLN) enables to expand professional knowledge of employees through collaborative efforts. PLNs are often specifically devoted to professional learning and development, and are keenly applicable to use the technology, which makes them as local or global in reach as the learner desires. PLNs are a collection of resources to go to when you want to learn new ideas, strategies and information.

3.2.5. Professional Interest and Other Psychological Factors

Professional interest plays a crucial role in workplace learning. It is a motive for learning. A self motivated learner in the workplace will be a good recipient of knowledge and skills. Such an attitude can be developed at individual level. The workers are characterised by the features of adult learners with open mind, ability to learn from experiences, active listening, initiative and self efficacy. Professional associations can nurture a feeling of professional attachment to create a positive approach for workplace learning of library professionals.

3.3. Formal Learning in Academic Libraries

Formal learning is the outcome of planned, structured, instructor-led courses and programmes that are specific to organisation. Formal learning environments are created purposively to educate or train library professionals to keep pace with the latest developments in the field which may take the form of seminars, workshops and are linked to HRD policies of the library system. A positive organisational approach will promote workplace learning, contributing to organisational learning to organisational efficiency and to better services to the users of the library.

3.3.1. Quality of Work Life (QWL) Programmes

Learning opportunities has a role in promoting work satisfaction and, specifically, in enhancing the Quality of Work Life (Chiara, 2010). Job designs in libraries coupled with job enrichment or job enlargement can promote more avenues for the workers to develop their workplace learning. Job rotation is a workplace learning tool (Malinski, 2002) and can be used to promote employee learning (in that it makes employees more versatile) as well as employer learning (employers learn about individual employee's strengths through rotation) (Eriksson and Ortega, 2006). However, it has been suggested that job rotation is better at building some skills over others; for example, it improves knowledge about the organisation more than technical expertise (Campion, M., Cheraskin, L. and Stevens, M. 1994). Activities to promote teamwork and to create a learning culture can be initiated in libraries.

3.3.2. Continuing Professional Development Programmes (CPD)

Continuing Professional Development Programmes (CPD) can be experienced in different ways, both on the job and away from the workplace. The term Continuing Professional Education (CPE) or 'professional continuing education' is also used, notably in the US (Corrall, 2010). CPD is a structured approach to ensure competence to practice, taking in knowledge, skills and practical experience. It can involve any relevant learning activity, whether formal and structured or informal and self-directed. CPD is one of the distinguishing characteristics of a professional practitioner, which is particularly important in the context of continuing rapid technology driven change in academic libraries. Staff development is a shared responsibility of individuals. Continuing education and training of staff will help to enhance their capacity for work performance. This may ensure efficiency, help to quickly adopt and properly adapt with new information handling methods, knowledge management tools and technologies. To maintain the competitive level of library professionals, continuing education and need-based trainings are essential.

Academic libraries as well as professional associations are interested in organizing seminars, conferences and workshops for library professionals. Moreover, libraries of all kinds are coming forward to conduct in-house training programmes for library professionals. Such trained learners in the workplace can develop and extend their expertise to other library professionals employed in various types of libraries. Libraries can play the role of facilitator as well as a learner in such workplace learning interventions.

3.3.3. User Education Programmes

Libraries have started user orientation programmes to educate users on information resources, search tools, scholarly communication and other aspects. The aim of user education is to make the user aware of different types of information resources available in libraries, and to educate them to develop skills to search for information on their own. It is important to take steps to improve the information consciousness of users and their ability to make the best use of library resources (Kannappanavar & Swamy, 2012). The role of librarian as a trainer cum learner is envisaged in the user education practices observed in libraries. Active participation in library orientation or user education or information literacy programmes will awaken the learner in library professionals.

4. CONCLUSION

Library professionals have active roles to play in formal as well as informal learning in libraries. As the workplace changes in libraries are so quick and inevitable, the library professionals need to develop a positive attitude towards workplace learning. The inbuilt learning environment in libraries provides ample opportunities for informal learning. More opportunities can be developed from the organisational point of view by creating proactive learning environments. However an investigation is required for thorough understanding of challenges and opportunities for workplace learning in academic libraries.

REFERENCES

1. Campion, M., Cheraskin, L. and Stevens, M. (1994). Career-related antecedents and outcomes of job rotation, *Academy of Management Journal, 37* (6) 1518-42.
2. Chiara Panari, Dina Guglielmi, Silvia Simbula, Marco Depolo, (2010). Can an opportunity to learn at work reduce stress: a revisitation of the job demand-control model", *Journal of Workplace Learning, 22* (3), 166-177.
3. Corrall, Sheila (2010). *Continuing Professional Development and Workplace Learning. In: University Libraries and Digital Learning Environments.* Ashgate , Farnham, 239-258.
4. Dora, Mallikarjun and Maharana, Bulu and Jena, Shasikanta(2008). *Open Source movement in Indian libraries: an analytical study.* In Emerging Trends and Technlogies in LIbraries and Information Services, JIIT University, Noida, 2008. [Conference Paper]
5. Doyle, W., & Young, J. D. (2007). Workplace learning strategies of managers in small and large firms in knowledge-based industries. Proceedings of the University Forum on Human Resource Development, Oxford, UK.
6. Eraut, M., Maillardet, F., Miller, C., Steadman, S., Ali, A., Blackman, C., & Furner, J. (2003). *Learning in the first professional job: The first year of full time employment after college for accountants, engineers and nurses.* Paper presented at the annual meeting of the American Educational Research Association, Chicago, IL.
7. Ellinger, Andrea D. (2005). Contextual factors influencing learning in the workplace setting: the case of reinventing itself company. *Human Resource Development Quarterly,* 16 (3). 389-415.
8. Eriksson, T. and Ortega, J. (2006). The adoption of job rotation: testing the theories. *Industrial and Labor Relations Review, 59* (4) 653-666.
9. Fontanin, Matilde (2010). E-learning contribution to the building of a multi-generational workplace learning community in an academic library: observations drawn from practice. *Library Hi- tech News, 2,* 15-19, doi. 10.1108/07419051011050439.
10. Han, Karla (2008). Publishing services: an emerging role for research libraries. *EDUCAUSE review,* 16-17.

11. Hicks, E., Bagg, R., Doyle, W., & Young, J. D., (2007). Canadian accountants: examining workplace learning. *Journal of Workplace Learning, 19*(2), 61–77.
12. Holliday, R. and Retallick, J. (1995). *Workplace Learning: module 2 – The workplace as a place of learning,* Open Learning Institute, Charles Sturt University, Wagga Wagga.
13. IFLA (2013). IFLA world library and Information congress. Retrieved July 20, 2013, from *http://conference.ifla.org/ifla79/calls-for-papers/libraries-as-learning-organisations-how-to-nurture-growth-in-our-staff-and-o*
14. Kannappanavar, B.U., Swamy, Chidananda (2012). User education in Agricultural Science University Libraries in India with special reference to South India. *Library Philosophy and Practice.* Retrieved July 29, 2013, from. *http://unllib.unl.edu/LPP*
15. Li, Xin., Bryan, Linda (2010). On Becoming an Employer of Choice: gauging Employee Satisfaction Through ClimateQUAL®, *Library Trends, 59* (1-2), 256-268.
16. Malinski, R. (2002) Job rotation in an academic library: damned if you do and damned if you don't! *Library Trends, 50* (4) 673-680.
17. Manorama Srinath, (1993). The organisational climate of university, *Library Management, 14(*1), 28 – 30.
18. Mathews, Pamela (1999). Workplace learning: developing a holistic model. *The Learning Organisation. 6* (1), 18–29.
19. Paula Crouse , Wendy Doyle & Jeffrey D. Young (2011). Workplace learning strategies, barriers, facilitators and outcomes: a qualitative study among human resource management practitioners, *Human Resource Development International,* 14(1), 39-55.
20. Sawant, Sarika (2011). Institutional repositories in India: a preliminary study. *Library Hi tech News* 10, 6-10.

11

Continuing Education for Professional Development : Necessity for nurturing Competent Professionals

Dr. Shabir Ahmad Ganaie

ABSTRACT

Library and information science profession is a dynamic and vibrant profession. From the very beginning it is being transformed due to the developments occurring in the universe of knowledge. Changes occurring in information landscape are influencing both library operations as well as library services. For facing the challenges posed by this turbulent information landscape needs professionals who are competent and capable. One method of generating and producing competent professionals in the discipline of library and information science is to motivate professionals for opting to continuous education programs whereby they can sharpen their existing skills and will develop a positive attitude towards the new developments. Present paper highlights the vibrant nature of library and information science profession. Concept of continuing education and different modes of such education is also deliberated in the paper. Modes applied by library professionals for updating their knowledge and skills are mentioned. It is suggested that library and information science departments must provide opportunity to working professionals for updating their knowledge.

Keywords : Library and Information Science, Continuing Education, Professional Development

1. INTRODUCTION

Human history has witnessed different revolutions. From the earliest years of mankind, until relatively recently in recorded history, we have lived entirely in an agrarian society. In this agrarian society man was wholly and solely dependent upon agriculture. Even at present, in some parts of the world, agriculture is still dominating the economic and social life. Agricultural societies were mostly dependent upon the muscle power of the individuals who were engaged in performing different activities related to agriculture. With the emergence of different machines, man established different industries and thus a new era ushered in which muscle power of human beings was replaced by the mechanical power of machines. Societies in different parts of the world realized the importance of industries and thus established different industries. Result of industrial growth was in terms of more production of goods at least cost and in short periods of time. Society witnessed another revolution brought about by industrialization and this society was labeled as industrial society. Yet, while the rest of the world struggles to take part in the Industrial Revolution some nations are already entering a new era, which we are calling the "information society". In information society, every aspect of our life is touched by the applications of information and communications technologies, and in which we are increasingly dependent on the information which we access through them (Johnson,1999).

Whether it is agricultural revolution or industrial revolution and even information revolution, information has and is playing a very important role. Libraries and information centers are acting as repositories of knowledge and information. Thus these are existing from time immemorial to serve the individuals for performing in an effective and efficient manner. Even in India, importance of knowledge has been realized by National Knowledge Commission (NKC) in following words:

"While making the recommendations we have been guided by how knowledge will impact the lives of ordinary people of India. We are conscious that knowledge is about farmers having access to accurate information about water, land, weather and fertilizers; students having access to quality education and jobs; scientists having access to laboratories; industry having access to skilled work force; and people feeling empowered with good governance in a vibrant democracy"(NKC, 2009).

It is in this context that NKC has recommended for strengthening the existing infrastructure of libraries and information centers in the country and is of the opinion that to revamp the Library and Information Services (LIS) sector NKC has recommended a comprehensive census of libraries, modernizing management of libraries to ensure greater community participation, including models for public private partnerships in LIS development and leveraging ICT for various applications. For sustained attention to the sector, NKC has recommended the setting up of an independent National Commission on Libraries which would streamline all development initiatives in the sector. Information in the present world has attained the status of an important resource. Information is treated as fuel for the overall progress and prosperity of any nation. Thus in order to make this information easily accessible to those who are in need of it, libraries must be redefined in the present information landscape. Libraries and information centers need to be equipped with modern electronic gadgets and information communication technology so that user will get prompt, pinpointed, exhaustive and expeditious information. This information when utilized by the users will generate new knowledge and information that is beneficial for the progress and prosperity of the nations of the world. Not only infrastructure of libraries is to be taken care of but also human resources employed in these libraries must be well educated for delivering information services efficiently and effectively.

2. LIBRARIANSHIP: A CHANGING PROFESSION

Librarianship has emerged as a profession and the mission of this profession is to provide right information to the right user at the right time. This mission can be achieved when library professionals working in the libraries are competent enough in managing the library's overall resources in a scientific manner and will deliver the information services in an effective and efficient manner. Libraries have existed in societies from time immemorial and in the past their mission was to take care of the documents stored in these libraries. More stress was given to the storage and preservation aspect and little concern of librarians was on the use of these documents by the library users. Librarians were just regarded as store keepers or even curators. Library professionals in these libraries have learned to select, acquire, organize, retrieve and circulate the documents to library users. But with the passage of time role of librarians changed as there were changes occurring in the information landscape and these changes were creating ripples touching every facet of library and information science profession. In the present world libraries are not only operating within the four walls of the library but have extended their existence beyond the physical collections and buildings to the virtual world of the internet. Libraries are witnessing transformation after transformation and thus we see emergence of electronic libraries, automated libraries, digital libraries and even virtual libraries. Libraries face a host of new challenges and one among these challenges is to find ways to stay relevant in the Information Age. In the present times of budget cuttings, libraries are required to do more with less, and the skills library professionals need continue to evolve. Librarian is no more a store keeper but is now treated as a facilitator who utilizes his capabilities for satisfying the information needs of the users in a professional manner. Library professionals are treated as information engineers. *Ward (1999)* describes an Information Engineer as someone who must have skills in "human communication and information behavior", "information resources", "information management", "multimedia systems", "information retrieval", "interface design", "multimedia programming", "hypertext and hypermedia", "distributed systems and product development and marketing". Thus it is clear that libraries are changing with the passage of time. Not only their modes of operations are changing but also these are providing multidimensional services to the library patrons using information and communication technology. Library science professionals are playing a vital role in creating knowledge societies. The role of librarian has evolved, the image of librarian has changed and the name has taken different denominations through time:

- Librarian
- Documentalist / Documentation officer
- Information mediator
- Information specialist
- Information manager
- Knowledge manager

At present, new librarian denominations are determined by new technologies. Emerging job titles in profession are:

- Technology consultant
- Electronic service librarian

- Digital librarian
- Web master librarian
- Metadata librarian
- Information architect
- Cybrarian (Martin, 2005).

This changing nature of library profession demands that Library and information professionals must develop new skills for facing the challenges. The best way to develop these new skills is to join the continuous education programs.

3. CONTINUING PROFESSIONAL DEVELOPMENT: BASIC CONCEPT

Education is the key enabler for the development of an individual and for the development of any profession. Education can be attained either in the formal manner (By joining any academic program) or through the non formal manner where there are no frequent contact between the learner and the teacher. After completing the education in any field, one can continuously learn different concepts evolving in that subject with the passage of time. If one will cease learning these new emerging concepts, then the result will be inability of that person to face the challenges posed by these new developments. Same is the case with any profession. If the professional is not keeping himself/herself up-to-date and abreast about the latest trends, professional will become unfit for performing professional obligations professionally and thus will be the reasons for defaming that profession in the society. In order to make professionals relevant for the all the times and avoid the chances of his / her rusting, continuous professional development is the best panacea. Continuing professional development (CPD) means maintaining, improving and broadening relevant knowledge and skills in one's subject specialism or in one's profession, so that it has a positive impact on practice and the learner experience.

CPD embraces a wide range of activities that are pursued to improve knowledge, skills and ability related to the performance of professional work and responsibilities. Examples of activities include training courses, professional reading, work exchanges and mentoring. CPD has been defined as learning activities designed to facilitate professionals' acquiring new competencies. This may take the form of in-person or distance education options, and could range from more informal formats, e.g., a lecture, or half-day or full-day workshop or seminar, to more formal education options, e.g., award of a certificate or other formal qualification. *Zepeda (2008)* offers a definition of successful professional development within the context of the public school environment, which includes a number of elements that are relevant to schools and to libraries. Some of those elements include collaborative planning by those who assist in the development, significant time and resources, focus on personal and institutional improvement and capacity for long-term maintenance. Staff training is defined as implementing programs to improve overall employee performance in order to be more innovative as an organization and try new things, and to "[bridge] a gap between present and desired performance" (*Saponaro et al., 2009*). Others define staff development as "change in individual's knowledge, understanding, behaviors, skills – and in values and beliefs" (*Southwest Educational Development Laboratory, 1994*). According to *Deiss (2001)*, "Staff development and continuing education will begin to take their places among the most strategically urgent activities in which libraries and the librarian profession engage". *Straatmann (2008)* emphasizes that staff development programs do not function solely to train and create resources, but that they exist to bridge the gap between paraprofessional staff and degreed librarians within academic libraries and to help repair any inequalities between the two groups.

4. MODES OF CONTINUING PROFESSIONAL DEVELOPMENT FOR LIS PROFESSIONALS

There are a number of modes whereby one can update his/ her capabilities, competencies and skills. Some of the methods adopted by library and information science professionals for keeping abreast about the latest trends are enumerated below:

a) Attending conferences: conferences are being organized at different levels and these events provide a platform to the professionals where they can exchange their views and ideas with each other. This sharing of ideas enriches all the participants and helps them to learn from each other.

b) Attending refresher courses organized by different agencies like university departments , Academic staff colleges of University grants commission for updating the knowledge base of individuals associated with higher education.

c) Reading latest professional literature like books, journals etc in both print and electronic format. Reading such types of literature will help the professionals to keep current and abreast about the latest trends in the profession.

d) Attending seminars and wok shops organized for providing opportunity to professionals to acquire more and more skills for performing different professional practices in a confident manner.

e) Writing articles and papers for conferences and journals or even for books will help professionals to refresh their ideas.

f) Attaining higher qualifications

g) Pursuing research

h) Mentoring new colleagues

i) Leading team/department self-assessment

j) Chairing team meetings

k) Constructing professional dialogue/learning conversation opportunities

l) Reading and reviewing books or journal articles

m) Updating knowledge through the internet/ TV (including teachers' TV)/other media and reviewing these with a group of professional colleagues

n) Sharing information on blogs, wikis and electronic lists or any other social media

o) Orientation for new employees

p) Sharing idea and resources with other

q) Designing innovative feedback mechanisms (learners and peers)

Badger (2001) is of the opinion that low-budget staff development activities include lunch talks, library newsletters, in-house staff-exchange programs, journal clubs, environmental scanning, mentor programs, orientation for new employees, and participation in library-related Internet lists.

5. CONCLUSION

In 21st century due to the revolution brought about by information and communication technology, libraries and information centers have become excellent centers for providing access to information that is available not only locally but also nationally and globally. Library professionals are supposed to equip themselves with the competencies that will help them to face the challenges posed by the developments in the existing information landscape. Whether it is computer, library software, internet, World Wide Web, web 2.0 or library 2.0, library and information professionals need both personal as well as professional competencies. Continuous professional developmental programs provide an opportunity to library professionals for enhancing their skills and competencies.

REFERENCES

1. Badger, L.C. (2001), "How to pay for programs", in Avery, E., Dahlin, T., Carver, D. (Eds),*Staff Development: A Practical Guide*, ALA, Chicago, IL, pp.42-5.
2. Deiss, K.J. (2001), "Introduction to staff development", in Avery, E., Dahlin, T., Carver, D. (Eds),*Staff Development: A Practical Guide*, ALA, Chicago, IL, pp.3-5.
3. Johnson,I.M (1999) "Librarians and the informed user: Reorienting library and information science education for the "information society"", Librarian Career Development, Vol. 7 (4), pp.29 – 42
4. Martin , S.G (2005), the information profession competencies. In Raina, R.L & Gaur, R.C (Ed), Library management :Trends and opportunities , New Delhi; Excell books , pp. 265-283
5. Saponaro, M.Z., Baughman, M.S., Kinniff, J. (2009), "You came for the snacks, but what have you learned? Evaluation of a staff learning program", in Connor, E. (Eds),*An Introduction to Staff Development in Academic Libraries*, Routledge, New York, NY, pp.205-19
6. Southwest Educational Development Laboratory (1994), *Staff Development and Change Process: Cut from the Same Cloth*, available at:
7. *www.sedl.org/change/issues/issues42.html*
8. Straatmann, M. (2008), "Addressing perceived inequalities between academic library faculty and paraprofessionals through staff development programs", *Nebraska Library Association Quarterly*, Vol. 39 No.1, pp.3-10.
9. Ward, S. (1999), "Information professionals for the next millennium", *Journal of Information Science*, Vol. 25(4), pp.239-47.
10. Zepeda, S.J. (2008), *Professional Development: What Works*, Eye on Education, Larchmont, NY

12

Role of Library Support in Academic Achievement of Postgraduate Students with special reference to Farook College Library and Information System

Sareef. K.
Dr. K.C. Abdul Majeed

ABSTRACT

The Farook College library and information system is one of the biggest of its kind in the state, with a collection of 82327 volumes and subscribing to 162 journals. The automated central library provides open access to its resources through quickly accessible web based online public access catalogue. There are separate sections for visually challenged students and teachers, with Braille literature and Digital Talking Book Library, and for electronic resource users. The digital library with e-resources was launched with the support of National Library and Information Service Infrastructure for Scholarly Content (N-LIST) programme of INFLIBNET. It provides access to more than 2100 e-journals and 100000 e-books. The library and information system provides a variety of services using latest technologies to the student community, teachers and administrative staff of the college and sister institutions as well as the public too. The college libraries influence in academic achievement of postgraduate students, extend of their use of library resources, opinion about the library collection and services are being studied.

Keywords : Library Support, Academic Achievement, Farook College Library and Information System

1. INTRODUCTION

Academic libraries are meant for supporting the teaching-learning process in academic institutions like schools, colleges and universities. The library is aimed to serve the students and teachers in doing their academic work properly. Support of library is very much necessary to fresh students and teachers. School libraries are supported to develop library culture and reading habit among students. Such students when they join colleges use the library properly. Without using the library these students can't move ahead. Unfortunately, such students are very few in number. Why this? It is to be studied separately.

There are very few students who visit and use the library regularly while some seldom visit the library; certain others are not visit the library at all. Compared to under-graduate level students, postgraduate students use the library more often. Every student, both under-graduate and postgraduate, use the library for obtaining a high academic achievement in studies. But how much the students are benefited from the library is yet to be measured.

The academic achievement of a student depends on many factors including social support, parental support, teacher-student relationships, motivation from friends, teaching methods, and caring from siblings and neighbours. But in a campus based education the curriculum design compel the students to make use of the library for their academic achievement.

The students depend on their teachers, parents, friends, Google, and textbooks for their studies. Moreover the support from a good library, staff of the library, calm and quite atmosphere of such a library, sound technologies and machines for reproduction and repackaging of information and knowledge are also required as they influence a student's academic achievement. This study is aimed at finding out the role of library in student's academic achievements.

2. BACKGROUND OF THE STUDY

The study was based on the support given by the library and information system of Farook College to the postgraduate students in their academic achievements. The Farook College library and information system is one of the biggest of its kind in the state, with a collection of 82327 volumes and subscribing to 162 journals. The automated central library provides open access to its resources through quickly accessible web based online public access catalogue. There are separate sections for visually challenged students and teachers, with Braille literature and Digital Talking Book Library, and for electronic resource users. The digital library with e-resources was launched with the support of National Library and Information Service Infrastructure for Scholarly Content (N-LIST) programme of INFLIBNET. It provides access to more than 2100 e-journals and 100000 e-books. The library and information system provides a variety of services using latest technologies to the student community, teachers and administrative staff of the college and sister institutions as well as the public too. The college libraries influence in academic achievement of postgraduate students, extend of their use of library resources, opinion about this libraries collection and services are being studied.

3. SAMPLE USED FOR THE STUDY

The present study is to find out whether there is any influence of library support in postgraduate students towards their academic achievement. The study was carried out among 180 postgraduate students of Farook College who joined the course after completing three year graduation course using the support and services of Farook College Library and Information System at Abussabah Library Complex. The details of the sample is shown in Table 1.

Table 1 : Sample Distribution among various categories

Variables	Category	N (180)	%	Total %
Gender	Male	54	30.00	100
	Female	126	70.00	
Faculty	Arts	93	51.67	100
	Science	78	43.33	
	Commerce	9	05.00	
Place of Residence	Hosteller	50	27.78	100
	Day Scholar	130	72.22	
Year of Study	First Year	98	54.44	100
	Second Year	82	45.56	

4. TOOLS USED FOR THE STUDY

The study was conducted administering a questionnaire to assess the influence of library support in the academic achievement of postgraduate students. The study is trying to find out the extent of students perception of the influence of library support in their academic achievement. It verifies other relevant factors affected their achievement. The study also tried to rate the library collection and services in the light of users opinion.

5. RESULTS AND DISCUSSION

The paper has attempted to study the extent of dependence of postgraduate students on the library services for their academic achievement, role of library support in their academic achievements, other aspects that influenced in their academic achievement, and opinion about library collection and services. The details are discussed below:

5.1. Extent of Library Use

The respondents were asked to mark whether they were using the library services for their study purpose or not. Most of the postgraduate students were found using the library collection and services for their academic purpose. Details are shown in Figure 1.

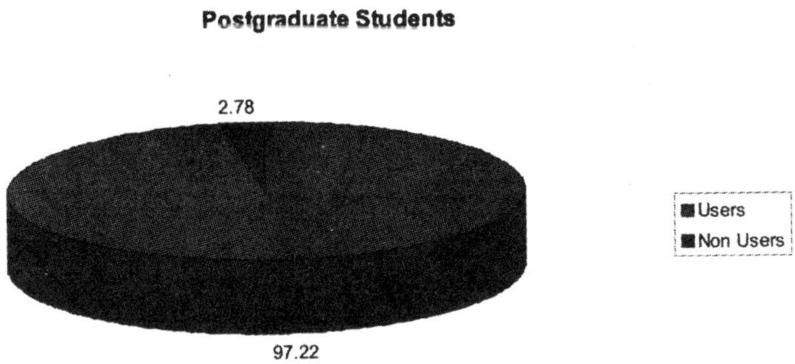

Fig. 1. Use of Library Collection and Services

The figure given above shows that almost all the postgraduate student community use the college library collection and services.

5.2. Role of Library support in academic achievement

These postgraduate students who are not using the library viewed that there was no role to college library in their academic achievement. Some of the postgraduate students also indicated that the library support didn't have any influence on their academic achievement.

Figure 2 shows that majority of the postgraduate students in the college believe that the college library collection and services had greatly influenced in their academic achievement.

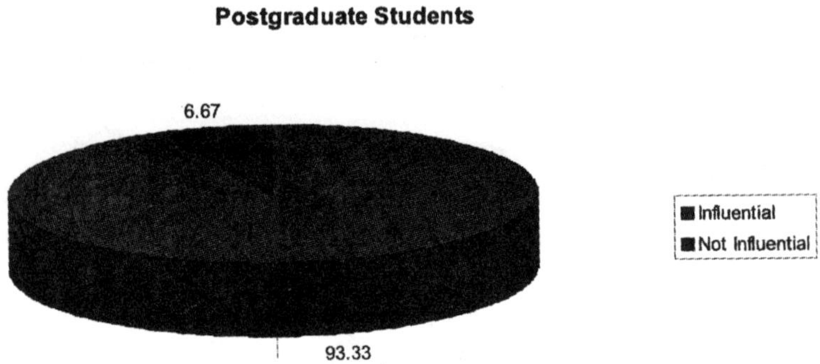

Fig. 2. Role of Library Support in Academic Achievement

5.3. Factors that influenced Academic Achievement of Postgraduate Students

Postgraduate students understand that there are many factors influencing their academic achievement. They may include library support, teacher's help, friend's support, support of parents and relatives, use of internet reading, etc. The respondents were asked to mention about these influencing factors.

Figure 3. provides the details of factors that influenced academic achievement. Majority of the postgraduate students opined that library support has a clear role in their academic achievement. The other factors such as directions from teachers and friends and classmates also have high influence in their academic achievement. Only a minor group opined that academic atmosphere of the campus, hostel living and self goal have some role in their academic achievement. Use of Internet, Parental support and lover's motivation, etc. also influence in academic achievement.

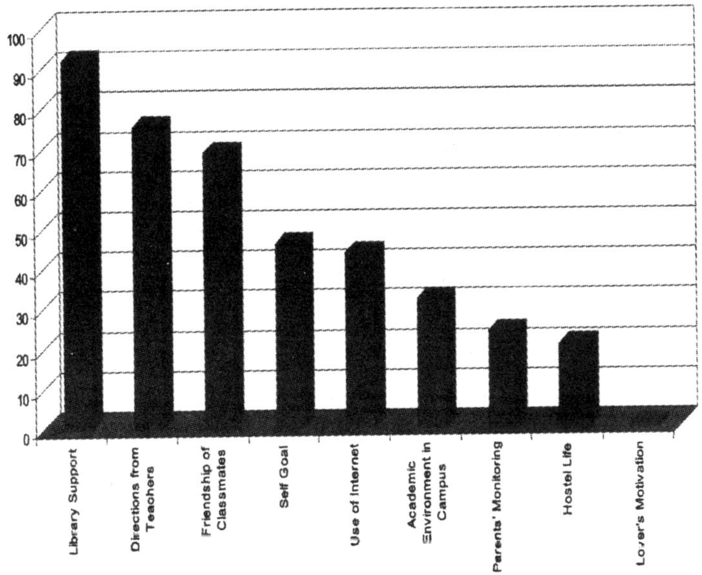

Fig. 3. Factors that Influenced Academic Achievement

5.4. Opinion about Library Collection and Services

College library collection and services are meant for supporting the academic exercise done by students and teachers. Use of the library resources and services have a direct impact on academic achievement of students. Therefore, the respondents were asked to rate the usefulness of the college library collection and services in their academic work. The data is summarized in Fig. 4.

Majority of Postgraduate students marked their response as very useful, but some students marked useful, no response, not useful and not at all useful. The responses given weighted scores like 5, 3, 0, -3 and -5 respectively. The cumulative score was divided by N (180). The obtained figure (3.79) is translated to verbal opinion. It is above 'useful level'.

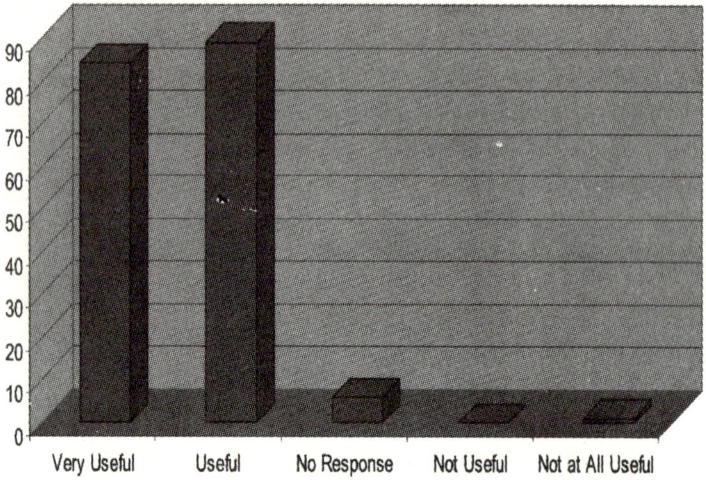

Fig. 4. Opinion about College Library Collection and Services

6. CONCLUSION

College library collection and services are vital part of student's academic achievement. Obtaining a good academic record is the wish of all students. Identifying such students and offering all possible help to them is the duty of college libraries. Students with ample motivation will use the library collection and services not only for their academic achievement, but also for their personal development and career development. The librarian and the teachers should work together for the proper and effective use of library resources and services.

REFERENCES

1. Allen, Mary Beth (1993). 'International Students in Academic Libraries: A User Survey'. *College & Research Libraries*. pp323-333.
2. Lance, Keith Curry (1994). 'The Impact of School Library Media Centers on Academic Achievement'. *SLMQ* 22(3).
3. Lance, Keith Curry (2010). *et. al.* 'The Impact of School

Libraries on Academic Achievement: A Research Study Based on Responses from Administrators in Idaho'. *School Library Monthly* 26(9).

4. Lonsdale, Michele (2003). Impact of School Libraries on Student Achievement: A review of the research. Victoria: Australian Council for Educational Research.

5. Rankin, J A (1992). 'Problem-based medical education: effect on library use'. *Bulletin of Medical Library Association.* 80(1). pp36-43.

13

Information Access through Internet for Managerial Decision Making

Mahjabeen Aydeed
Dr. Jalaja V

ABSTRACT

Internet is providing unprecedented opportunities to access information, improve decisions, and enhance communication among decision-makers and the people affected by their decisions. This study provides an understanding on the information access through internet for managerial decision making. The questionnaire was distributed to higher, middle and lower level managers of Info Park, Kakkanad. The analysis of data is presented in the form of tables with description. The study revealed that internet had a great role in decision making and IT managers depend on internet to a great extent for managerial decision making.

Keywords : Internet, managerial decision making, Managers

1. INTRODUCTION

Managers need information available at their

fingertips in today's dynamic market place. The Internet can provide this information at little cost and with little training, eliminating the "middleman" effect present today in most organizations. Internet is a "network of networks" that consists of millions of smaller domestic, academic, business, and government networks. It carries together various information and services, such as electronic mail, online chat, file transfer, and the interlinked Web pages and other documents of the World Wide Web. The Internet has an ever-increasing importance in business. Businesses rely heavily on the Internet for all aspects of their functioning, from reaching out to clients, contacting and ordering from suppliers, marketing, as well as carrying out financial transactions. The Internet is a very important means of communicating, researching, marketing and conducting business.

The Internet is introducing new ways for humans to interact with machines and to communicate with each other. Internet users, regardless of their role, background or knowledge, can experience confusion and anxiety because of the virtually unlimited amount of information available, information that is often poorly organized and of highly variable quality and relevance.

Internet helps to easily retrieve, digest, manipulate, and utilize information relevant to the decision making process. The internet, like the mind, has the potential to store vast amounts of information; the problem with both, of course, lies within the process of retrieving that information. Vast amounts of data are transmitted in seconds, and Internet access offers unimaginably large amounts of information, data, and interpreted materials. As a powerful and dynamic tool for communication, it is the largest single source of information at the global level.

Information to have a real value to decision making, it must be accurate, timely, relevant and complete. Information is a vital part of every manager's job.

Managers use information to make decisions and conduct their work, and create new information used by others. Information has always been a key element in the performance of a business and the effectiveness of management, and information technology can now transform the use of this information to give managers substantial benefits in business planning and decision making.

2. INFOPARK, KOCHI

InfoPark, located at Kochi is an IT infrastructural development program being developed by the Government of Kerala in 2004. Info Park Kochi is located in 100.86 acres of land at Kakkanad village, Kanayannur Taluk, Ernakulum district. Around 80 acres has been notified as an IT sector Specific Economic Zone by Ministry of Commerce, Government of India. Info Park Phase I is spread over a 101 acres campus with more than 3,200,000 sq. ft. of built up area housing over 80 companies which employ around 17,000 professionals. The park is currently in expansion mode and is adding another 160 acres as part of the Phase II expansion. The park is built on the 'Hub and Spoke model' for the development of the Information Technology industry in Kerala

3. OBJECTIVES OF THE STUDY

The following are the main objectives of the study:

1. To find out the level of dependence on internet for managerial decision making.
2. To understand the type of information sought from internet by the IT managers for managerial decision making.
3. To examine the use of internet tools by the IT managers for managerial decision making.
4. To find out the problems faced by the IT managers

while accessing information for managerial decision making.

4. METHODOLOGY

The present study is conducted on a sample of 69 IT managers of Info Park, Kochi in Kerala who responded positively to the questionnaire distributed among higher, middle and lower level managers.

5. ANALYSIS

The responses obtained from the managers are presented in the following tables. Percentage method has been used for analysing the responses.

Table 1. Distribution of respondents

Level of managers	Questionnaires distributed	Questionnaires received
Higher	30	21
Middle	40	35
Lower	20	13
Total	90.00	69.00

A total of 90 questionnaires were distributed to the IT managers in Info Park. Out of 90 only 69 questionnaires were returned back from the managers of which 21 from the higher level, 35 from middle level managers and 13 from the lower level managers. Hence the response rate was 86.25 per cent.

Table 2. Time spent on Internet daily

Opinion	Higher	Middle	Lower	Total
1-2 hours	6(28.57)	6(17.14)	3(23.08)	17(24.64)
2-3 hours	9(42.86)	7(20.00)	6(46.15)	22(31.89)
3-4 hours	4(19.05)	17(48.57)	4(30.76)	23(33.33)
Above 4 hours	2(9.52)	5(14.29)	-	7(10.14)
Total	21(100.00)	35(100.00)	13(100.00)	69(100.00)

Table 2 describes the time spent by the IT managers on Internet daily. A good number of higher level managers (42.86 per cent) spend 2-3 hours on Internet daily whereas a good number of middle level managers (48.57 per cent) and lower level managers (33.33 per cent) spend 3-4 hours daily on internet.

Table 3. Level of use of Internet for managerial decision making

Opinion	Higher	Middle	Lower	Total
To great extent	14(66.67)	17(48.57)	6(46.15)	37(53.62)
To some extent	7(33.33)	13(37.14)	5(38.46)	25(36.23)
To lesser extent	-	5(14.29)	2(15.39)	7(10.15)
Total	21(100.00)	35(100.00)	13(100.00)	69(100.00)

* The figures in brackets show the respective percentages.

It can be observed from the Table 3 that the majority of the higher level managers (66.67 per cent), about half of middle level (48.57 per cent) and lower level managers (53.62 per cent) depend on internet to great extent for managerial decision making.

Table 4. Extent of information obtained from Internet for managerial decision making

Opinion	Higher	Middle	Lower	Total
To great extent	10(47.62)	12(34.29)	4(30.77)	26(37.68)
To some extent	8(38.09)	17(48.57)	9(69.23)	34(49.28)
To lesser extent	3(14.29)	6(17.14)	-	9(13.04)
Total	21(100.00)	35(100.00)	13(100.00)	69(100.00)

Table 3 furnishes the details of the extent of information obtained from internet for managerial decision making .It is evident that a good number of the higher level managers (47.62 per cent) obtain information to a great extent from internet for managerial decision making and good number of middle level managers (48.57 per cent) obtain information to some extent from internet for managerial decision making.

Table 5. Type of Information sought from Internet for managerial decision making

Information Types	Information for software design	Information on HRM	Sales/ marketing information	Financial information	Govt. policies & regulations
Higher	16(76.19)	8(38.09)	17(80.95)	9(42.86)	11(52.38)
Middle	31(88.57)	18(51.42)	25(71.42)	14(40)	13(37.14)
Lower	6(46.15)	3(23.07)	8(61.54)	5(38.46)	8(61.54)

* The figures in brackets show the respective percentages

Table 5 shows the type of information sought from internet for managerial decision making. Managers need different types of information for taking different decisions. Here it is clear that a large majority of the higher level managers (80.95 per cent) and a majority of the lower level managers (61.54 per cent) depend on internet for sales/ marketing information and a large majority of the middle level managers (88.57 per cent) depend on internet for information on software designing.

Table 6. Use of different Internet tools for managerial decision making

Opinion	Higher	Middle	Lower
E mail	21(100.00)	33(94.29)	13(100.00)
Blog	9(42.86)	18(51.43)	3(23.07)
Social networking	12(57.14)	15(42.86)	-
Wikis	8(38.09)	21(60.00)	5(38.46)
Webinars /web conferences	9(42.86)	10(28.57)	-
Industry portals	19(90.48)	31(88.57)	10(76.92)

Table 6 depicts the use of different internet tools for managerial decision making .Managers especially IT managers always use various internet tools like e mail, blog, wikis etc for information support .Cent per cent of the higher level and middle managers depend use e mail the middle level managers. A good number of middle level managers (51.43 per cent) use blog than higher and lower level managers. Majority of the middle level managers (60.00 per cent) use blog than higher and lower level managers. None of the lower level managers depend on Webinars /web conferences for information for managerial decision making. A large majority of higher level managers (90.48 per cent), majority of middle level (88.57 per cent) and lower level managers depend on Industry portals for information for managerial decision making.

Problems faced by the managers while depending on internet for decision making

The above table shows that majority of the higher level managers (42.86 per cent) face the problem of overload of information. About half of the middle level managers (48.57per cent) face the problem of lack of organized information and half of the lower level managers (46.15 per cent)) finds it difficult to judge relevant information from the internet which may be due to large amount of information available on the internet.

Table 7

Level of managers/ Problems	Lack of organized information	Confidential status of required information	Difficulty in judging relevant information	Too long to download/view web pages	Overload of information	Total
Higher	2(9.52)	5(23.81)	5(23.81)	-	9(42.86)	21(100.00)
Middle	17(48.57)	5(14.29)	6(17.14)	3(8.57)	4(11.43)	35(100.00)
Lower	3(23.08)	1(7.69)	6(46.15)	3(23.08)	-	13(100.00)
Total	22(31.88)	11(15.94)	17(24.64)	6(8.69)	13(18.85)	69(100.00)

Table 8. Ways in which Internet improved managerial decision making

Internet	Higher		Middle		Lower	
	Agree	Not agree	Agree	Not agree	Agree	Not agree
Led to better-informed decision making.	16 (76.19)	5 (23.81)	27 (77.14)	8 (22.86)	13 (100.00)	-
Increased confidence in decision or recomme-ndation	14 (66.67)	7 (33.33)	22 (62.86)	13 (37.14)	6 (46.15)	7 (53.85)
Improved the efficiency of manufac-turing product	13 (61.91)	8 (38.09)	19 (54.29)	16 (45.71)	9 (69.23)	4 (30.77)
Identified new markets and marketing strategies	9 (42.86)	12 (57.14)	14 (40.00)	21 (60.00)	5 (38.46)	8 (61.53)
Helped to improve advertising pattern of the product	10 (47.62)	11 (52.38)	15 (42.86)	20 (57.14)	7 (53.85)	6 (46.15)
Helped to allocate funds into profitable ventures	5 (23.81)	16 (76.19)	21 (60.00)	14 (40.00)	9 (69.23)	4 (30.77)

The above table furnishes some data on the role of internet in enhancing managerial decision making. The manager's opinion regarding the usefulness of internet for decision making have been sought. Majority of the higher level managers (76.19 per cent) and middle level managers (77.17 per cent) and cent per cent of the lower level managers agreed that internet led to better-informed decision making. Majority of the higher level managers (66.67 per cent) and middle level managers (62.86 per cent) agree and a about half of the lower level managers (53.85 per cent) not agree that internet increased confidence in decision or recommendation. Majority of the higher level managers (61.91 per cent) and lower level managers (69.23 per cent) and about half of middle level managers (54.29 per cent) agreed that internet improved the efficiency of manufacturing product. Majority of the higher level managers (61.91 per cent) and lower level managers (69.23 per cent) and about half of middle level managers (54.29 per cent) agreed that internet improved the efficiency of manufacturing product. Majority of the higher level managers (57.14 per cent) and lower level managers (61.53 per cent) not agree that internet helped to identify new markets and marketing strategies.

6. RESULTS AND DISCUSSION

The analysis of the data collected from higher, middle and lower level managers revealed that internet is very essential for higher and middle level managers for decision making. It is true that more decisions are made by these categories of managers and hence they need more information which can be obtained without any time limit from internet. This is supported by the higher frequency of the dependence on internet for managerial decision making by the higher and middle level managers. Managers who have to take higher level decisions feel that internet is very essential and has impact on all the areas of management.

7. CONCLUSION

Information is vital for managerial decision making. Those who hold higher managerial positions need more information. Managers must consequently take a critical view about information. In recent years, micro processing technology has radically transformed the ability to acquire, analyse and produce information of various kinds, much of it in quantified form. Since decision making is information-based the practicing managers must not merely understand the role of information for informing, instructing and motivating, but ensure that it contributes constructively to decision making through being timely, relevant, available and intelligible. The Internet is providing unprecedented opportunities to access information, improve decisions, and enhance communication among decision-makers and the people affected by their decisions.

REFERENCES

1. Leigh, Andrew. (1983). Decisions, decisions! a practical management guide to problem solving and decision making. Germont USA: Gower.
2. http://www.infopark.in/
3. http://en.wikipedia.org/wiki/InfoPark,_Kochi

PART III
COLLABORATIVE LIBRARY SERVICES

14

Use of Cloud Computing in Libraries

Ashokkumar A. Suthar

ABSTRACT

Latest technological development has brought a dramatic change in every field, and library science is no exception to it. The libraries have been automated, networked and now moving towards paper less or virtual libraries. The libraries increasingly adopt cloud computing, a new model for Information Technology services. Cloud computing is a new technique of computing that is extensively used in today's industry as well as society. It allows them to avoid locally hosting multiple servers, housing massive equipment and constantly dealing with hardware failure, software installs, upgrades and compatibility issues. Cloud computing can simplify processes and save time and money. Cloud computing brings innovative changes in the world of Information and Communication Technology because of its potential benefits such as reduced cost, access from anywhere and anytime as well as its flexibility. Cloud computing technology helps in bridging the gap between digital libraries and IT. Sharing of data among the libraries will in principle reduce the overall cost and increase the efficiency. This paper describes the concept and definitions of the cloud computing, characteristics, types of cloud computing, its architecture and its advantages in new generation libraries. The use of cloud computing in libraries and how cloud computing actually works is communicated in this paper.

Keywords : Cloud Computing, Cloud Libraries, Library-Cloud, Cloud Computing Services, Cloud Computing Models

1. INTRODUCTION

The term "Cloud Computing" became famous from the past few years. "Cloud computing" is used to describe web based operating systems and Sharing of data through the internet. Cloud computing allows consumers and businesses to use application without installation and access their personal files or data at any computer with use of internet access. Its acceptance is growing very quickly. It is newly emerged method which is broadly used in IT industries. The idea of cloud computing is based on a very fundamental principle of reusability of IT capabilities. The difference that cloud computing brings compared to traditional concepts of "grid computing", "distributed computing", "utility computing", or "autonomic computing" is to broaden horizons across organizational boundaries. Cloud computing is a computing paradigm, where a large pool of systems are connected in private or public networks, to provide dynamically scalable infrastructure for application, data and file storage. With the advent of this technology, the cost of computation, application hosting, content storage and delivery is reduced significantly. Cloud computing is a practical approach to experience direct cost benefits and it has the potential to transform a data center from a capital intensive set up to a variable priced environment. Cloud computing has the potential to transform a large part of the IT industry, making software even more attractive as a service and shaping the way IT hardware is designed and purchased.

In internet environment, it is a normal thing you store your files or photos online instead of on your home computer, or use webmail or a social networking site, you are using a "cloud computing" service. Cloud computing is often proposed as the biggest revolution since the internet. Users who have had the experience of using Web 2.0 services like Wikipedia, Blogger, and Flickr etc have already experienced about cloud computing, may be unknowingly. Cloud Computing is a completely new IT technology and it is known as the third revolution after PC and Internet in IT. To be more specific, Cloud Computing is the improvement of Distributed Computing, Parallel Computing, Grid Computing and Distributed Databases. And the basic principle of Cloud Computing is making tasks distributed in large numbers of distributed computers but not in local computers or remote servers. We can say that, by collecting large quantities of information and resources stored in personal computers, mobile phones and other equipment, Cloud Computing is capable of integrating them and putting them on the public cloud for serving users. Cloud computing refers to the delivery of computing resources over the Internet. Instead of keeping data on your own hard drive or updating applications for your needs, you use a service over the Internet, at another location, to store your information or use its applications. This technology allows users to access much more efficient computing by centralizing storage, memory and processing. Cloud computing is a technology that uses the web (Internet) and central remote servers to maintain data, software and application. Cloud computing allows users to use applications without installation in their local machine to access their personal and official files on any computer with internet access.

This is not a new technology; it's associated since inception of the web. In the libraries cloud computing is used to build a digital library and to automate housekeeping operations using third party services, software and hardware. Cloud computing refers to both applications delivered as a service over the internet and the systems software in the data centers that provide services. In simple words the datacenters, hardware and systems software is what we can call a cloud. A simple example of cloud computing is Yahoo mail, Gmail etc. One does not need any software or server to store them. These services are free to all users till some limit, any extra storage capacity and advanced services are available at cost.

The interesting thing about cloud computing is that we've redefined libraries with its use in libraries, to provide platform- infrastructure and to include everything that we already do. Today, its huge use has been seen in libraries which have shown new horizons to knowledge based societies. With the advent of Information technology, libraries have become automated which is the basic need towards advancement followed by networks and more effort are towards virtual libraries. The latest technology trend in library science is the use of cloud computing for various purposes and for achieving economy in library functions. Since cloud computing is a new and core area the professionals should be aware of it and also the application of cloud computing in library science.

2. CONCEPTUAL APPROACH: CLOUD COMPUTING

Cloud computing means cloud based networking environment. Cloud computing contains set of software and hardware resources which are available on the internet and its services are managed by third-party. These services provide access to advanced software applications and high configured servers. Service provider performs role of consultant.

Cloud computing is a web based computing where shared resources, applications and information are provided to the set of computers and other devices on demand using web technology. Cloud computing is based on internet; generally the internet is commonly visualized as a cloud. Therefore, the process of cloud computing is being done through set of web enabled applications loaded on the server with proper access rights.

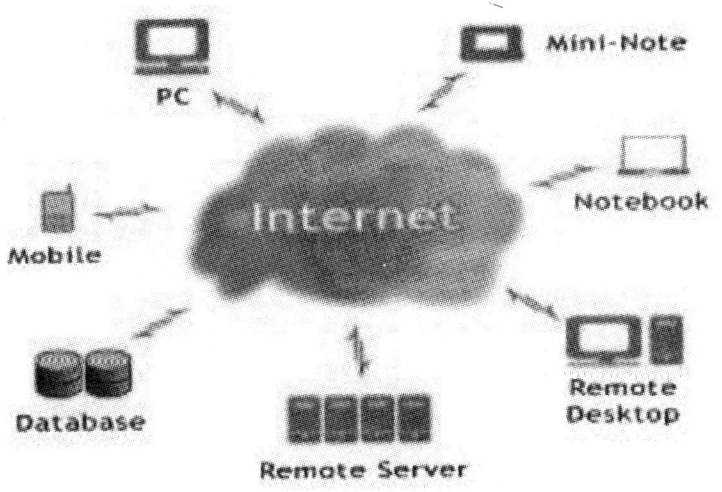

Fig. Cloud Computing

"Internet based computing in which large group of remote servers are networked so as to allow sharing of data-processing tasks, centralized data storage and online access to computer services or resources." [1]. Cloud computing is the delivery of computing services over the Internet. Cloud services allow individuals and businesses to use software and hardware that are managed by third parties at remote locations. Examples of cloud services include online file storage, social networking sites, webmail, and online business applications. The cloud computing model allows access to information and computer resources from anywhere that a network connection is available. Cloud computing provides a shared pool of resources, including data storage space, networks, computer processing power, and specialized corporate and user applications.

The following definition of cloud computing has been developed by the U.S. National Institute of Standards and Technology (NIST): Cloud computing is a model for enabling convenient, on-demand network access to a shared pool of configurable computing resources (e.g., networks, servers, storage, applications, and services) that can be rapidly provisioned and released with minimal management effort or service provider interaction. This cloud model promotes availability and is composed of five essential characteristics, three service models, and four deployment models.[2]

We see Cloud Computing as a computing model, not a technology. In this model "customers" plug into the "cloud" to access IT resources which are priced and provided "on-demand". Essentially, IT resources are rented and shared among multiple tenants much as office space, apartments, or storage spaces are used by tenants. Delivered over an Internet connection, the "cloud" replaces the company data center or server providing the same service. Thus, Cloud Computing is simply IT services sold and delivered over the Internet. [3]

3. CHARACTERISTICS OF CLOUD COMPUTING

Following are the main characteristics of the Cloud Computing:

3.1. On demand self services

Computer services such as email, applications, network or server service can be provided without requiring human interaction with each service provider. Cloud service providers providing on demand self services include Amazon Web Services (AWS), Microsoft, Google, IBM and Salesforce.com.

3.2. Broad network access

Cloud Capabilities are available over the network and accessed through standard mechanisms that promote use by heterogeneous thin or thick client platforms such as mobile phones, laptops and PDAs.

3.3. Resource pooling

The provider's computing resources are pooled together to serve multiple consumers using multiple-tenant model, with different physical and virtual resources dynamically assigned and reassigned according to consumer demand.

3.4. Rapid elasticity

Cloud services can be rapidly and elastically provisioned, in some cases automatically, to quickly scale out and rapidly released to quickly scale in. To the consumer, the capabilities available for provisioning often appear to be unlimited and can be purchased in any quantity at any time.

3.5. Measured service

Cloud computing resource usage can be measured, controlled, and reported providing transparency for both the provider and consumer of the utilized service. Cloud computing services use a metering capability which enables to control and optimize resource use. This implies that just like air time, electricity or municipality water IT services are charged per usage metrics – pay per use.

3.6. Multi Tenacity

It is the 6th characteristics of cloud computing advocated by the Cloud Security Alliance. It refers to the need for policy driven enforcement, segmentation, isolation, governance, service levels, and chargeback/ billing models for different consumer constituencies.

3.7. Security

Security is obviously essential in all systems dealing with potentially sensitive data and code. The cloud is managed and administered by the team of IT expert. Therefore, the data will be secure in terms of data loss and system crash.

4. SEGMENTS OF CLOUD COMPUTING

There are three segments in Cloud Computing which are inter-related to each other and out of three if, anyone is missing then a concept of cloud will remain unfulfilled.

4.1. Application

The application segment is the part of internet technology which is proved already as the constructive and helpful model. When many individual applications are accessed through the central server of cloud, the library (Institute) will demand severe cost. On the other hand, the applications of on-demand are not similar in the price scheme and delivering process to the users. In short an application is the first segment without which a concept of cloud computing cannot be survived.

4.2. Storage

The backbone of the main concept of Cloud Computing is called infrastructure or storage. All the vendors will permit the users to create their own cloud applications within the limited space. The popular S3 of Amazon is considered as a storage segment.

4.3. Connectivity

Most important part of the cloud is connectivity. Without high speed internet connectivity there will be no use of application and storage. Therefore, the high speed leased line internet connectivity is necessary to connect with the cloud.

5. TYPES OF CLOUD COMPUTING

5.1. On the basis of Usage

On the bases of the cloud computing usage by individuals/among different groups, it can be divided mainly in four types.

5.1.1. Public cloud

Public cloud applications, storage, and other resources are made available to the general public by a service provider. These services are free or offered on a pay-per-use model. Generally, public cloud service providers like Amazon AWS, Microsoft and Google own and operate the infrastructure and offer access only via Internet (direct connectivity is not offered).

5.1.2. Community cloud

Community cloud shares infrastructure between several organizations from a specific community with common concerns (security, compliance, jurisdiction, etc.), whether managed internally or by a third-party and hosted internally or externally. The costs are spread over fewer users than a public cloud (but more than a private cloud), so only some of the cost savings potential of cloud computing are realized.

5.1.3. Hybrid cloud

Hybrid cloud is a composition of two or more clouds (private, community or public) that remain unique entities but are bound together, offering the benefits of multiple deployment models. By utilizing "hybrid cloud" architecture, companies and individuals are able to obtain degrees of fault tolerance combined with locally immediate usability without dependency on internet connectivity. Hybrid cloud architecture requires both on-premises resources and off-site (remote) server-based cloud infrastructure.

Hybrid clouds lack the flexibility, security and certainty of in-house applications. Hybrid cloud provides the flexibility of in house applications with the fault tolerance and scalability of cloud based services.

5.1.4. Private cloud

Private clouds are available only to the members of the organization. The cloud will facilitate user to store and disseminate their data on respective cloud (e.g. Institutional cloud, ebay). Undertaking a private cloud project requires a significant level and degree of engagement to virtualise the business environment, and it will require the organization to reevaluate decisions about existing resources. When it is done right, it can have a positive impact on a business, but every one of the steps in the project raises security issues that must be addressed in order to avoid serious vulnerabilities.

5.2. On the basis of Service

Cloud Providers offer services that can be grouped into three types:-

5.2.1. Software as a Service (SaaS)

In this model, a complete application is offered to the customer, as a service on demand. A single instance of the service runs on the cloud & multiple end users are serviced. On the customers' side, there is no need for upfront investment in servers or software licenses, while for the provider, the costs are lowered, since only a single application needs to be hosted & maintained. Today SaaS is offered by many companies such as Google, Sales force, Microsoft, Zoho, etc.

5.2.2. Platform as a Service (Paas)

In Paas, a layer of software, or development environment is encapsulated & offered as a service, upon which other higher levels of service can be built. The customer has the freedom to build his own applications, which run on the provider's infrastructure. To meet manageability and scalability requirements of the applications, PaaS providers offer a predefined combination of OS and application servers, such as LAMP platform (Linux, Apache, MySql and PHP), restricted J2EE, Ruby etc. Google s App Engine, Force.com, etc are some of the popular PaaS examples.

5.2.3. Infrastructure as a Service (Iaas)

IaaS provides basic storage and computing capabilities as standardized services over the network. Servers, storage systems, networking equipment, data centre space etc. are pooled and made available to handle workloads. The customer would typically deploy his own software on the infrastructure. Some common examples are Amazon, GoGrid, 3 Tera, etc.

6. USE OF CLOUD COMPUTING IN LIBRARIES: ADVANTAGES

There are many possibilities offered by Cloud computing in libraries that assists to decrease technology cost and increase capacity reliability, and performance in automated activities run by libraries. Cloud computing has made strong applications inroads into other commercial sectors and is now beginning to find more application in library science. The cloud computing pushes hardware to more abstract levels. In cloud computing data is saved into cloud environments. The things we do on computer likely for even on MS word application is saved through internet. So it becomes new paradigm of computer applications or systems. Cloud Computing in Libraries is user centric, openness, interoperable and its access is round the clock available anytime anywhere. It is flexible and innovative. It provides highly secured infrastructure and resilient in disaster recovery. It reduces hardware and maintenance cost. It is very economical thing and more capacity of servers is expected compare to local servers. Also we can store more data and information too. The same may be retrieved very speedy and easily. In cloud based services, we need not to worry to update or upgrade our software and application packages and make us free from licensing issues. The vision of using cloud computing in libraries is to deliver library resources, services and expertise at the point of need, within user workflows and in a manner that users want and understand. It will free and ease libraries from managing technology so that they can focus on collection building, improved services, innovations and initiatives practices. The basic benefits of implementing Cloud Computing in libraries may be considered for the following aspects.

6.1. Reduced Cost

There are a number of reasons to attribute Cloud technology with lower costs. The billing model is pay as per usage; the infrastructure is not purchased thus lowering maintenance. Initial expense and recurring expenses are much lower than traditional computing.

6.2. Increased Storage

With the massive Infrastructure that is offered by Cloud providers today, storage &maintenance of large volumes of data is a reality. Sudden workload spikes are also managed effectively & efficiently, since the cloud can scale dynamically.

6.3. Flexibility

This is an extremely important characteristic. With enterprises having to adapt, even more rapidly, to changing business conditions, speed to deliver is critical. Cloud computing stresses on getting applications to market very quickly, by using the most appropriate building blocks necessary for deployment.

7. CLOUD COMPUTING, EXAMPLES

- **OCLC :** OCLC Online Computer Library Center is a nonprofit, membership, computer library service and research organization dedicated to the public purposes of furthering access to the world's information and reducing the rate of rise of library costs.
- **Library Thing :** It is one of the sites that combine aspects of social networking and Cloud computing

is Library Thing, originator of which is Tim Spalding. Library Thing offers services which are just like social networking site, authorizes people to contribute information and suggestion about books and allows them to interconnect globally to share interests.

- **Reed Elsevier :** Reed Elsevier is a service provider for scientific information working with hospitals to provide point in time information to medical technicians as they need the information. It is capitalizing on the cloud computing model.
- **Amazon and Google :** These are among the leading enterprises also providing solutions for libraries by having partnerships between library automation vendors. Amazon has been developing for many years large web services architecture and they now offer hosting services for data which are priced at gigabytes-month and CPU hour rates. We basically pay what we actually use. Google for years is working for the dissemination of information also taking interest in library solutions, going to implement "APP Engine" which provides a hosted service for application within their server farms and on massive and highly redundant storage system.
- **Kindle and Mobile Me services :** In the electronic book arena Amazon is providing some reading services with Kindle. If one have wireless connection, can purchase and read a rapidly growing list of books and periodicals from the Kindle no matter for the location. With this service largest text can be downloaded in seconds. Another like this service is "Mobile Me" provided by Apple computing. The concept is distributed calendaring and messaging no matter what device you are using. Modifications made via one device are instantly reflected on all of the devices and computers that are tied into "Mobile Me".

- **DuraSpace :** A hosted service and open technology to help organizations and end users effectively utilize public cloud services built upon existing cloud services. The service can work on Amazon, Atmos, Sun, Rackspace, and other cloud services.LOCKSS in the cloud based on DuraCloud.
- **Chronopolis Project :** Designed primarily as a preservation storage system. Chronopolis Tools also monitors files and does auditing. (http://surferblue.wordpress.com)
- **TerraPod :** Digital video library. It allows you to outsource upload and data creation to the creators of the content. (http://surferblue.wordpress.com)

8. DISADVANTAGES OF CLOUD COMPUTING

There are some disadvantages of Cloud Computing too. These are:

- Risk or data loss
- Failure in compliance
- Constant connectivity required
- Dependency
- Quality problems with cloud service provider
- Time and Budget Constraints
- Since all the development and deployment have been done by Cloud service provider, it is very difficult to get good grip on overall system.

9. CONCLUSION

In conclusion, we can say that cloud computing service is a blazing topic which is giving new dimensions to computer systems. The Cloud computing offers numerous benefits for different organizations, individuals and in libraries also. It is vital for the libraries due to various reasons. We can access data and information from anywhere at any time scenario. Its services are available from remotely. It helps in renovating data centers so we can say cloud computing services is like uprising in the field of library and Information Science. There are also privacy and security concerns. The libraries have the opportunity to improve their services with the help of Cloud computing. It is one path for this move into the future which brings numerous advantages for libraries.

REFERENCES

1. Abidi, F., & Abidi, H. J. (2012). Cloud Libraries: A Novel Application of Cloud Computing. International Journal of Cloud Computing and Services Science (IJ-CLOSER) , 1 (3), 79-83.
2. Gosai, A., & Raval, R. (2012-13). Cloud Computing: A New Paradigm for E library. Journal of Information, Knowledge and Research in Computer Science and Applications , 02 (02), 124-127.
3. Gosavi, N., Shinde, S. S., & Dhakulkar, B. (2012). Use of Cloud Computing in Library and Information Science Field. International Journal of Digital Library Services , 2 (3), 51-60.
4. Goyal, L. C., & Jatav, P. K. (2012). Cloud Computing: an Overview and its Impact on Libraries. International Journal of Next Generation Computer Applications (IJNGCA) , 1 (1), 9-15.
5. Mayank, Y. (2013). Cloud Computing Applications in Indian Central University libraries: A study of librarians' use . Library Philosophy and Practice (e-journal). Paper 992.
6. Reddy, T. R. (2012). Digital Era: Utilize of cloud computing technology in digital Library. International journal of Digital Library Services , 2 (3), 92-106.
7. Suthar, A. A. (2013). An Overview of Using Cloud Computing in Libraries. Indian Journal Of Applied Research , 3 (6), 303-306

8. Pandya, M. (2012). Cloud Computing for Libraries: A SWOT Analysis. 8th Convention PLANNER-2012 Sikkim University, Gangtok, March 01-03, (pp. 387-394). Ahmedabad: INFLIBNET.
9. http://commons.wikimedia.org/wiki/File:Cloud_computing.svg (Accessed on 06.11.2013)
10. http://csrc.nist.gov/groups/SNS/cloudcomputing/(Accessed on 05.11.2013)
11. http://www.dictionary.reference.com/ (Accessed on 08/11/2013)
12. http://en.wikipedia.org/wiki/Multi-tenancy (Accessed on 09.11.2013)
13. *http://www.dummies.com/how-to/content/cloud-computing-models.html*(Accessed on 12.11.2013)
14. http://www.gartner.com/it/page.jsp?id=1035013 (Accessed on 09.11.2013)
15. http://www.ijecse.org/wp-content/uploads/2012/06/Volume-1Number-3PP-1214-1219.pdf (Accessed on 09.11.2013)
16. http://www.oclc.org/content/dam/oclc/events/2011/files/IFLA-winds-of-change-paper.pdf (Accessed on 09.11.2013)
17. http://www.priv.gc.ca/resource/fs-fi/02_05_d_51_cc_e.pdf (Accessed on 05.11.2013)
18. http://www.slideshare.net/goodfriday/amazon-web-services-building-a-webscale-computing architecture (Accessed on 09.11.2013)
19. http://www.youtube.com/watch?v=0swJCYLH2C (Accessed on 09.11.2013)

15

Cloud Computing: Applications in Library Domain

Aswathy S

ABSTRACT

Cloud computing is the buzz word of the time and it is an emerging concept that endeavor to decentralize the computing power by making the possibility of location and device independent free use of the library resources as well as services. Cloud computing impacts the library routine by providing the opportunity to users over dispersed locations. An attempt has been made to depict the true picture of cloud components, nature and potential of cloud computing, devices, service provides the areas of application in libraries and also the advantages and disadvantages.

Keywords: Cloud Computing; security, privacy, reliability, Saas, Paas, Iaas

1. INTRODUCTION

Rapid transformations and advancements in technology has made its impact in every aspect of life like power grids, traffic control, medical and health care, water supply, food and energy and all the financial transaction of the world and the introduction of cloud computing is not an exception in revolutionizing world.

Cloud computing provides unlimited, on – demand computing resources us virtually. With "Virtualization" and "Remote hosting" as the key technology, Cloud computing is a natural advancement to meet needs that have been obvious for numerous years. A cloud, of course, is a visible mass of droplets or frozen crystals floating in the atmosphere above the surface of the Earth or another planetary body and also a visible mass attracted by gravity, exerting a strong gravitational pull all of its own— one that has been attracting a mass of money. The big performers in cloud computing are Google, Amazon, and, of late, Microsoft and IBM. Private (often on premise) clouds can provide increased utilization compared with deploying, installing, and maintaining traditional farms of servers deployed on a task per- server basis. Public clouds offer increased efficiency, but are perceived as being less secure. Newer hybrid solutions, such as IBM Cloudburst, Eucalyptus, and Windows App Fabric provide a consistent development experience for easy migration, redundancy, and scalability.

As a result of huge increase in connectivity and data, many providers including data centres started employing larger infrastructures with dynamic load and access balancing and by distributing and reproducing the data on demand from servers across the world, the significant utilization of the resources made possible. The term "cloud" dates back to the 90's established in reference to the capability of dynamic traffic switching to balance utilization ("telecom clouds") and to indicate that the telecoms infrastructure is virtualized and at the same time the end user does not know or care over which channels her data is routed. By the advent of Amazon, who published the internal resources and their management mechanisms for the use by customers the term "cloud" associated with "on demand" access. Following Amazon, many companies have rebranded their infrastructures to this system.

Thus the concept and even technological approaches behind "cloud computing" cannot be considered a novelty and in cloud systems are, not driven by research first and then being taken up by industry, but instead originates directly from commercial requirements and solutions. It is hence not surprising, that the term "cloud computing" and its current understanding only really became popular with Amazon's publication of the Elastic Compute Cloud EC2 in 2006. Barr, J. (2006), giving rise to a small boom of "cloud offerings" which mostly consisted in a rebranding of their existent in-house solutions and techniques, as well as a potential exposition of these capabilities to consumers.

2. WHAT IS CLOUD COMPUTING?

In simple expression, cloud computing is the dynamic delivery of information technology resources and capabilities as a service over the Internet and a computing approach in which dynamically scalable, virtualized resources are provided as a service via Internet. It generally incorporates infrastructure as a service (IaaS), platform as a service (PaaS), and software as a service (SaaS).

3. DEFINITIONS

According to National Institute of Standards and Technology (2009), Information Technology Laboratory, Cloud computing "is a model for enabling convenient, on-demand network access to a shared pool of configurable computing resources (e.g., networks, servers, storage, applications, and services) that can be rapidly provisioned and released with minimal management effort or service provider interaction. This cloud model promotes availability and is composed of five essential characteristics, three service models, and four deployment models."

Cloud computing has evolved by addressing the QoS

(quality of service) and reliability problems and provides the tools and technologies to build data/compute intensive parallel applications with much more affordable prices compared to traditional parallel computing techniques. Cloud computing shares characteristic with Client–server model, Grid computing, Mainframe computer and Utility computing.

4. FEATURES OF CLOUD SERVICES

National Institute of Standards and Technology, Information Technology Laboratory has provided the following features of cloud services.

4.1. On-demand self-service

A consumer can unilaterally provision computing capabilities, such as server time and network storage, as needed automatically without requiring human interaction with each service's provider.

4.2. Broad network access

Capabilities are available over the network and accessed through standard mechanisms that promote use by heterogeneous thin or thick client platforms (e.g., mobile phones, laptops, and PDAs).

4.3. Resource pooling

The provider's computing resources are pooled to serve multiple consumers using a multi-tenant model, with different physical and virtual resources dynamically assigned and reassigned according to consumer demand. There is a sense of location independence in that the customer generally has no control or knowledge over the exact location of the provided resources but may be able to specify location at a higher level of abstraction (e.g., country, state, or datacenter). Examples of resources include storage, processing, memory, network bandwidth, and virtual machines.

4.4. Rapid elasticity

Capabilities can be rapidly and elastically provisioned, in some cases automatically, to quickly scale out and rapidly released to quickly scale in. To the consumer, the capabilities available for provisioning often appear to be unlimited and can be purchased in any quantity at any time

4.5. Measured Service

Cloud system automatically controls and optimizes the resource use by leveraging a metering capability at some level of abstraction appropriate to the type of service (e.g. storage, processing, bandwidth, and active user accounts). Resource usage can be monitored, controlled, and reported providing transparency for both the provider and consumer of the utilized service

5. SERVICE MODELS OF CLOUD

Cloud services are based on quite a few elementary models such as Software as a service (Saas), Platform as a service (Paas), Infrastructure as a service (Iaas). Adding to this a few other models are also available which are Data as a Service (Daas) and Network as a service (Naas), Collaboration as a service, Communication as a service and Strategy as a service.

5.1. Cloud Software as a Service (SaaS)

The capability provided to the consumer is to use the provider's applications running on a cloud infrastructure. The applications are accessible from various client devices through a thin client interface such as a web browser (e.g., web-based email). The consumer does not manage or control the underlying cloud infrastructure including network, servers, operating systems, storage, or even individual application capabilities, with the possible exception of limited user-specific application configuration settings. Here users are provided access to application software and databases while the cloud providers handle the infrastructure and platforms that run the applications which are sometimes referred to as "on-demand software" and is usually priced on a pay-per-use basis. SaaS providers generally price applications using a subscription fee. The cloud providers install and operate application software in the cloud and cloud users access the software from cloud clients and the cloud users do not manage the cloud infrastructure and platform where the application runs which eliminates the need to install and run the application on the cloud user's own computers, which simplifies maintenance and support. Some of such services are Google Apps and Salesforce.

5.2. Cloud Platform as a Service (PaaS)

In this model the consumer is provided the capability to deploy onto the cloud infrastructure consumer- created or acquired applications created using programming languages and tools supported by the provider. The consumer does not manage or control the underlying cloud infrastructure including network, servers, operating systems, or storage, but has control over the deployed applications and possibly application hosting environment configurations. The cloud providers deliver a computing platform, typically including operating system, programming language execution environment, database, and web server in Paas model were application developers can develop and run their software solutions on a cloud platform without the cost and complexity of buying and managing the underlying hardware and software layers. With some PaaS offers, the underlying computer and storage resources scale automatically to match application demand so that the cloud user does not have to allocate resources manually. Some of the examples for Paas are Windows Azure, Google AppEngine, and Force.com.

5.3. Cloud Infrastructure as a Service (IaaS)

The consumer is provided with the provision to processing, storage, networks, and other fundamental computing resources where the consumer is able to deploy and run arbitrary software, which can include operating systems and applications. The consumer does not manage or control the underlying cloud infrastructure but has control over operating systems, storage, deployed applications, and possibly limited control of select networking components. Providers of IaaS offer Computers – physical or (more often) virtual machines – and other resources. IaaS clouds often offer additional resources such as a virtual-machine disk image library, raw (block) and file-based storage, firewalls, load balancers, IP addresses, virtual local area networks (VLANs), and software bundles on demand from their large pools installed in data centers and for wide-area connectivity, customers can use either the Internet or carrier clouds i.e. dedicated virtual private networks. The best example of this service is Amazon's web services viz. Simple Storage Services (S3) for data storage and elastic compute cloud (EC2) for computing resources.

5.4. Network as a service (NaaS)

Naas is a category of cloud services where the capability provided to the cloud service user is to use network/transport connectivity services and/or inter-cloud network connectivity services and involves the optimization of resource allocations by considering network and computing resources as a unified whole. Usually, NaaS services include flexible and extended VPN, and bandwidth on demand.

6. CLOUD DEPLOYMENT MODELS

Similar to diverse services available in cloud computing, there are different models for delivering those services. Mell and Grance (2009) identify the following four cloud "deployment" models:

6.1. Private cloud

Infrastructure operated solely for an organization is named as private cloud which may be managed by the organization or a third party and may exist on premise or off premise. Undertaking a private cloud project requires a noteworthy level and degree of engagement to virtualize the business environment, and requires the organization to re-examine decisions about existing resources which can improve the business when done right but every step in the project raises security issues that must be addressed to prevent serious vulnerabilities. Cloud bursting is an application deployment model in which an application runs in a private cloud or data center and "bursts" to a public cloud when the demand for computing capacity increases. According to Rouse, Margaret (2011), a primary advantage of cloud bursting and a hybrid cloud model is that an organization only pays for extra compute resources when they are needed.

6.2. Community cloud

The cloud infrastructure is shared by several organizations and supports a specific community that has shared concerns such as mission, security requirements, policy and compliance considerations) which is managed by the organizations or a third party and may exist on premise or off premise and the costs are spread over fewer users than a public cloud, so only some of the cost savings potential of cloud computing are realized.

6.3. Public cloud

Public cloud infrastructure is made available to the general public or a large industry group and is owned by an organization selling cloud services. Technically there may be little or no difference between public and private cloud architecture, however, security consideration may be substantially different for services like applications, storage, and other resources that are made available by a service provider for a public audience and when communication is effected over a non-trusted network. Generally, public cloud service providers like Amazon AWS, Microsoft and Google own and operate the infrastructure and offer access only via Internet.

6.4. Hybrid cloud

The composition of two or more clouds i.e. private, community, or public resulted in hybrid cloud that remain unique entities but are bound together by standardized or proprietary technology that enables data and application portability (Metzler, Jim & Taylor, Steve. (2010). By utilizing "hybrid cloud" architecture, companies and individuals are able to obtain degrees of fault tolerance combined with locally immediate usability without dependency on internet connectivity and require both on-premises resources and off-site (remote) server-based cloud infrastructure. Hybrid cloud provides the flexibility of in house applications with the fault tolerance and scalability of cloud based services.

7. CLOUD CONCEPT IN LIBRARY APPLICATIONS

Cloud-based applications offer libraries new ways to present information or offer services. Libraries are using computers for running services such as Integrated Library Management Software (ILMS), website or portal, digital library or institutional repository, etc which is maintained by computer division of the parent organization or by library itself. Also the implementation and maintenance involves investment on hardware, software, and staff and effort should be put for undertaking backup and up-gradation as and when new version of the software gets released. Even though privacy, security, etc are some concerns in using cloud services, few libraries have already embraced this new technology to run various services. Kroski (2009) argues that, "libraries are experimenting with all types of cloud computing services including that of infrastructure services, i.e., IaaS".

Mitchell (2010) is of the view that cloud computing given their service-oriented mission which needs to find appropriate solutions using limited resources. One of the key pressures that pushes libraries to cloud solutions and proves to be an impediment to the migration is the availability of IT support services. The goals and policies of organisation might also force libraries in making use of cloud computing services (Fox, 2009).

8. AREAS OF CLOUD IN LIBRARY SERVICES

Libraries are using cloud computing in several of areas which begins from federated search, website hosting, digital libraries, library automation, etc. Some of these are:

8.1. Information Search Services

In this era of information explosion and digital document revolution, search service is a major task of libraries and cloud services is a solution to the problem. Various federated search service providers (both open and paid) which provides resource discovery service which is also named as web-scale discovery emerged with their valuable service. Exlibris, K-nimbus etc are providing such services in which the library can route their subject queries through their web-scale discovery / resource discovery tools that provide links to the subscribed / unsubscribed journals / articles. Google Scholar also provides this service free of cost.

8.2. Website Hosting

Many organizations including library prefer to host their website by a third party service provider rather than to host and maintain their own in-house servers. Google Sites serves as an example of a service for hosting websites outside of the library's servers and allowing for multiple editors to access the site from varied locations.

8.3. Library Automation

In the present scenario most of the libraries work

in an automated environment and till now, this is being undertaken on in-house servers using different proprietary as well as free / open source library management software. OSS Labs and Ex-libris are offering this service. The introduction of software as a service in cloud services has possibilities of budget reduction in the investment and maintenance of the hardware / software and many software vendors started providing these types of services which makes libraries free from updating the software and maintenance of daily backups.

8.4. Digital Library Services

Along with the paradigm shift in the form of publishing from print to electronic institutional repositories / digital libraries has also become the part of present libraries. In the present situation these services are being offered by locally hosted softwares like Greenstone, Dspace, Eprints etc which involves the painstaking task of maintenance cost of servers and it also need to update the software and maintain regular backups. In cloud based services vendors like OSS Labs and Duraspace offer these kinds of services.

8.5. Storage

With the introduction of digital library services, a vast amount of storage space is needed for the computers which serve as the digital library servers. Also the daily transaction of the library is to be stored in backups which need a huge amount of storage space and the situation warrants a server with high storage capacity. In cloud services new service has introduced which provides storage space like Windows Sky Drive, Amazon, DropBox etc. Google Drive also provides space for digital storage.

9. SERVICE PROVIDERS OF CLOUD COMPUTING FOR LIBRARIES

Various service providers exist who are hosting diverse types of services to libraries which provide solutions on paid basis and also free. A few among them are the following:

9.1. Ex Libris

Ex Libris, a cloud service provider in USA provides cloud solution in the field of library with all the software and hardware support needed to provide services to the users including cutting-edge interface to the library collection, maintaining the usage statistics of the scholars, electronic resource management, preservation of digital collection, etc including the management of print collections. Ex Libris is available for all type of libraries and also for consortia which is built on various standard and contains number of features like compatibility with Unicode font, flexibility, migration of data, customization etc.

9.2. Polaris Library Systems

Polaris is a cloud based library automation system who provides standard acquisition and processing system including cataloguing, circulation and patron services. Also, with a Polaris ILS Client License, the library can integrate various PC and print management systems at no extra cost. Polaris Library Systems offers full suite of products including services like inventory management system, outreach services software, self-check technology etc. The service includes the virtual private cloud hosting which is effective in managing the network monitoring and troubleshooting.

9.3. Dura Cloud

Dura Cloud, a sister concern of the Duraspace which is a collaboration of the Dspace digital library software and Fedora Commons provides cloud solution for digital library services. Fedora Commons is a framework for digital repository which tender complete solution for digital library with standard software and hardware solution. Dura cloud also provides open source code and the code needs to be installed on your machine.

A library's institutional repository can live in the cloud through DuraCloud services.

A cloud-based platform for running Koha, which is an open-source ILS, is one popular option. OCLC has recently arrived with its new web-scale Management Services (WSM) which it describes as "the first cooperative management service for libraries." Biblios.net is an open-source, cloud-based cataloging system. Keeping reference statistics, which formerly was most easily accomplished with a pencil and paper, is streamlined in the cloud with applications such as "Desk Tracker", which offers customizable data entry forms and flexible reporting for reference statistics. Hash marks can be entered electronically from any computer, so librarians who field phone calls, e-mails, or instant messages can easily enter information from their own computers.

Cloud applications offer new training opportunities for libraries looking for ways to increase their visibility and relevance. In an effort to increase outreach and gain a higher presence without investing in software, many libraries are offering training on web-based services such as Google Docs. A variety of cloud applications are illustrated below which can be easily incorporated into a library website or can become the website itself.

- Library calendars – Google and Zoho
- Forms –Google and Zoho Docs.
- Blogs – Wordpress.
- Surveys – SurveyMonkey.
- Organising presentations: LibGuides and Subjects Plus.
- Virtual Reference Management – QuestionPoint and Knowledge Tracker
- Instant Messaging – Services such as Meebo and Digsby
- Remote Support –Zoho Assist and Glance

- Remote Group Training – Fuze Meeting, Yuuguuand Glance
- Bibliographic Management – RefWorks, EndNote Web, Mendeley, and Zotero
- Professional Networking –SciVal and Researcher ID
- Storing Searches and More – My NCBI and Ovid
- Social Networking for Readers –GoodReads or LibraryThing
- Browser plugins - LibX and Facebook

10. SECURITY ON CLOUD ENVIRONMENT

Reliability, Availability, and Security (RAS) are the three most concerns about migrating to the cloud. "Reliability" is covered by a service level agreement (SLA) and "Availability" addresses the matters about the sufficient resources are available and how long provisioning of new resources can take and how quickly they can be deprovisioned as needs scale back down. The main goal of Security is to limit access only to those approved, to let those with approved see and/or modify only the data they are entitled to see and no other data, and to ensure that no one can requisition resources beyond their budget. "Cloud Security Alliance" has been developing cloud-specific standards that will improve the available standards. "CloudAudit" is developing an open, extensible, and secure interface that allows cloud computing providers to expose Audit, Assertion, Assessment, and Assurance information for cloud infrastructure (IaaS), platform (PaaS), and application (SaaS) services to authorized clients.

11. SUSTAINABILITY

According to Berl, Andreas...et al. (2010), it is often assumed that cloud computing is in a form of "green computing", till now there is no way to measure the proportion of "green" in these computers and energy use is the most important environmental problem associated with the cloud. To tackle the situation, a few companies have come forward by shifting to use clean and renewable energy to power its own operations. Farrahi Moghaddam, Fereydoun... et al. (2011) is of the view that energy efficiency in cloud computing can result from energy-aware scheduling and server consolidation and in the case of distributed clouds over data centers with different sources of energy including renewable energy, the use of energy efficiency reduction could result in a significant carbon footprint reduction.

12. ADVANTAGES

Switching to cloud means various activities are outsourced and there are various benefits and also drawbacks. There are many advantages and disadvantages to cloud versus desktop computing in this age of high-speed Internet access, in which the following are a few:

12.1. Scalability

Increase in access to computing resources are possible without acquiring new hardware and Organizations can make on-the-fly adjustments to increase or decrease capacity since a vast array of SaaS options is available on demand. It also increases agility i.e. increase in speed of deployment.

12.2. Reduced Expenses

IT support costs are lowered; since fewer programs are hosted locallyand hardware costs are also reduced. Charges for computing power and storage are generally inexpensive. By reducing the expense, the customer needs to pay only for what they actually use, not for the upper limit of what they might use. It Eliminates capital expenditures by paying only for what you used. And also there is a reduction in arranging the in-house training for the staff and the maintenance cost is also reduced. It also reduces unused computing capacity.

12.3. Access and Portability

Because there is no requirement other than an Internet connection and a browser, files can be available at work, at home, and on mobile devices. In the cloud environment, E-mailing files back and forth or carrying flash drives around is no longer necessary.

12.4. Reliability

Reliability varies according to the cloud provider, but, barring disaster, using a trustworthy company means that files and services will be as expected.

12.5. Ease of Collaboration

Documents can be made available to everyone those who involved in a project and shared in real time without e-mailing and copying changes.

12.6. Program Updates

Automatic updating of software is possible from the source, eliminating the need for manual updates and also enables adoption of latest technology and encourages standardization. It also gives opportunity to carry experiment with newer technologies.

13. DISADVANTAGES

Cloud computing offers many benefits, but is also vulnerable to threats. As the use of cloud computing increase, it is likely that criminals find new ways to exploit system vulnerabilities. To mitigate the threat, heavy investment on risk assessment which ensures encryption methods which protect the data, establishment of trusted foundation to secure the platform and infrastructure, and the building up of higher assurance into auditing to strengthen compliance is necessary. Trust should be assured by the security systems. Data breach is a big concern in cloud computing which should be addressed well according to Bowen, Janine Anthony (2011). The observance of the critics of cloud computing is that transition to remote and subscription based resources opens up organizations to new legal and operational challenges and also they raise the uncertainty about the trust on the cloud computing platforms (Truitt, 2009) and argues that new regulations and policies are required to ensure openness and sustainability (Nelson, 2009).

Cloud computing is an uncertain area of concern and debate among the library profession. There are justifiable concerns about trusting one's data to a third-party vendor in which Librarians will have to decide where to wallop the balance between storing and preserving information on-site versus in the cloud. Various other issues which will be of major apprehension of libraries are:

13.1. Security

The data provider should assure about the necessary precautions taken to protect the data. Although reliability is usually high with reputable companies, there is always a risk of losing data and it is crucial to understand what protections against loss of data are offered by a cloud service provider. To avoid the data loss, storing a backup copy is just as important as ever.

13.2. Privacy

Concerns about cloud computing, including the effect on privacy laws by a cloud provider's location, the terms and conditions set by vendors, jeopardized legal privacy protections, and easier access to records by government agencies has been cited by the World Privacy Forum, a nonprofit research and education organization.

13.3. Access

Even though access is one of the selling points of cloud computing, it is not a guarantee. One way that access may change is that formerly free providers may start charging for service and there is also the risk of a provider going out of business and leaving its customers without access to their data.

Also in cloud environment, the risk of increased delegation to third parties and data security risks are involved. There is also a chance of reduced ability to limit physical access, control over compliance and reduced control over disaster recovery control. Fear of increased overall costs, reduced control over performance and availability is also a concern about the cloud services. Risk of vendor business failure and vendor lock-in and lack of portability are also the disadvantages involved in this kind of services.

14. CONCLUSION

Libraries should have an apparent consciousness about the trade-offs they must make in order to take advantage of the benefits of cloud computing, but not all disadvantages have been submissive with the philosophical reinforcement of librarianship. Journal licensing and fair use are one of the serious issue for the libraries in the cloud model, with librarians which has been successfully resisted by the licensing that compromises the fair sharing of information. The vanishing of print versions of journals and books is another problem confronted by the libraries. Despite the disadvantages, the cloud offers countless prospects through which libraries may offer service to their users by reduced cost, greater reliability, and ease-of-use benefits. Ex Libris, VTLS, CyberTools, the Serials Solutions e-resource management suite which provides "Summon" etc are major ILS vendors that provide various service models.

More over fascination in the cloud seems inevitable for any service-oriented organization. The benefit of the cloud i.e. "any time any where device agnostic access" can be utilised by the end users. Before switching over to the new environment a thorough investigation should be conducted in order to sort out all the merits and demerits.

Cloud Computing has emerged with powerful panorama in all most all the areas, and the libraries are also not in exception and it can be used in various areas like collection development, selection procedures, organization and dissemination of information.

REFERENCES

1. Berl, Andreas...[et al.]. (2010). Energy-Efficient cloud computing. *The Computer Journal*
2. Bowen, J. A. (2010). Cloud computing: issues in data privacy/ security and commercial considerations. *Computer and Internet Lawyer Trade Journal*, *8* (8).
3. Farrahi, Moghaddam Fereydoun...[et al.]. (2011). Low carbon virtual private clouds. *IEEE International Conference on Cloud Computing (CLOUD)* (pp. 259-266). Washington DC: IEEE Explore.
4. Fox, R. (2009). Libraries in a cloud. *OCLC Systems and Services*, *25* (3), 156-61.
5. Kroski, E. (2009). Library cloud atlas: a guide to cloud computing and storage/stacking the tech. *Library Journal*.
6. Margaret, R. (2011). *Definition: cloudbursting.* Retrieved October 2013, from SearchCloudComputng.com: http:// definition/cloud-bursting
7. Mell, P and Grance T. (2009). *The NIST definition of cloud computing.* National Institute of Standards and Technology, Information Technology Laboratory.
8. Metzler, Jim and Taylor, Steve. (2010). *Cloud computing: reality vs. fiction.* Retrieved 2013, from http:// www.networkworld.com/newsletters/frame/2010082310 wan1.htnl/
9. Mitchell, E. (2010). Using cloud services for library IT infrastructure. *Code4Lib Journal*.
10. Nelson, M R. (2009). The cloud, the crowd and public policy. *Issues in Science and Technology*, *25* (4), 71-76.
11. NIST. (2010). *NIST.gov.* Retrieved November 2013, from Computer Secutiry Division - Computer Security Resource Center: http://csrc.nist.gov/groups/SNS/cloud-computing/ index/html
12. Truitt, M. (2009). Computing in the "cloud". *Information Technology and Libraries*, *28* (3), 107-108.

16

Role of Cloud Computing in Libraries

Leena Khullar

ABSTRACT

Cloud computing is a latest technology of IT (Information technology) services.Now a days, severa organizations are adopting it due to its advantages. The term"cloud computing" means new generation of computing where distant servers areused for data storage and management. Cloud computing help libraries to move away from owning and operating local servers to Web-based services. Its mainadvantage is that it simplify processes and saves time and money. Its examplesinclude Google's suite of apps, Amazon's S3 and EC2 services. Cloudcomputing came into focus when a need is felt to increase capacity and capability of institution in terms of IT but without investing in new infrastructure, training new personnel, and licensing new software. This service is very economical, as application and hardware is provided service provider. Users are required to pay only for the services they require and use. This paper is an attempt to discuss the concept of cloud computing, its types, advantages, disadvantages and its use in libraries.

Keywords : Cloud Computing, Organizational Computing, Cloud Services, Utility Computing.

1. INTRODUCTION

Cloud computing is off-premise, on-demand computing in which user is provided with applications, infrastructure and services by cloud service provider via Internet. Cloud computing changes the way applications are delivered, managed and integrated. Compared to traditional computing, cloud computing operates on a larger scale and attracts a variety of users. Mostly service providers provide cloud computing in the form of shared hosting and SaaS (software as a service).The most simple example of cloud computing is Yahoo e-mail, Gmail, or Hotmail .You just need an internet connection and you can start sending e-mails. The server and e-mail management software is all on the cloud (internet) and is totally managed by the cloud service provider.

2. DEFINITION

According to Wikipedia "Cloud computing is internet-based computing, where by shared resources, software, and information are provided to computers and other services on demand, like the electricity grid". The Gartner Group defines cloud computing as "a style of computing in which massively scalable and elastic ITenabled capabilities are delivered as a service to external customers by using Internet technologies". Eric Mitchell defines cloud computing as the act of "storing, accessing, and sharing data, applications and computing power in cyberspace."

3. FEATURES OF CLOUD COMPUTING

Now a days concept of cloud computing is gaining lots of popularity, because of its features. Some of these features are:

3.1. Utility computing

Utility computing has significantly contributed to the advancement of cloud computing. It is in great demand as it provides storage and virtual servers that IT can access on demand. Organizations not only use utility computing for their supplementary needs, but they can also replace parts of the datacenter while using it.

3.2. Web services in the cloud

Closely related to SaaS(Software as a service), Web service providers offer APIs(application program interface) that enable developers to have functionality over the Internet, rather than delivering full-blown applications. They offer discrete business services —like Strike Iron and Xignite — to full range of APIs offered by Google Maps, ADP payroll processing, Bloomberg, and even conventional credit card processing services.

3.3. MSP (Managed Service Providers)

This is one of the oldest form of cloud computing. This application is more related to IT rather than to end-users, like virus scanning service for e-mail. Managed security services delivered by SecureWorks, IBM, Verizon and cloud-based anti-spam services as Postini, recently acquired by Google falls into this category.

3.4. Service commerce platforms

This service is a hybrid form of SaaS and MSP and it provides a service hub for users to interact with. This type of service is mostly used in trading environments, such as expense management systems which allow users to order travel or secretarial services from a common platform. Examples are Rearden Commerce and Ariba.

3.5. Internet integration

The integration of cloud-based services is in its early days. OpSource, mainly concerned with serving SaaS providers, recently introduced the OpSource Services Bus, which employs in-the-cloud integration technology from a little startup called **Boomi**. SaaS provider Workday recently acquired another player in this space, CapeClear, an ESB (enterprise service bus) provider that was edging toward b-to-b (business –to-business) integration. (extremely flexible mapping tool).

4. CLOUD COMPUTING MODELS AND CONCEPTS

Generally there are three types of clouds.These are:

4.1. Community Cloud

Community cloud shares infrastructure between several organizations from a specific community with common requirements or interests and are hosted internally or externally. Costs are shared by fewer users as compared to public cloud.

4.2. Public Cloud

A public cloud is established where several organizations have similar requirements and they share infrastructure as well as services.

4.3. Private cloud

Private cloud enables you to remote access the applications of organization via private means like smartphones, tablet etc anywhere and anytime. This kind of cloud-based services and resources are made available on one single platform, which providing high performance, security, and user experience. You can access the desktop, run applications, change settings, and access data exactly as you are sitting in front of the local PC, using its keyboard and mouse.

5. CATEGORIES OF CLOUD COMPUTING

Cloud computing can be divided into three categories:

Software-as-a-Service (SaaS)

Platform-as-a-Service (PaaS)

Infrastructure-as-a-Service (IaaS)

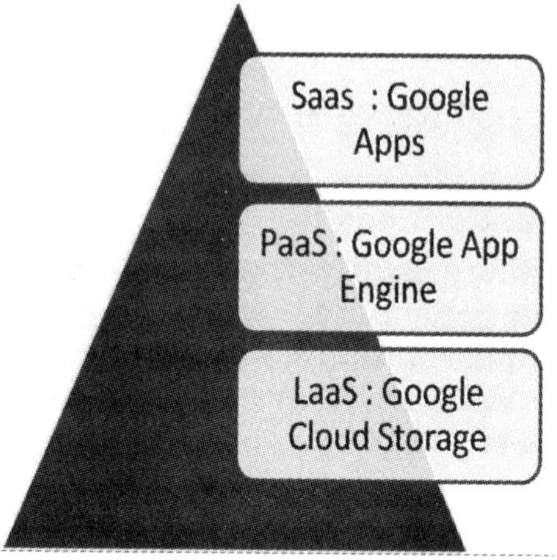

Fig. 1

5.1. SaaS (Software service)

In a SaaS concept, organizations use an application through hosted service. They do not have access to the underlying infrastructure (i.e. network or server elements) and are not responsible for managing the underlying software. This type of cloud computing delivers a single application through the browser to thousands of users using a multitenant architecture. On the users side, it means no investment in servers or software licensing; on the organizations side, with just one app to maintain, costs are low as compare to conventional hosting. Example is Google apps and electronic journal subscription management systems.

5.2. PaaS (Platform service)

This form of cloud computing provides hosted platform on which a specific application can be deployed. One can build its own applications which runs on the provider's infrastructure and are delivered to users through Internet from the provider's servers. For example Legos. But its negative aspect is that these services are constrained by the vendor's design and capabilities, thereby restricting complete freedom to user like Google App Engine. PaaS is mostly done by using an application such as cPanel or Plesk.

5.3. IaaS (Infrastructure-as-a-Service)

IaaS computing provides user with provision servers, storage space, and networking components to meet the computing needs. In an IaaS environment, the organization is responsible for starting and sizing a server, managing its network access, and ensuring that the core server components (e.g. operating system, web server, firewall) are configured correctly. Now a days cloud computing is also called "sky computing".

6. EVALUATION OF CLOUD COMPUTING SERVICES

Services of cloud computing can be evaluated on the following three points :

6.1. Quality and stability of service.

6.2. Impact on organization (library) services.

6.3. Utility computing and cost comparison.

6.1. Quality and stability of the services

Cloud computing services have sorted out some common problems like server configuration, backups, and archives. As all these problems are sorted out effectively, so many institutions including libraries have started using SaaS-style Services with ease.

6.2. Impact on Library Services

By using an infrastructure level service we are able to bring library applications online. But some SaaS and PaaS solutions are difficult to be implemented in libraries, as core applications require specialized software that are either localized or simply application specific. By using laas (an infrastructure level service) one can bring library applications online without finding a service that supported the correct versions of the underlying technology. By moving key application infrastructure outside the campus network means that during Internet connectivity we will have none of key services (e.g. website,ILS).Ability to mount new applications quickly without having focus on available server space means that technology-based library services can be provided much more quickly by cloud computing as compared to local hardware.

6.3. Utility computing and cost comparison

This form of cloud computing is being offered by Amazon.com, Sun, IBM, and others offering storage and virtual servers that IT can access on demand. Earlier utility computing was used for supplemental, non-mission-critical needs, but now a days one can even think of replacing parts of the datacenter. Various companies and providers offer solutions that help IT to create virtual datacenters from commodity servers. Some examples are 3Tera's AppLogic and Cohesive Flexible Technologies' Elastic Server on Demand. Even liquid Computing's LiquidQ offers similar capabilities, enabling IT to stitch together memory, I/O, storage, and computational capacity as a virtualized resource pool available over the network.

7. ADVANTAGES OF CLOUD SERVICES

Some of the advantages of cloud computing are as follows:

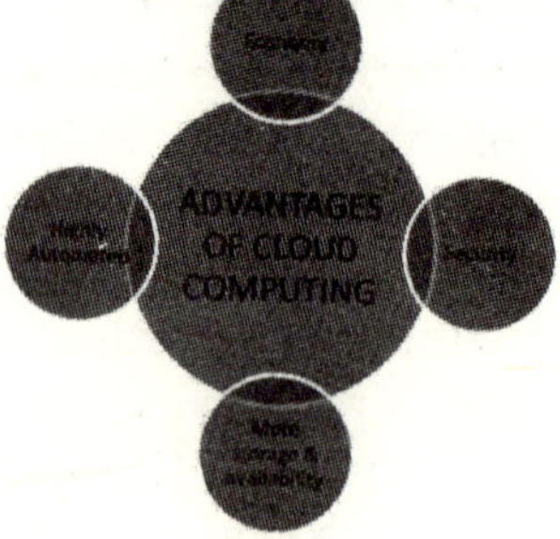

Fig. 2

7.1. Economy

The whole point of cloud computing is economy. It saves the money of organization. Organization can pay only for what it(organization) is using. This means that there is no need to pay for servers and their storage. It's more cost effective for any organization to outsource the computation. In an era of shrinking budgets, it gets harder with each passing year to justify the purchase and maintenance of servers that aren't in use almost all the time.

7.2. Security

Security is an another important component in cloud computing. A security-conscious computing services provider would provide each user with its own processors, caches, and memory at any given moment. A secure data center which is administered externally, allowing a very limited group of employees physical access to the computers is a great boon. Even operators won't be able to access any of the clients data, while supervising the scheduling and provisioning of computations.

7.3. More Storage and availability

Cloud computing has very efficient and effective storage and computing services. Organisations can store much more data as compare to data stored on private computer systems. Moreover services are highly reliable and redundant. Another plus point is a widespread availability of its services irrespective of geographical locations.

7.4. Highly Automated

Now a days, there is no need to come to the particular organization or library to view its holdings. Users can access information from anywhere or where they are sitting. For example OPAC (Online Public Access Catalogue) of Punjab University is available on net on P.U Website and one can easily access it from anywhere. Libraries and other organisations are free to concentrate on innovation and other facilities without worrying about constant server updates and other computing issues. Thus we can say that advantages of using cloud computing include cost savings, speed, access to greater computing resources, high availability, and scalability.

8. DISADVANTAGES OF CLOUD COMPUTING

8.1. Legal and operational challenges

In cloud computing transition to remote and subscription based resources can land organizations in legal and operational challenges. It is also not clear whether the major cloud-computing platforms are trustable or not. Some times new government policies are required to ensure openness and sustainability in cloud computing solutions to avoid legal challenges.

8.2. Technical concerns

In addition to these legal and operational challenges, several other technical concerns exist like how to include cloud-based applications within the organizational network, how to take back up and archive information located in the cloud and how to manage services in decentralized environment. There are some important legal, privacy and security considerations also which must be followed while opting for cloud computing.

9. LIBRARIES AND CLOUD COMPUTING

Libraries are adopting cloud-computing for performing various services including electronic journal access management, statistics tracking, digital library hosting, and even integrated library system (ILS) hosting. It has allowed libraries to provide better services and to make appropriate choices regarding the allocation of resources. The use of SaaS in libraries started in early 2000 with the establishment of companies like Serials Solutions. At that time much of the work regarding electronic journals has been focused on SaaS platform.

In the IaaS arena, Amazon Elastic Computing Cloud (EC2) offers IT infrastructure for organizations to launch different sized servers using a variety of operating systems, including several versions of Linux and Windows. EC2 provides libraries with essentially unlimited storage, while S3 service, provides the ability to take snapshots of both data and servers. Libraries having Twitter, Youtube or Flickr account or a facebook page are supposed to be in cloud. In 2009 OCLC took a step to develop a library management system in the cloud, which includes circulation and acquisitions modules also. Now libraries will be in a unique position to experiment cloud computing by using limited resources. Key pressures which push libraries to cloud solutions is the availability of IT support services. Libraries are often supported by external or organization level IT services and do not have internal expertise on advanced IT management. The cloud can be used for collaboration and working more efficiently.

10. SPECIAL FEATURES OF CLOUD IN RELATION TO LIBRARY SERVICES

10.1. Broad, general IT skills vs. deep, specialized skills

Cloud computing increases the pressure on library professionals to become allrounder employees having IT and managerial skills too. Knowing how to configure and network a server isn't enough. Systems librarians have to manage complex projects and evaluate competing vendors on variety of criteria. They also have to see and find out the accountability of the vendor to whom the significant chunk of the online data has been allocated. Therefore, as long as cloud security remains a significant concern, techies may be called upon to hold vendors to certain standards with regards to reliability and security of their services. Furthermore, techies will likely be part of the teams which periodically audit cloud vendors and ensure they're performing up to the contractual standards.

10.2. Cloud OPAC(Online Public Access Catalogue) and Cloud ILS (Integrated Library System)

Now a days many ILS vendors have started offering cloud-hosted versions of their products. OCLC joined several other vendors a year before when they began offering a cloud-based ILS tools that complement their existing cataloguing tools (e.g. WorldCat and FirstSearch). In both ways whether individuals or members of organizations, one has to choose between desktop applications and cloud applications regarding e-mail, RSS, file storage, word processing and other applications.

10.3. Private Clouds, hybrid Clouds and community Clouds

Libraries in future will build and manage their own data centers. The three major concerns: Security, Privacy and Reliability are compelling libraries to build their own private or hybrid clouds. A hybrid cloud is primarily based on a privately-owned and operated data center, but it can shift some of its data processing requests to public cloud vendors like Amazon or Rackspace on need or request basis. This hybrid model will help libraries to have major control over the applications and data stores which contains private information about users. Moreover, with cloud computing, libraries can adjust and fine-tune the balance between the tight control of a private IT infrastructure, and the flexibility and savings of cloud-hosted infrastructure. If reliability or security of one vendor becomes a concern, library is not committed to one particular company or one model of computing services. It can straight away switch over to another vendor. Secondly if one finds building and managing data center difficult, one can have a community cloud. As libraries are presently cooperating with one another to buy IT equipment, bandwidth and the services of IT professionals, libraries will soon be cooperating in the building and management of data centers also. Alternately, if enough libraries express interest, a company such as Google, Amazon, Microsoft or another cloud vendor can also create a Library Cloud for them.

11. CONCLUSION

Cloud Computing is a service in which internet and central remote servers are used to preserve data and applications. Cloud computing allows users to use applications without installation and access the personal files at any computer with internet access. This technology allows much more effective computing by centralizing storage, memory, processing and bandwidth. Cloud computing can be financially good for libraries because libraries pay for what they use. Moreover thcy have to spend significantly less for local IT services and software. So, it can be said that cloud computing is an abstract of information technology (IT) software and services from the hardware from where they run. When we are using Gmail, Wikipedia, Flickr or Twitter, we are using cloud computing because these applications are hosted in the large online data centers which are hallmarks of cloud computing. In nutshell it can be said that the cloud computing has started gaining mass appeal as it can be used for collaboration and for increasing the efficiency, output and working of Information centres and libraries.

REFERENCES

1. Borko, Furht . Handbook of Cloud Computing, Springer, 2010.
2. Buyya, Rajkumar, Broberg, James (Ed.), Cloud Computing : Principles and Paradigms, Wiley Press, New York,USA, 2011.
3. Corbato,Fermando J "An Experimental Time Sharing System" SJCC Proceedings MIT. Retrieved 2012.03.07.
4. "Defining "Cloud Services" and "Cloud Computing" IDC 2008.09.23. (Accessed on 07.06.2012)

5. George Reese, Cloud Application Architectures – Building applications and infrastructure in the cloud, Shroff Publishers & Distributers Pvt. Ltd., 190 p, Mumbai, 2010.
6. N.Leavitt,"Is Cloud Computing Ready for Prime Time?". Computer, vol.42,no1,2009,pp15-20.
7. Dr. Saurabh kumar, Cloud Computing – Insights Into New Era Infrastructure, Wiley India Pvt. Ltd., New Delhi, 2011
8. http://www.infoworld.com/d/cloud-computing/what-cloud-computing-reallymeans- 031 (Accessed on 21.08.2013).
9. http://en.wikipedia.org/wiki/Cloud_computing (Accessed on 27.08.2013)
10. Wilson,S. AppEngine Outage. CIO Weblog (June 2008). http://www.cioweblog. com/. (Accessed on 11.09.2013).

17

Cloud Computing Technologies and Libraries

Seena S. T.
Dr. K.G. Sudhier

ABSTRACT

The aim of this paper is to present and elaborate the new IT trend – Cloud Computing. Cloud computing represents the move from desktop applications toward Web applications and services. In cloud computing the actual computing is moved into the cloud so the users are using third-party services and paying for them on pay per- use model. The cloud (data and services) can be accessed from any device connected to the Internet. This paper explores an overview of cloud computing, types and deployment models of cloud computing, and benefits as well as issues of cloud computing. It also discusses the application of cloud computing in libraries and some of the cloud computing initiatives taken over the globe. The paper concludes that the establishment of shared public cloud can save manpower and material resources greatly among academic libraries.

Keywords: Cloud Computing, Public Cloud, Private Cloud, Community Cloud, Hybrid Cloud

1. INTRODUCTION

Information and Communication Technologies (ICT) have become common place entities in all aspects of life.

ICT has made a huge impact on library users and the way they need information. There are drastic increase in the use of Cloud-based services and applications i.e. Online mailbox service, Online photo-video storage, Online Document Creation, Online Calendar and many more for their daily use. Information Management / Knowledge Management is entering a new era making significant contribution to knowledge generation, creation and management helped by new thinking, tools, web 2.0 and cloud computing. Cloud computing is an emerging area within the field of Information Technology (IT). Cloud computing is the use of computing resources (hardware and software) that are delivered as a service over a network (typically the Internet). The name comes from the use of a cloud-shaped symbol as an abstraction for the complex infrastructure it contains in system diagrams (Wikipedia). The basic principle of cloud computing entails the reduction of in-house data centers and the delegation of a portion or all of the Information Technology infrastructure capability to a third party. This new approach is expected to herald a new knowledge and information rich world. Libraries can certainly improve their services with the help of cloud computing and web collaboration.

2. CLOUD COMPUTING

Cloud computing is a buzz word now a days in the world of ICT. If you use a web-based e-mail account (e.g. Gmail) or a social networking web site (e.g. Facebook), then you have already experienced cloud computing. To use these services you don't have to install any software or save data on your computer – the software and storage for your account are in "the cloud". Cloud computing uses the Internet as a platform to run applications and store data on servers. Data and services can be accessed from any connected device over the Internet through Web browsers or specialized applications. The core concept of cloud computing is, quite simply, that the vast Computing resources that we need will reside somewhere out there in the cloud of computers and we will connect to them and use as and when needed. You just login, customize and start using it. Some of the Cloud Computing Providers are:

- Amazon Elastic Compute Cloud EC2
- Google App Engine
- Windows Azure
- IBM Blue Cloud
- Salesforce Force.com
- Rackspace

3. HISTORY OF CLOUD COMPUTING

Cloud Computing is considered as the fifth generation of computing after Mainframe, Personal Computer, Client-Server Computing, and the web. Everywhere there is a talk about Cloud Computing and it feels that it has newly born technology, but the reality is that it has gone through decades of slow evolution. Computing can be described as any activity of using and/ or developing computer hardware and software.

Computing started off with the mainframe era which is Centralized & Monolithic. There was a kind of freedom in the use of personal computers. Now we come back to the centralized computing infrastructure. But this time it is something which can easily be accessed via the internet and something over which we have all the control. eg web 2.0, cloud, virtualization, software as service etc. About the emergence of Cloud computing, Salesforce.Com came into existence in 1999, Amazon web services came into 2002 and with the emergence of Web 2.0, Google and others started introducing browser based enterprise applications through services such as Google Apps.

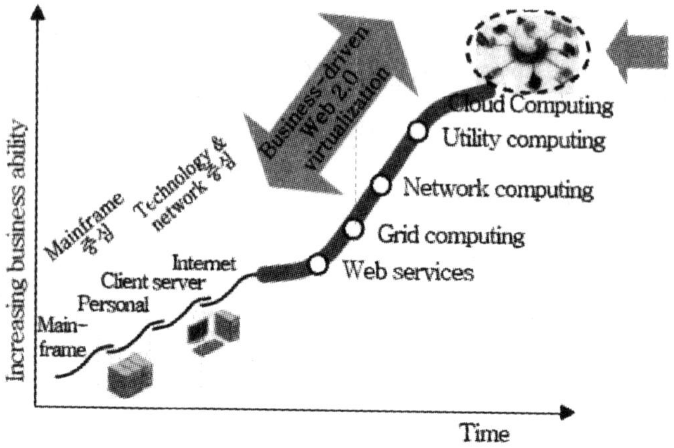

Fig 1. Paradigm Shift of computing over time - Adapted from Das, K. C. (2013)

4. DEFINITION

Cloud computing is a recent concept that is still evolving across the information technology industry and academia. Several definitions have evolved so far. The Gartner Group defines cloud computing as "a style of computing in which massively scalable and elastic IT-enabled capabilities are delivered as a service to external customers using Internet technologies."(Gartner Group, 2010)

National Institute of Standards and Technology (NIST) had provided a universally acceptable definition of 'cloud-computing, as follows: "cloud computing is a model for enabling convenient, on-demand network access to a shared pool of configurable computing resources (e.g., networks, servers, storage, applications, and services) that can be rapidly provisioned and released with minimal management effort or service provider interaction. This cloud model promotes availability and is composed of five essential characteristics, three service models, and four deployment models."

5. WORKING OF CLOUD COMPUTING

Cloud computing system can be divided it into two sections: the front end and the back end. They connect to each other through a network, usually the Internet. The front end is the side the computer user, or client, sees. The back end is the "cloud" section of the system. On the back end there are various computers, servers and data storage systems that create the "cloud" of computing services. A central server administers the system, monitoring traffic and client demands to ensure everything runs smoothly. It follows a set of rules called protocols Servers and remote computers do most of the work and store the data. (Gosavi and Shinde,2012)

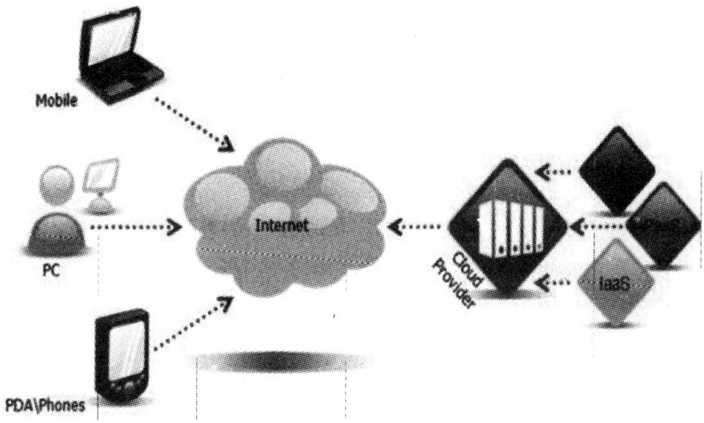

User terminal **Internet** **Data center**

Fig. 2. Working of Cloud Computing

6. CHARACTERISTICS

NIST prescribed essential characteristics

On-demand self-service : A consumer can unilaterally provision computing capabilities, such as server time and network storage, as needed automatically without requiring human interaction with each service provider.

Broad network access : Capabilities are available over the network and accessed through standard mechanisms that promote use by heterogeneous thin or thick client platforms (e.g., mobile phones, tablets, laptops, and workstations).

Resource pooling : The provider's computing resources are pooled to serve multiple consumers using a multi-tenant model, with different physical and virtual resources dynamically assigned and reassigned according to consumer demand.

Rapid elasticity : Capabilities can be elastically provisioned and released, in some cases automatically, to scale rapidly outward and inward commensurate with demand.

Measured service : Cloud systems automatically control and optimize resource use by leveraging a metering capability at some level of abstraction appropriate to the type of service (e.g., storage, processing, bandwidth, and active user accounts) (Mell & Grance, 2010).

7. CLOUD COMPUTING SERVICE MODELS

Software as a Service (SaaS) : When you purchase any software and installed on a personal computers, is something called Software-as-a-Product. Software-as-a-Service is a software distribution model in which applications are hosted by a vendor and made available to customers over a network. SaaS applications are generally priced based on the number of users that can have access to the service. You might have to pay extra fees for the use of help desk services, extra bandwidth or sometimes for storage, if used. Examples: Gmail, Dropbox and Citation Management Software (Mendeley).

Platforms as a Service (PaaS) : Cloud Computing has evolved to include platform for building and running web-based applications, a concept known as Platform-as-a-Service. It offers a faster, more cost effective model for application development and delivery, and provides the entire infrastructure needed to run applications over the internet. PaaS is based on subscription based, so you have to pay only for what you use. Example: Microsoft Azure, Force.com, Google Apps Services, Google Doc, and Worldcat.

Infrastructure as a Service (IaaS) : According to Wikipedia, Infrastructure as a Service (IaaS) is the delivery of computer infrastructure as a service. It leverages significant technology, services, and data center investments to deliver IT as a service to the users. IaaS service providers manage the transition and hosting of selected library applications on their infrastructure. Librarians maintain ownership and management of their application(s) while off-loading hosting operations and infrastructure management to the IaaS service provider. The following things are entrusted by the IaaS service providers:

- Computer hardware, Computer network (including routers, firewalls, internet-users load balancing etc.)
- Internet connectivity
- Service level agreements and many more.

Rather than purchasing servers, software, network equipment etc., librarian can rent those resources as a fully outsourced service. Usually, the service is billed on a monthly basis, just like your telephone or electricity bills. Example: Amazon Elastic Compute Cloud (Amazon EC2), Amazon Simple Storage Service (S3) (Joshi & Prajapati, 2013).

8. CLOUD DEPLOYMENT MODELS

There are four primary cloud deployment models. The basic differences lie in the scope and access of cloud services, as they are made available to end users.

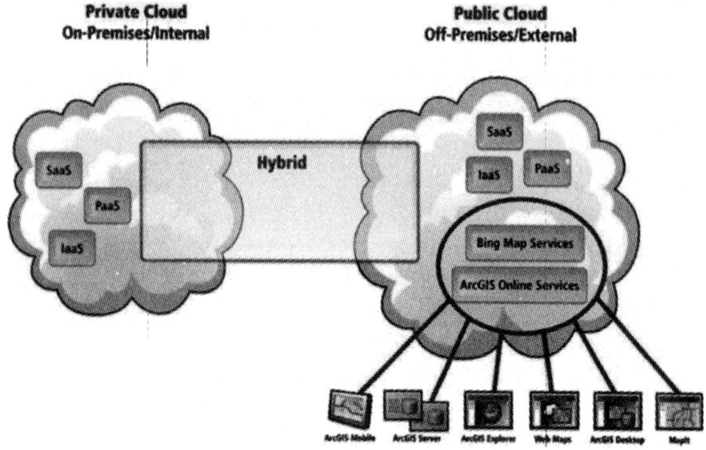

Fig. 3. Cloud Deployment models

Public Cloud : A public cloud is a publicly accessible cloud environment owned by a third-party cloud provider. In this model the vendor or service provider controls the whole cloud system and offers service on demand over Internet on pay-per-use basis. It is also known as provider cloud. Examples: Google App Engine, Microsoft Windows Azure, IBM Smart Cloud, Amazon EC2

Community Cloud : A community cloud is similar to a public cloud except that its access is limited to a specific community of cloud consumers. Examples: Google Apps for Government, Microsoft Government Community Cloud

Private Cloud : A private cloud is owned by a single organization. Private cloud is also known as "internal cloud". Example: eBay, Amazon VPC (Virtual Private Cloud)

Hybrid Cloud : A hybrid cloud is a cloud environment of two or more different cloud deployment models. Hybrid clouds combine both public and private cloud models. It is also known as combined cloud. Examples: Windows Azure (capable of Hybrid Cloud) (Joshi & Prajapati, 2013).

9. ADVANTAGES

Reduced Cost : Cloud technology is paid incrementally (you pay only for what you need), saving organizations money in the short run. Money saved can be used for other important resources.

Increased Storage : Organizations can store more data than on private computer systems.

Highly Automated : IT or library personnel not needed to keep software up to date as maintenance is the job of the service provider on the cloud.

More Mobility : Employees can access information wherever they are, rather than having to remain at their desks.

Allows IT to Shift Focus : No longer having to worry about constant server updates and other computing issues. Organizations will be free to concentrate on research output and development of innovative services.

Shared Resources : One of the important components of cloud computing is that one can share the resources and intensify the power of cooperation.

Program Updates : Software is updated automatically from the source, eliminating the need for manual updates.

Back up and Restoration : Back up of the Cloud can protect all kinds of your library data from loss of owing to fire, flood, or any other natural or man-made computer related disaster that could cause data to disappear. You can easily restore your data if back is done and placed at the safest place.

Green library : Cloud computing will help the libraries to go green by centralizing all resources and efficient utilization. It can reduce the carbon footprints, power consumption, the air-conditioning and electronic waste that can be caused by number of datacenters.

10. CHALLENGES

Main issue is internet and electricity is must. Following are some of the main issues of cloud computing:

Privacy and Security : A primary concern that cloud computing adopters have is the security of enterprise information. End users' information and data can easily be hijacked unless companies keep these data carefully with secure firewalls. Data placed in storage clouds, can potentially be located in, and sent across the communication channels of different country, with potentially different data privacy laws, and therefore expose data to unauthorized individuals.

Performance and Availability : Experiments that are required for research endeavors require extensive computing power. Some of the concerns include how to guarantee such performance from an outside vendor. Availability of services is another related concern in terms of the possibility of massive vendor outages.

Limited flexibility : Flexibility may be limited in terms of special customization as services on the cloud will be common for all the customers.

Service Unavailability due to Power Outage : If there is no power supply it is difficult to get access to application and services.

Cloud interoperability with external Services : No universal and standardized interfaces.

Dependence on outside agencies

Licensing issue : Virtualization of the platform can lead to licensing problems at the customer.

11. CLOUD COMPUTING IN LIBRARIES

Most common library services can be divided into following three categories:

Data : Bibliographic, Technical, Access, License

Content : Collection, Subscription, Digital, Print, Publishing

Services : Library as a place, content-access, content-creation, research, preservation

As libraries are having service-oriented mission they are in a position to adopt cloud computing. Many library patrons are already using cloud products such as Gmail and Google Docs. As more patrons become familiar with these tools, libraries will be able to transition away from installing traditional office software. Libraries have been adopting cloud-based solutions services like electronic journal access management, statistics tracking, digital library hosting and now trend is coming up for hosted library management systems. The use of SaaS in libraries dates back to early 2000 with establishment of companies like SerialsSolutions (http:// serialssolutions.com) (Patel, 2011).

A Library could do the following on cloud infrastructure:

- Library Management Services - access to OPAC and other modules of the library for circulation, acquisition, serials control, issue of books etc.
- Libraries can build digital library, content management system, institutional repository, Inter Library Loan (IIL) system and Integrated Library System (ILS) from locally-managed to vendor-hosted environment, of their own with the help of cloud technology
- Libraries can use cloud technology like Google Docs to collect responses to web forms, Google Calendar for instruction and meeting rooms, and Google Analytics to collect statistics about their website, catalogue and blogs. Cloud technology can be applied for backing up of media collections and storing and accessing of bibliographic data. (Bhattacharjee and Sarmah, 2009).
- Cloud-based content management systems like Ex Libris's bX can combine usage data from millions

of researchers to create a scholarly recommendation service. Online documents such as Google Drive can be used to create and share documents in support of collaborative work (Luo, 2013).

- Bibliographic management is another area where cloud-based tools are rapidly becoming the norm. The ability to access and manage citations from anywhere and share them among multiple users is one of the key features driving this expansion.

12. APPLICATION OF SAAS, PAAS, AND IAAS IN LIBRARIES

Saas and libraries

SaaS is often used in virtual reference and research guides. Virtual reference software such as LibChat and QuestionPoint, and research guides such as LibGuides, is all hosted on the cloud. There are SaaS tools from which reference librarians can benefit, such as cloud-based video services (e.g., YouTube), information collection services (e.g., Google Forms), and file sharing services (e.g., Dropbox) (Luo, 2013). Western State College of Colorado is using Google Apps for hosting its E-Library.

Paas and libraries

PaaS allows libraries can create applications in an online environment. These environments allow a library to - build, test, and deploy Web-based applications (Kroski, 2009). Examples: Social networks which help to marketing the resources in the libraries. Wordpress is another platform which is beneficial for libraries. LibraryThing is platform for cataloguing the document (Ashkar, 2012).

Iaas and libraries

By using IaaS, a library can purchase server space and computing power. One of the major players in this arena is Amazon which offers the -Elastic Compute Cloud (EC2), which provides computing resources and Simple

Storage Services (S3) for data storage (Kroski, 2009). By using an IaaS, a library gains the benefit of only paying for the resources you actually use. Potential datasets that could be moved to the cloud include educational resource repositories, institutional repositories, institutional archives, corporate datasets, data backup, archiving and disaster recovery, and research datasets.

Following is a (non-exhaustive) list of available library focused SaaS offerings:

ILS

- Ex Libris Alma
- OCLC Web-scale Management Services
- SirsiDynix
  - Horizon
  - Symphony
- CyberTools for Libraries
- EOS International EOS.Web
- Auto-Graphics AGent Verso
- VTLS Virtua
- Kuali Foundation Kuali OLE

Content management/Subject Guides

- Springshare LibGuides & CampusGuides

Discovery

- SerialsSolutions Aqua Browser
- VTLS Visualizer
- EBSCO Discovery Service
- Ex Libris Primo
- OCLC WorldCat Local

Reference

- OCLC QuestionPoint
- Springshare LibAnswers
- Compendium Knowledge Tracker

E-resource management

- SerialsSolutions 360 suite
- SwetsWise ERM as a Service
- EBSCONET (Prince, 2012).

13. CLOUD COMPUTING INITIATIVES FOR LIBRARIES

Some of the cloud computing initiatives for libraries are:

- OCLC WorldShare Management Services
- Worldcat
- OSS Labs
- Ex Libri
- Dura Cloud
- Polaris
- LibLime
- Springshare
- Library of Congress (LC)
- Scribd
- Encore

13. Challenges in Indian Perspective

- Many foundations, establishment and government agencies are not aware about the cloud benefit.
- Government grant and assistance towards cloud based model is an emerging issue.
- Many cloud services are costly so for developing countries like India this is another issue.
- University library has not yet embraced the idea of the virtual reality of a library in the digital age.
- Unwillingness to change, funding and finance are important challenges.
- University should evolve an ICT development plan in order to improve the on-the-job performance of

the automated services personnel. Regular training of staff through seminars, workshops, conferences, refresher courses and in-service training should be institutionalized as part of the development plan.

14. CONCLUSION

Cloud computing is being used to describe the act of storing, accessing, and sharing data, applications, and computing power in cyberspace. This technology is relatively new in the field of library and utilization of cloud computing in the library depends upon the efforts of library professionals. Dr. S. R. Ranganathan's fourth principle very much applied when we say Cloud Computing, save the time of reader by providing information anytime anywhere. So now it is time for librarian to concentrate on providing pro-active services and move from general service to personalize information services to the users for the benefit of academic community rather than hunting for technology to deliver the services.

REFERENCES

1. Balakrishna, B. (2012). Evolution of libraries: a walk through emerging and developing aspects. In Osswald, Achim and Ahmed, Zabed S.M. (Eds), *Dynamics of librarianship in the knowledge society,* (312-321). B.R. Publishing Corporation: Delhi.
2. Bansode, S.Y. & Pujar, S.M. (2012). Cloud computing and libraries. *DESIDOC Journal of Library & Information Technology,* 32 (6), 506-512.
3. Bhanti, Prateek., Lehri, Sushma., & Kumar, Narendra. (2011). Cloud computing: a new paradigm for data storage in Indian universities. *Indian Journal of Computer Science and Engineering,* 2(5), 680-683. Retrieved from http://www.ijcse.com/docs/INDJCSE11-02-05-018.pdfý
4. Bhattacharjee, Deepshikha Sen Nilratan. & Sarmah, Mukut. (2009). Cloud computing: a boon for library services. Retrieved from http://www.slideshare.net/ksatpathy/cloud-computing-a-boon-for-library-services

5. Choukimath, Puttaraj A., Agadi, K. B., & Koganuramath, Muttayya M. (2013). Cloud-based services: prospects for the university libraries. *Paper presented at 9th International Conference of CALIBER.* Gandhinagar: INFLIBNET Centre.

6. Gartner Group (2010): *http://www.gartner.com/it/page.jsp?id=1035013*

7. Gital, Abdulsalam Ya'u. & Zambuk, Fatima Umar. (2011). Cloud computing: solution to ICT in higher education in Nigeria. *Advances in Applied Science Research,* 2 (6), 364-369. Retrieved from http:// *www.pelagiaresearchlibrary.com*

8. Goldner, M. (2010). Winds of change: Libraries and cloud computing. Retrieved from *http://www.oclc.org/multimedia/2011/files/IFLA-winds-of-change-paper.pdf*

9. Gosavi, Nandkishor., Shinde, Seetal S. & Dhakulkar, Bhagyashree. (2012). Use of cloud computing in library and information science field. *International Journal of Digital Library,* 2(3), 51-60. Retrieved from *http://www.ijodls.in/uploads/3/6/0/3/3603729/vol._2_july_-_sept._2012_part-2.pdf*

10. Joshi, Namrata S. & Prajapati, Saurabh K. (2013). Academic libraries and cloud computing. *Paper presented at 9th International Conference of CALIBER.* Gandhinagar: INFLIBNET Centre.

11. Kroski, Ellyssa. (2009). Library cloud atlas: a guide to cloud computing and storage/stacking the tech. *Library Journal.* Retrieved from http://www.libraryjournal.com/article/CA6695772.html

12. Luo, Lili. (2013.) Reference librarians' adoption of cloud computing technologies: an exploratory study. *Internet Reference Services Quarterly,* 17(3-4), 147-166. doi: *http://dx.doi.org/10.1080/10875301.2013.765824*

13. Mell, Peter. & Grance, Timothy. (2010). NIST definition of cloud computing. Retrieved from *http://csrc.nist.gov/publications/nistpubs/800-145/SP800-145.pdf*

14. Natarajan, M. (2012). Innovative use of cloud computing in library and information centres. In Osswald, Achim and Ahmed, Zabed S.M. (Eds), *Dynamics of librarianship in the knowledge society,* (312-321). B.R. Publishing Corporation: Delhi.

15. OCLC. OCLC Worldshare management services. 2012. Retrieved from *http://www.oclc.org/webscale/overview.htm*

16. Patel, Yatrik. (2011). Cloud computing and its impact on library services. *INFLIBNET Newsletter, 18(1),* 17-20. Retrieved from *http://www.inflibnet.ac.in/publication/newsletter/Vol.18,No.1%28Jan-Mar2011%29.pdf*

17. Prince, J. Dale. (2012). Climate change in libraries: library functions move to the cloud. *Journal of Electronic Resources in Medical Libraries,* 9(1), 87-93. doi: *http://dx.doi.org/10.1080/15424065.2012.651575*

18. Seena, S.T. & Sudhier, K.G. (2013). From Desktop to Cloud: Cloud Computing Technologies for Libraries. *Paper presented at the National Seminar on New Information Technology Interfaces in libraries and information centres (NITILIC).* Thiruvananthapuram: Kerala Library Association.

19. Singh, Shashi Prabha & Veralakshmi, R.S.R . (2012). Cloud computing: a promising economic model for library and information centers. *DESIDOC Journal of Library & Information Technology,* 32(6), 526-532.

20. Wang, Xiaocan (Lucy) and Huang, Jie. (2011). What coud computing means to libraries and information services. *Journal of Library and Information Science,* 37(2), 166-174. Retrieved from *http://ir.lib.ntnu.edu.tw/retrieve/73138/*

21. Wikipedia. Cloud computing. Retrieved from http://en.wikipedia.org/ wiki/Cloud_computing

22. Xiaona, Feng. & Lingyun, Bao. (2010). Application of cloud computing in university library user service model. *Paper presented at 3rd International Conference on Advanced Computer Theory and Engineering (ICACTE).* Retrieved from *http://ieeexplore.ieee.org/xpl/articleDetails.jsp?reload=true&arnumber=5579681*

PART IV
INNOVATIVE LIBRARY SERVICES

18

E-Learning, Information Literacy and the Librarian

Dr. Vijayakumar K. P.

ABSTRACT

The paper discusses the role of Library and Information Professionals in India in the context of the widespread use of information technology in education and the resultant increase in e-learning and information literacy instruction. It starts with a portrayal of the mammoth higher education scenario in India. By citing forecast studies, it establishes the preponderance of e-learning programmes over the conventional regular courses and establishes what librarians can do in such a situation. Then the paper highlights the need for information literacy instruction which has become all the more necessary in the digital context. Here also the mandate of the libraries and the stake of the LIS professionals in the venture is highlighted. It also discusses the skills to be imparted through the IL instruction and concludes with the prerequisites needed for organizing such programmes.

Keywords : E-learning, Information Literacy, Role of librarians, India

1. THE CHALLENGE OF MASSIVE EDUCATION IN INDIA

Georges Clemenceau, the French Prime Minister

who led the nation in the First World War, had commented that *war is too serious a matter to entrust to military men.* In the same vein, we have to say that Education is too important to be left to the educationists alone. Since Information Technology is coming in a big way in the educational process, we cannot say that education is something which can be left to IT specialists alone. It is especially true in India since Education in the country is a mammoth enterprise.

India has about 1 000 000 educational institutions, 200 000 000 (20 crore) students and more than 3.5 million teachers. India's higher education system is the third largest in the world, next to the United States and China. With 700 universities and more than 35,000 affiliated colleges enrolling more than 20 million students, Indian higher education is a large and complex system (Rahul Choudaha, 2013). The structure of degree-granting institutions is cumbersome primarily due to "affiliation" and funding sources. The sheer size of the system makes its modernization a Herculean task. The effort is more complicated because of the fact that there is a co-existence of world class institutions on the one side and schools which do not have a single teacher or black board or chalk piece.

At the same time, we witness a shift from industrial economy to knowledge economy. This change gives us challenges and great opportunities. ICT can be effectively used to leapfrog from the brick and mortar structures to information hubs where information can be created, stored, analyzed and disseminated to the needy. It is in this context that e-learning and information literacy assume significance. By using the fast emerging technologies in these spheres, our teachers, students and information professionals can be made active participants in the creation and dissemination of information.

2. E-LEARNING

E-learning (or electronic learning) refers to the use of electronic media and information and communication technologies (ICT) in education. E-learning encompasses:

— multimedia learning
— technology-enhanced learning (TEL)
— computer-based instruction (CBI)
— computer-based training(CBT)
— computer-assisted instruction or computer-aided instruction (CAI)
— internet-based training (IBT)
— web-based training(WBT)
— online education
— virtual education
— virtual learning environment
— m-learning, and
— digital educational collaboration.

E-learning encompasses forms of technology-enhanced learning (TEL) or very specific types of TEL such as online or Web-based learning. There are also arguments that e-learning is: pedagogy empowered by digital technology. E-learning has different meanings to different people. In industrial organizations, it often refers to the strategies that are used through the organization's network to deliver training courses to employees. In most of the universities, e-learning is used to define a specific mode to attend a course or programme of study where the students study online.

It can be seen that e-learning is moving rapidly from the margins to being a predominant form of post-secondary education, at least in the USA. It is calculated that by 2015, 25 million post-secondary students in the United States will be taking classes online. As a result, the number of students who attend classes exclusively on physical campuses would come down drastically from 14.4 million in 2010 to just 4.1 million five years later, according to a new forecast released by market research specialist firm Ambient Insight. (Ambient Insight Research)

3.1. Growth of Online Learning

The Report by Ambient Insight Research predicted a five-year compound decline of 22.08 percent per year in students attending traditional classrooms exclusively. The number of post-secondary students taking some (but not all) classes online will grow at a compound annual rate of 11.08 percent over the same five-year period, from 12.36 million in 2010 to 21.13 million in 2015. By that time, the number of students taking classes exclusively online will be nearly equal to the number taking classes exclusively on a physical campus. Further, according to the report, "If this trend continues, by 2018, there will be more full time online students than students that take all their classes in a physical classroom."(Ambient Insight Comprehensive Report).

The report by Ambient Insight Research states that Asia has the highest growth rate worldwide for online learning and revenues are predicted to top $11.5 billion (£7.2 billion) by 2016. It found the growth rate for digital education on the continent - focusing on countries such as India, China, Japan, Malaysia and South Korean - is currently at 17.3 percent. The two countries with the highest growth rate are Vietnam and Malaysia, at 44.3 percent and 39.4 percent respectively. (Ambient Insight Regional Report, 2012).

3.2. Five Stage Model of E-learning

Salmon (2002) defines a five-stage model of e-learning which describes the stages that the learner goes through:

- Access and motivation

- Online socialization
- Information exchange
- Knowledge construction, and
- Development.

E-Learning pioneer Luskin (2010) argues that the "E" must be understood to have broad meaning if e-Learning is to be effective. Luskin argues that the "e" should be interpreted to mean exciting, energetic, enthusiastic, emotional, extended, excellent, and educational. Later, in a presentation made by him at the Annual EDEN Conference in Valencia in 2010, he has added the epithets extra, emerging, exceptional, early, ephemeral, effortless, electronic, eclectic, engaging, external, elastic, empirical, everywhere, eloquent, epoch, epic, evangelistic and effective.

3.3. Advantages of E-learning

E-learning has a number of advantages over conventional learning. Some of them are:

1. Wide availability of browsers and internet connections
2. Cross-platform support
3. Inexpensive worldwide distribution
4. Flexibility, accessibility and convenience to learners
5. Savings in travel cost and time
6. Improved performance
7. Ease of updates
8. Helpful to develop the skills and competencies needed by the employees in the 21st century.

More information on this aspect can be seen in web sites like http://www.dso.iastate. edu/asc/academic/elearner/advantage.html and *http://www.kineo.com/resources/new-to-elearning/the-benefits-of-elearning.*

4. E-LEARNING 2.0

The term Learning 2.0 is used to refer to new ways of thinking about e-learning inspired by the emergence of Web 2.0. From an e-Learning 2.0 perspective, conventional e-learning systems were based on instructional packets that were delivered to students using Internet technologies. The role of the student consisted in learning from the readings and preparing assignments. Assignments were evaluated by the teacher.

In contrast, the new e-learning places increased emphasis on social learning and use of social software such as *blogs, wikis, podcasts* and virtual worlds such as *Second Life.*

A learning management system (LMS) is software for delivering, tracking and managing training/education. LMSs range from systems for managing training/ educational records to software for distributing courses over the Internet. A learning content management system (LCMS) is software for authoring, editing and indexing e-learning content (courses, reusable content objects). An LCMS may be solely dedicated to producing and publishing content that is hosted on an LMS, or it can host the content itself (remote AICC content hosting model). E-learning is naturally suited to distance learning and flexible learning, but can also be used in conjunction with face-to-face teaching, in which case the term Blended Learning is commonly used.

5. SCREENCASTING

The recent trend in the e-Learning sector is screencasting. A screencast is a digital recording of computer screen output, also known as a video screen capture, often containing audio narration. In other words, it is the capture all of the action on a computer screen while you are narrating. The term screencast compares with the related term screenshot. While screenshot is a picture of a computer screen, a screencast is essentially a movie of the changes over time that a user sees on a computer screen, enhanced with audio narration. There are many *screencasting* tools available. Eg: Camtasia, Screencast-o-matic, ScreenFlow, iShowU. (Centre for Learning and Performance Technologies) The latest buzz is all about the web based screencasting tools which allow the users to create screencasts directly from their browser and make the video available online so that the viewers can stream the video directly. With the combination of video and audio, the expert can mimic the one on one experience of the classroom and deliver clear, complete instructions.

6. E-LEARNING AND THE LIBRARY

As is well known, libraries can play a major rolc in personalized content delivery and learning process. Modern libraries try to provide personal library experience through Library portal. In addition, library's space – both physical and virtual – serves as 'information common' and repository of e-learning objects for enhanced learning experience.

At the heart of the learning/technology nexus are learning objects. Learning objects is a concept that does not have a standard definition or application. Churchill (2007) states that the learning object remains as an ill-defined concept, despite numerous and extensive discussions in the literature. However, he describes it as a representation designed to afford uses in different educational contexts. In order to make things clear, he makes a typology of several kinds of learning objects. He includes presentation objects, practice objects, simulation objects, conceptual models, information objects and contextual representations in its fold. Whatever be the standard definition of a learning object, its use and reuse, its discovery and ability to share, its existence as a digital entity and the context in which it can be used are the key elements to creating broader, inter-institutional applications of technology and learning and teaching.

In order for learning objects to have any kind of value, they first require the use of semantically consistent, easily created metadata that allows for the objects themselves to be easily found. In fact, the management of digital asset repositories, learning object repositories and the metadata governing their use are inextricably linked with the LIS profession.

7. INFORMATION LITERACY (IL)

Information literacy is a continuum of skills, behaviour, approaches and values that is so deeply entwined with the uses of information. It is a fundamental element of learning, scholarship and research. The epitome of Information Literacy is embodied in the Chinese Proverb"Give a man a fish and he eats for a day; teach a man to fish and he eats for life."

The main purpose of Information Literacy is to empower customers/ citizens for life with transferable skills. Information literacy is knowing when and why you need information, where to find it, and how to evaluate, use and communicate it in an ethical manner (CILIP). It is the ability to recognize when information is needed, to identify, to locate, evaluate and use effectively information needed for a particular decision or issue at hand. It *is the ability to evaluate information across a range of media; recognize when information is needed; locate, synthesize, and use information effectively; and accomplish these functions using technology, communication networks, and electronic resources.*

7.1. Purpose of Information Literacy

IL provides the foundation for lifelong learning which is increasingly viewed as a fundamental human right. The purpose of IL is:

— to help inculcate a lifelong habit of identifying an information need

— to efficiently search for and use indigenous oral, print, electronic and other sources of information to satisfy that need, and

— to enhance personal, community and national socio-economic interests.

Its major objective is *to produce students who are actively literate* (term used by Michael Holzman), who are able to take the techniques useful in one environment and apply them to unfamiliar environments. In other words, IL aims at the *creation of critical thinkers.*

7.2. Dimensions of IL

Information literacy covers a large number of areas like:

i. Tool Literacy
ii. Resource literacy
iii. Social-structural literacy
iv. Research Literacy
v. Publishing Literacy
vi. Emerging Technology Literacy, and
vii. Critical literacy

With successive developments in ICT, various authors have included many other forms of literacy within the fold of IL. They are:

i. Computer literacy
ii. Digital literacy
iii. IT literacy
iv. Internet literacy
v. Library literacy
vi. Media literacy
vii. Network literacy
viii. Visual literacy etc.

7.3. IL through Academic Institutions

Developing lifelong learners is central to the mission of higher education institutions. Colleges and universities should provide the foundation for continued growth throughout their careers. IL is a key component of and contributor to lifelong learning. IL competency extends learning beyond formal classroom settings. Because IL augments student's competency in evaluating, managing and using information, it is now considered by many accreditation associations as a key outcome for college students. For students not on traditional campuses, information resources are often available through networks and other channels. Distributed learning technologies permit teaching and learning to occur when the teacher and the student are not in the same place at the same time. IL competencies for distance learning students should be comparable to those for "on campus" students. Incorporating IL across curricula, in all programmes and services, requires the collaborative effort of the faculty, librarians and academic administrators. (Kaplowitz, 2012)

7.4. Mandate of Libraries

The library is an academic division within the College/University which has a mandate to serve the knowledge and information needs of the academic Community. It is the principal campus resource for human creativity and memory in traditional and electronic formats providing a truly global information environment(Godwin & Parker, 2012). The university/ college library has:

- a vast array of information resources,
- access to advanced technology on the web,
- the experience in IL instruction, and
- advantages in proving a sound learning and research environment.

Therefore, the university/college library should become the incubation center of Research Literature competency and should develop the necessary instruction for this competency.

7.5. Stake of LIS Professionals in IL

As custodians of information, or documents information skills have been taught very much within the library context. Terms like initiation of freshmen, bibliographic instruction, library orientation and user education are used to denote these efforts. But in the context of the availability of information in different formats – print, audio-visual, digital etc. – these techniques need reorientation and further augmentation. Compared with any other stakeholders in the field of information, Librarians are better equipped to offer IL programmes because:

a. They have a long history and experience of teaching library skills.

b. They are highly convinced of the need for IL education.

c. They are well aware of the methods adopted by students for literature search.

d. They have intimate knowledge about the various tools and sources of information.

e. They, more than any other group, keenly keep track of the developments in ICT.

To cap it all, the spread of the message of IL was taken by major professional associations of the world. A few examples are:

- American Library Association (ALA)
- Association of College and Research Libraries (ACRL)
- Chartered Institute of Library and Information Professionals (CILIP)
- Society of College, National and University Libraries (SCONUL)

- Canadian Library Association (CLA)
- Australian Library and Information Association (ALIA), and
- Scholarly Publishing and Academic Resources Coalition (SPARC).

7.6. Partnership Role with the Faculty

Librarians, libraries, and IL have limited effectiveness without a change in relationships between teaching faculty and librarians. Librarians can work to inform teaching faculty of the need for change, especially in the arena of IL. Librarians can work to inform teaching faculty of the need for change, especially in the arena of IL. For instance, librarians and teaching faculty can begin building partnerships by collaborating in the design of IL courses. Such collaboration can provide a sense of cohesion for both parties because the design and delivery of IL sessions will not be constructed in isolation. Curriculum enrichment is the process whereby librarians assist faculty to broaden their curriculum resources beyond the standard textbook. Librarians can provide research assistance to faculty as they develop their courses and create their reading and reserve lists. Some simple strategies employed adopted are:

i. meeting regularly with faculty to discuss the courses and library involvement;
ii. reading copies of course syllabi and offering ideas;
iii. attending classes to get a real sense of the courses; and
iv. consulting regularly with faculty for input on library acquisitions.

Librarians have identified Internet resources for faculty as part of web demonstrations and teaching sessions, and have created World Wide Web (WWW) pages with links to important Web sites. They, mostly in western countries, also used to provide faculty with student handouts on copyright, subject bibliographies, citation style, and the research process. Association for College and Research Libraries (ACRL) reinforces this idea, noting that shared leadership and collaboration with effective planning is necessary for a successful IL teaching model.

7.7. IL through Academic Libraries: Objectives

The objectives of imparting IL instruction through academic libraries can be described as:

- To acquaint the users with the academic power of Internet;
- To provide an indication as to what is there on Internet related to the area of study and research;
- To show how web resources could be of immense use in their academic pursuit and research;
- To show the usefulness of various multimedia resources on web in Science/Social Science/ Humanities Research;
- To promote the use of subscribed databases in academics and research;
- To describe specific features of various databases subscribed by the Library;
- To acquaint the users with the use of various search techniques to retrieve relevant information;
- To recognize the need for information, and to evaluate, organize, interpret and communicate information in all its formats;
- To promote that Information Literacy is for participants' academic and vocational success and for lifelong learning;
- To provide research-integrated instruction in collaboration with the faculty and in alignment with research objectives;
- To establish a direct interaction between users and library professionals;

- To explain the necessity of bibliographical citations and its usefulness;
- To promote the use of standardized citations of bibliographical references.
- To describe specific features of various databases being subscribed by the Library;
- To acquaint the users with the use of various search techniques to retrieve relevant information;
- To recognize the need for information, and to evaluate, organize, interpret, and communicate information in all its formats;
- To promote that Information Literacy is for participants' academic and vocational success and for lifelong learning.

7.8. Skills to be Imparted through IL Instruction

It is very difficult to make a list of the training programmes to be organized to develop the necessary skills in the faculty members, research scholars and students to make them lifelong learners. These skills keep on changing with the developments in the information scenario (Flashpohler, 2012). Moreover, they are also incremental in nature with the stage of growth of the target group. Nonetheless, a few areas of instruction to start with are indicated below:

- Distinguish between scholarly and popular sources
- Know how to integrate primary and secondary sources in research
- Understand the structure of scholarly publications in a discipline
- Use fundamental reference sources
- Identify and use databases (bibliographic, numeric, or full text) in a discipline by formulating successful search strategies.
- Be able to navigate electronic resources, including the WWW, and apply critical evaluation to selection

of appropriate sources for a specific assignment.

- Know how to locate sources in a library.
- Be familiar with procedures for obtaining materials from remote locations by interlibrary lending or other document delivery services.

8. CONCLUSION

For the LIS professionals in academic libraries to play a meaningful role in e-learning and information literacy instruction, a number of pre-requisites are necessary. Firstly, this can be done only by partnering with colleagues across the campus to integrate information literacy into academic programs. The collaboration can be achieved by promoting the use of library resources in all formats, in as much as familiarity with both print and electronic formats. This can be done by providing instruction formally and informally, to individuals and to classes, in person and online. The best means of achieving this is by providing programmatic instruction that addresses the needs of the college/ university community. The library professionals should strive to make every interaction at the library, especially reference questions, a learning opportunity for users. This inevitably calls for the constant evaluation of the effectiveness of the approaches and regular renewing of one's own skills.

REFERENCES

1. Ambient Insight Comprehensive Report. *The US Market for Self-paced eLearning Products and Services: 2010 - 2015 Forecast and Analysis*. Retrieved from http://www.ambientinsight.com/Resources/Documents/AmbientInsight_2006_US_eLearning_Market_Snapshot.pdf.
2. Ambient Insight Regional Report. The Asia Market for Self-paced eLearning Products and Services: 2011-2016 Forecast and Analysis. Retrieved from *http://www.ambientinsight.com/ Resources/Documents/AmbientInsight-2011-2016-Asia-SelfPaced-eLearning-Market-Abstract.pdf*

3. Ambient Insight Research. International eLearning Market Research. Retrieved from http://www. ambientinsight.com/ Reports/eLearning.aspx
4. Centre for Learning and Performance Technologies. 30 screencasting tools. Retrieved from *http://c4lpt.co.uk/ directory-of-learning-performance-tools/screencasting-tools/*
5. CILIP. Information literacy – definition. Retrieved from *http:/ /www.cilip.org.uk/cilip/ advocacy-campaigns-awards/ advocacy-campaigns/information-literacy/information-literacy*
6. Churchill, Daniel (2007). Towards a useful classification of learning objects, *Educational Technology Research and Development,* 55 (5). Retrieved from *http://dx.doi.org/10. 1007/s11423-006-9000-y*
7. Flashpohler, M.R.(2012). *Engaging first year students in meaningful library research: a practical guide for teaching faculty.* Oxford: Chandos Publishing.
8. Godwin, P. and Parker, J. (2012) *Information literacy beyond library 2.0.* London: Facet Publishing.
9. Kaplowitz, J.R. (2012). *Transforming information literacy instruction using learner-centered teaching,* London: Facet.
10. Luskin, Bernard (2010). Think exciting: E-Learning and the Big "E". Retrieved from *http://www.educause.edu/ero/ article/think-exciting-e-learning-and-big-e*
11. Rahul Choudaha (2013). Statistics on Indian Higher Education 2012 – 13. Retrieved from *http:// www.dreducation.com/2013/08/data-statistics-india-student-college.html*
12. Salmon, Gilly (2002). *E-tivities: The key to active online learning.* London: Kogan Page.

19

Marketing Plan for the Kerala Studies Collection of Kerala University Library

Dr. P. K Suresh Kumar

ABSTRACT

Libraries are facing rising costs and dwindling budgets due to technological advances and today's dynamic economic climate. As a result, marketing concepts are increasingly adapted within the library environment. Libraries are discovering that by using marketing principles and techniques, they can understand better their users' needs, justify funding, communicate more effectively with a variety of external audiences, and achieve greater efficiency and optimal results in delivering products and services that meet the identified needs of their clients, for developing marketing plans and strategies. This paper is based on a survey conducted in the Kerala Studies Section of the Kerala University Library since it is considered as a prestigious collection by the academic community. The main objective of the study is to dig out the market potentiality of information products and services of the Kerala Studies Section through SWOT analysis and marketing mix variables. The data collected randomly from 75 Research Scholars, who are conducting research on various aspects of the Kerala State under the University of Kerala through a structured questionnaire. Based on the analysis this study formulated a strategic marketing plan for the products and services of the Kerala Studies Section of the Kerala University Library.

Keywords: Kerala Studies, University Library, Information products and services, SWOT analysis, Marketing mix, Market plan

1. INTRODUCTION

The main objectives of the libraries today are to obtain self-sufficiency in their resources and to provide an optimum level of services to reach more potential users and encourage the use of library resources. The marketing of information in the university libraries happens to be a recent phenomenon. In India, the universities are being funded by the UGC and State Governments. This may be the reason that the information providers in the university libraries are not seriously thinking in terms of marketing their products and services. The university libraries until now depended upon common sense standards for the acquiring of information and disseminating of the same to the users. Their efforts in this direction can at best be described as casual or immature. The result is that information services provided by the libraries have not proved very beneficial to the scholars. The libraries have failed to provide the required information support to the users because the services provided by them are often not user-oriented or need based. The reason for this sad state of affairs is that users are not involved in the design of services and they are not made aware of the potentialities of information services and how these services can benefit them in their pursuits. The result is that whatever services are available, remain either unutilized or underutilized. However, this state of affairs can be activated by adopting suitable marketing strategy.[1]

One of the most important steps a business or community can take to improve the effectiveness and efficiency of its marketing effort is to develop an appropriate marketing plan. Marketing planning involves deciding on marketing strategies that will help the institution attain its overall strategic objectives. A detailed marketing plan is needed for each service, product or brand. This plan will guide their marketing decisions and assist them in allocating marketing resources such as money and personal time[2]. The plan should include the overall business objectives; an assessment of the market environment; a business/community profile; market identification (segmentation); the marketing objectives of each segment; the marketing strategies (mixes) for different markets; an implementation plan; and a method for evaluation and change. Marketing planning helps to inject the philosophy of consumer orientation into the total business system and serves as a guide to the organizational effort.[3] University libraries should sec marketing as a tool needed by library and thus, should employ suitable marketing strategies to attract users' to make maximum use of available information products and services.

1.2. Relevance of Kerala Studies Section

Kerala Reference Collection is maintained by the Kerala Studies section of the Kerala University Library. This area studies collection on Kerala was formed by the Kerala University library in 1973. Now the research scholars consider this section as a prestigious section of the library. The collection includes books especially Malayalam books, bound volumes of periodicals, personal collections, study reports, Gazette, and rare books having research value on all aspects of Kerala. It is having a big treasure of rare materials on Kerala. The collection, though not so adequate, provides a central source to those who seek information on Kerala. The academic community in Kerala and also renowned scholars from outside including foreign countries has made extensive use of the section. Rare materials are digitized for the use of present and future generations as part of the modernization programme of the library. Now this is the only institutional repository available in the University of Kerala named under the brand name "*LIDAS*". The objectives of the Kerala Studies section are :

- To build up a comprehensive, exhaustive and up to date collection of reading materials on different aspects of Kerala;
- To preserve and protect old and rare materials;
- To procure all materials related to Kerala and if they are out of print and not available, they are to be procured using other means like photocopying, microfilming, Digitations etc.;
- To be a depository of all materials on Kerala;
- To provide central sources to all those seeking information on Kerala;
- To prepare Union Catalogue of books, periodicals and other materials pertaining to Kerala available in different libraries, which are rich in such materials so that, the section is in a position to give necessary guidance to scholars regarding the location of such materials; and
- To enhance the use of the Kerala Reference Collection by foreign tourists, since a large number of them visit the library.

1.3. Present status of the section

The section occupies a floor area of about 2500sq.ft. of the library building. Admission to this section is restricted to the teachers ad research scholars of the Kerala University. Other members of the library can make use of this section with permission from the university librarian. The collections of this section can be accessed by temporary members also by paying an amount of Rs. 40/- for three days. It functions from 8a.m to 8 p. m. except on Sundays. This section follows closed access system. Users are allowed to consult the documents for reference only.

This section was started with a collection of 2000 books transferred from different sections of the University Library. The collection includes some very old publications such as almanacs, directories, reports, serial publications, proceedings, manuals, gazettes etc. Bound volumes of periodicals are also available in this section. The section also houses publications of the Govt. of Kerala, its allied bodies and also the publications of some autonomous institutions. As regards to books the section contains many rare and old books such as *Hortus Indicus Malabaricus (1684), Hindu Sastra Samgraham (1877), Lectures of Corruption (1868), Land of Charity (1870), A descriptive Memoir of Malabar (1906), Memoir of the Survey of Travancore (1908), The Forest Trees of Travancore (1908), Kerala Society Papers (1933), Fishes of Malabar (1910), Flowering Plants of Travancore (1914)* etc. Most of these rare books are now digitized and available in the repository, "LIDAS".

Despite a large collection of materials both in terms of quantity and quality, retrieval and dissemination of information would be difficult unless there exists proper tools which would be helpful for this purpose. Keeping this in view, the section took up the compilation of bibliographies has been transferred to the Documentation Section. Some of the bibliographies compiled are Asan Granthassoochi (1973), Select bibliography of Lexicography (1977). Kerala- A bibliography of books on Kerala (1977), Vallathol Bibliography, Ezhuthachan Bibliography (1985), Ulloor Bibliography (1987), Feminism and literature (1987) etc.

Kerala University Library is the oldest and the richest university library regarding resources in Kerala. The library maintains a comprehensive and balanced collection of reading materials in all field of knowledge. It is a matter of gratification that the section is found useful by the scholars and others in meeting their information requirements. Despite its strength, the Kerala Studies section also has its weakness regarding its collection and services. Efforts should be made to overcome the weakness by producing new information products and services and applying modern marketing techniques, in order to enable it to serve the scholarly community more effectively and efficiently.

2. REVIEW OF RELATED LITERATURE

Bamigbola[4] analyzed the websites of Nigerian University libraries and identified some of the information products and services such as CD-ROM, internet search, open access institutional repositories (OAIR), e-resources, e-books, e-journals, online reference services, and computer laboratory. The marketing strategies employed in theses libraries are users' orientation, demonstration, exhibition, display, email messages, telephone, library websites, and word of mouth during the departmental/ faculty meetings, and selective packaging of relevant information to users. Schmidt [5] suggested the ways of marketing library services effectively to today's users. Marketing should be focusing on users, the library's products, and the appropriate place for service delivery, an appropriate pricing strategy and effective promotional strategies. Baltes and Leibing [6] gave an introduction to 'guerrilla marketing' principles and discussed its suitability for information services. They examined whether guerrilla marketing strategies may be suitable for introducing information services and found that guerrilla marketing strategies may be applied for information services whenever a product-like representation for such a service can be developed and a link to emotional values be established. Liu and Shu[7] argued that for academic libraries to achieve maximum efficiency in its electronic resources it was necessary to seek the most effective marketing strategies. The paper suggested that the library can market their resources through different channels, such as the use of e-mail, posters, guided tours, online bulletin, and other educational means. In an article Shukla and Tripathi [8] discussed a set of principles in the field of marketing strategy and various factors that will influence the information market. Various methodologies for promoting information services of a university library were discussed. The article pointed out that in university libraries, a huge amount invests on collection development, processing and storage of information resources. Effective utilization of these resources and services can be achieved thorough new marketing approach and such tools are assisting in the university in developing and delivering appropriate services and information products.

Kennedy and Hannon[9] identified the marketing activities that libraries are using to promote electronic resources and examined how libraries are measuring the successes or failures of their marketing plans by analyzing the literature published in library science on marketing techniques for electronic resources in use at libraries. Makori[10] highlighted various marketing initiatives of making university libraries in Kenya and explored recent innovative strategies for marketing information products and services. It was found that marketing helps university libraries to market and promote information products and services, provide innovative products and services, understand the needs and demands of the information audience or user population, plan service provision, and provide efficient and effective information products and services. Alford, Emily[11] suggested that marketing electronic resources is now a necessary task for librarians and libraries. In order for libraries to successfully market their e-resources, they must first understand what such an undertaking entails through user studies, working creatively and collaboratively, and using many lines of communication to disseminate the message. Reiners and

Thompson[12] narrated how the library at the University of Lincoln in the UK developed a marketing plan for its services. Duke and Tucker [13] suggested that marketing should be a part of the library's overall strategic planning process and libraries must develop a marketing plan that incorporates the library's strategic plan as well as the mission and vision statements.

3. OBJECTIVES OF THE STUDY

The specific objectives of the study are:

i) To find out new information services and products suitable for different user groups, so as to increase the rate of use of the resources and services.

ii) To dig out the possibility of marketing of information products and services of the Kerala Studies Section through SWOT analysis.

iii) To identify the extent of use of information products and services and its satisfaction level by various user segments.

iv) To find out whether the research scholars are ready to buy the information products and services.

v) To formulate a marketing plan for the products and services of the Kerala Studies Section of the Kerala University Library.

4. ANALYSIS AND DISCUSSIONS

Data collected from 75 Research Scholars, who are conducting research on various aspects of the Kerala State under the University of Kerala through a structured questionnaire. Out of 75 samples selected 56 percentage are females and 44 percentages are males. All the respondents opined that they visited the Kerala Studies section for referring to Malayalam books, periodicals, reports and digital resources pertaining to Kerala. Majority of the respondents (88.57 percent) reported that Kerala Studies section is very helpful for their research work out of which 95% are females and 80% are males. It reveals the importance of this section in promoting information for the specialized community.

4.1. Level of satisfaction

Identifying satisfaction level of users is an important index for assessing the quality of services provided. Researchers were requested to respond to the satisfaction level regarding the information products and services of the section and the responses are given in Table 1.

Table 1. Level of Satisfaction of information products and services of Kerala Studies Section of the Kerala University Library

Level of satisfaction	Respondents		
	Male	Female	Total
Very Satisfied	6 (18.18)	8(19.05)	14(18.67)
Satisfied	10(30.30)	14(33.33)	24(32.00)
Less Satisfied	8(24.24)	9(21.43)	17(22.67)
Not at all Satisfied	6(18.18)	7(16.67)	13((17.33)
No Opinion	3(9.10)	4(9.52)	7(9.33)
Total	33(100.00)	42(100.00)	75 (100.00)

Table shows that 32 percent of the researchers were satisfied with the services provided by the section. A good number of researchers (30 percent) were either less satisfied or not at all satisfied with the information products and services. Only 18.67 percent opined that they were very satisfied with the products and services of the section. Gender wise analysis shows that more males are less satisfied or not at all satisfied (42.42 percent) than females (38.1 percent).

4.2. Usefulness of Information products and services

Table 2 reveals that the most useful information product is the digital resources (46.67 percent) followed by Kerala Index (17.33 percent). Also, Index to Journal of Kerala studies, index to Travancore Information

Listener and Journal of Kerala History and Culture are either most useful or useful to more than 50 percent of the research scholars which shows the market potentiality of these products. The Malayalam literature documents available are useful to 46.66 percent of the researchers shows the importance of this specialized collection in the Kerala Studies section. Gazettes and Bibliography available in the section are the less useful items in the Kerala Studies section. It may be due to lack of promotional activities. This also strengthens the need for marketing information products and services of the Kerala University Library.

Table 2. Percentage Distribution of Usefulness of Information Products and and services of Kerala Studies Section of the Kerala University Library

Information products	Most useful	Useful	Least Useful	Not useful	No opinion	Total
Kerala Index	13 (17.33)	31 (41.33)	7 (9.33)	4 (5.33)	20 (26.67)	75 (100.00)
Index to Journal of Kerala Studies	9 (12.00)	30 (40.00)	10 (13.33)	4 (5.33)	22 (29.33)	75 (100.00)
Index to Travancore Information Listener	11 (14.67)	29 (38.67)	9 (12.00)	6 (8.00)	20 (26.67)	75 (100.00)
Journal of Kerala History and Culture	9 (12.00)	29 (38.66)	11 (14.67)	5 (6.67)	21 (28.00)	75 (100.00)
Digital Resources (LIDAS)	35 (46.67)	18 (24.00)	10 (13.33)	6 (8.00)	6 (8.00)	75 (100.00)
Gazettes	6 (8.00)	21 (28.00)	15 (20.00)	6 (8.00)	27 (36.00)	75 (100.00)
Malayalam Literature documents	10 (13.33)	25 (33.33)	12 (16.00)	5 (6.67)	23 (30.67)	75 (100.00)
Bibliography	12 (16.00)	10 (13.33)	18 (24.00)	22 (29.34)	13 (17.33)	75 (100.00)

4.3. Attitude towards marketing of products of Kerala Studies section

Table 3 shows that only 44 percent agreed, 26.67 percent strongly agreed, and 18.67 percent not sure about the specific user oriented services rendered by the Kerala Reference section. Only 17.33 percent strongly agree or agree with the statement that "Kerala Studies section regularly collect information on the wishes and needs of researchers". It shows the need for regular user study and the introduction of Selective Dissemination of Information (SDI) services in the Kerala Studies section. Only 6.67 percent agreed or strongly agreed with the promotional or marketing activities of the Kerala Studies section and it implies the need for adopting various channels of promotion and marketing of information products and services. Regarding the marketing segmentation, 9.33 percent are agreed and 2.67 percent strongly agreed and another 33.33 percent are neither agreed nor disagreed. User oriented information products and services offered by the library is agreed and strongly agreed by only 6.67 percent. The cooperation of the staff in rendering services is agreed by 32 percent and strongly agreed by 26.67 percent.

The instruction regarding the use of information products and services is accepted and agreed by only 6.67 percent and strongly agreed by 8%. The analysis clearly indicates that the present marketing application is less accepted by most of researchers.

4.4. Scope for the introduction of new information products and services

The main purpose of a library is to satisfy the information requirements of its potential users. In order to identify the marketing possibility in Kerala Studies section, the researchers were asked to mention the information products and services to be introduced in the section and their responses are given in Table 4.

Table 3. Researcher's attitude towards the marketing of products of Kerala Studies

Application of Marketing	Strongly disagree	Disagree	Not sure	Agree	Strongly agree
Kerala Studies section tries to adapt as much as possible services to the specific needs of each user	2(2.67)	6(8.00)	14(18.67)	33(44.00)	20(26.67)
Kerala Studies section regularly collect information on the wishes and needs of researchers	26(34.67)	21(28.00)	15(20.00)	10(13.33)	3(4.00)
Promotes its services according to a well planned marketing program by the type of users and the level of use	28(37.33)	16(21.33)	26(34.67)	3(4.00)	2(2.67)
It has differen-tiated offers and different plans for the various user segments	28(37.33)	13(17.33)	25(33.33)	7(9.33)	2(2.67)
Products/Services (P/S) offered are not user oriented	5(6.67)	5(6.67)	20(26.67)	30(40.00)	15(20.00)
Library staff are very cooperative and are always pay due attention to our problems.	4(5.33)	6(8.00)	15(16.00)	30(32.00)	20(26.67)
Library clearly gives instruction regarding the uses of its P/S from time to time	29(38.67)	13(17.33)	23(30.67)	4(6.67)	6(8.00)

Table 4. Suggestions regarding new Information Products and services

Information Products/Services	Number of Respondents Male	Female	Total
Index of periodicals	26(86.67)	38(90.48)	64(85.33)
Content Page service	30(90.90)	40(95.23)	70(93.33)
Digital Library Service	32(96.97)	39(92.86)	71(94.67)
Tourism information Bulletin	26(78.79)	32(79.19)	58(77.33)
CD-Writing	31(93.94)	41(97.62)	72(96.00)
SDI service	23(69.70)	34(80.95)	57(76.00)
Reprographic/ Printing service	32(96.97)	42(100.00)	74(98.67)
Abstracting service	24(72.73)	32(79.19)	56(74.67)

Table 4 indicates that the most important information service identified was reprographic/ printing service (98.67 percent) followed by CD-writing (96 percent) and Digital Library service (94.67 percent). All the female researchers proposed reprographic/printing service as the most important service. All these information products and services are useful to more than 75 percent of the researchers indicates its market potentiality.

4.5. Pricing

Pricing is one of the most important components of market mix. Researchers were asked whether they were ready to pay for the information products and services and their responses is provided in Table 5.

Table 5 shows that majority of the research scholars (84 percent) were ready to pay for information products and service. More female researchers (92.85 percent) were willing to pay for information products and services than their counterparts (72.72 percent). This shows the urgency of new information products and services in Kerala Studies section and the potentiality of marketing, if introduced, which can improve the revenue of the Kerala University Library.

Table 5. Willingness of the Researchers to pay forthe information products

Response	Number of Respondents		
	Male	Female	Total
Yes	24(72.72)	39(92.85)	63(84.00)
No	9(27.28)	3 (7.15)	12(16.00)
Total	33(100.00)	42(100.00)	75(100.00)

4.6. Level of Pricing

Pricing of the product or service is aimed at gaining a profit for cost recovery for the organizations. A library as a non-profit organization does not sell their products or services for profit but for recovery, maintenance and other related costs. The respondents who are willing to pay for information products or services reported their extent of sharing the cost and are provided in Table 6.

Table 6. Extent of payment

Response	Number of Respondents		
	Male	Female	Total
Half of the actual cost	13(39.34)	18(42.86)	31(41.33)
Actual cost	8(24.24)	10(23.81)	18 (24.00)
Actual cost plus marginal profit for the library	3(9.09)	5(11.90)	8(10.67)
Free of cost	9(27.28)	3(7.14)	12 (16.00)

Table 6 shows that 41.33 percent of the research scholars are willing to pay half of the actual incurring cost for information products. Only a marginal number of research scholars (10.67 percent) are ready to pay the actual cost plus marginal profit for the library. This reveals that though they were differed in their views regarding pricing, majority of them are willing to pay for information products and services. There is urgency for more information products and services among the research scholars.

5. MARKETING PLAN

On the basis of the survey a detailed marketing strategy to be adopted for Kerala Studies section of the Kerala University library is provided below by analyzing the strengths and weakness of the Kerala studies

5.1. Strengths

a. It occupies a floor area of about 2500 sq. ft.;

b. Unique collection - comprehensive collection on all aspects of Kerala and Malayalam language and literature in particular. Some of the rare materials are available in digital form;

c. Personal collections of Dr. K. M George, Shri. Sooranadu Kunjan Pillai, Dr. A.V Varghese which contain some rare documents;

d. Separate manual card catalogue in Malayalam as well as OPAC facility;

e. Qualified, dedicated and expert staff; and

f. Infrastructure – 10 computers, 4KV UPS, air-conditioned digitization room, seating arrangement for research scholars etc.

5.2. Weaknesses

a. Brittle state of the old publications;

b. Antique look and dust;

c. Open shelves with closed access;

d. Lack of publicity;

e. Lack of media coverage for the documentation services based on this section;

f. Restrictions on photocopying the documents;

g. Access restriction- this section is open to the research scholars only; and

h. Absence of a well-written acquisition policy in building up the collection.

5.3. Segmentation

The target groups consist of research scholars, teachers, public and foreign tourists.

5.4. Marketing Objectives

- To generate new information products and services;
- To increase the rate of use of the rare collection;
- To attach price tag to the services;
- To increase press, media and web coverage; and
- To enhance the reputation of the Kerala University Library.

5.5. Target groups

Research scholars of the parent university and outside universities, foreign tourists, individual researchers, and authors.

Objective : To enhance the use of the collection and to raise the market potential

Segment : Researchers and tourists- both Indian and foreign

Demand : Large number of research scholars in Arts and Humanities and Social Science faculty from the universities in Kerala and there are many occasional users from India or even from abroad. The tourists visiting the Gods own country, Kerala needed information about Kerala, its history, culture and tourism information.

Competition : Nearby libraries especially State Central library, Trivandrum. From publishers, mass media and internet.

5.7. Marketing mix

Products

a. Bibliographies both author and subject;

b. Kerala Index, the monthly indexing periodical;

c. Content page service of Malayalam periodicals;

d. Digital library service using digitized rare materials;

e. Tourism information bulletin;

f. Application of Library 2.0 technology in computerized information services; and

g. Selective Dissemination of Information service is to be introduced.

Place : Library will be the place for delivering service. Provide online login facility to access from remote locations. To facilitate queries, telephone, fax, and e-mail facilities have to be provided. Also, all the services should be made available through Campus library, Department libraries and Study centre libraries and libraries of affiliated colleges.

Pricing : The actual cost incurred for the services are to be found out and 50% subsidy is to be provided for research scholars, teachers and student members of the university library. 25% subsidy to be given for the public and academic community from other universities. Also, 25% subsidy is to be provided to public members. Full cost is to be levied from others. Actual cost plus a 50% margin is to be levied from foreigners.

Promotion : An e-brochure containing the details of the services is to be sent by e-mail to each research scholar of the university irrespective of membership. Printed brochures should be given to new members at the time of taking membership. Notify the updating of the products and services in the library and university website. News and press releases and feature articles will be able to attract other researchers and public. Efforts are to be made to advertise the products and services in the travel guides published by the Kerala Tourism Development Corporation and Tourism Promotion Council. Publish Tourism information bulletin by the library.

6. CONCLUSION

Kerala Studies is one of the exclusive collections of the Kerala University Library which attracts a large number of scholars from all parts of our country. Satisfaction of the potential users is most important on the part of the University Library. The reputation of the library is based on the usage of library services, products and resources. In the present situation library and information professionals have to play an important role to identify the user groups and provide them with necessary information, not only within, but also outside the library and information centres. The study shows the Kerala Studies Section with its strengths and opportunities can easily overcome the threats and weakness with appropriate positioning and marketing strategies. An intensive effort is required from the part of the top management of the library, staff, and authorities of the university to overcome the listed weakness. The Kerala Studies collection has enough potential to market through a strategic marketing approach. Hence Kerala University Library has to adopt appropriate marketing plans, strategies and techniques in marketing of its information products and services.

REFERENCES

1. Kendadamath, G.C.(2000). Marketing of library and information services. In Dipak De and Basavaprabhu Jirli (Eds.). *Communication support for sustainable development.* Varanasi: Ganga Kavery Publishing House. Available from *http://www.bhu.ac.in/InstituteofAgriculturalSciencesBHU/EXTENSIONEDUCATION/ Winter%20 School/ WS_13.pdf* (14 April 2013).
2. Kotler, Philip and Armstrong, Gray (1995). *Principles of marketing.* Ed.9. Prentice Hall of India: New Delhi, 49.
3. Gupta, C.B. and Rajan Nair, N. (2007). *Marketing management.* Sultan Chand & Sons: New Delhi, 2.16.
4. Bamigbola, Alice A.(2013). Application of Marketing Strategies and Mix to Digital Information Services (DIS):

Nigerian University Libraries Perspectives. *Library Philosophy and Practice (e-journal)*.Paper 961. Available from *http:// digitalcommons.unl.edu/ libphilprac/ 96 (10* June 2013)

5. Schmidt, Janine.(2007). Promoting library services in a Google world. *Library Management.* 28(6/7), 337-346.

6. Baltes, Guido and Leibing, Isabell.(2008). Guerrilla Marketing for Information services. *New Library World.* 109(1/2), 46-55.

7. Liu, Huang_yu and Shu,Jung-Huei.(2008). A study of demand analysis and marketing strategy of electronic resources in University Library. *Journal of Educational Media & Library Science.* 45(3), 331-356.

8. Shukla, Anil Kumar and Tripathi,P.K. (2009).New marketing strategies of information services in university libraries. *University News.* 47(42), 19-25.

9. Kennedy, Marie and Hannon, William H. (2011).What are we really doing to market electronic resources? *.Library Management* .32(3), 144-158.

10. Makori, Elisha Ondieki. (2010).Making University Libraries in Kenya the Destination for the User Population *.Library Review* .59(7), 548-557.

11. Alford, Emily.(2009).Promoting and Marketing E-Resources *.The Serials Librarian* .57(3), 272-277.

12. Reiners, Lys Ann and Thompson, Lesle (2007).Why market? Introducing a marketing approach at the University of Lincoln Library. *SCONUL Focus.* 42 (January), 61-63.

13. Duke, Lynda M. and Tucker, Toni (2007). How to develop a marketing plan for an academic library. *Technical Services Quarterly* 25.1, 51-68.

20

Information Literacy for Distance Learners : Issues and Challenges

Dr. Nasirudheen T.P.O.
Dr. M. Bavakutty

ABSTRACT

Information literacy is a set of abilities requiring individuals to recognize when information is needed and have the ability to locate, evaluate, and use effectively the needed information. Information literacy forms the basis for lifelong learning. It is common to all disciplines, to all learning environments, and to all levels of education. It enables learners to master content and extend their investigation, and to become more self-directed and assume greater control over their own learning. Information literacy is a key component of and contributor to lifelong learning. Information literacy competency extends learning beyond formal classroom settings and provides practice with self-directed investigations as individuals move into internships, first professional positions and increasing responsibilities in all arenas of life. The paper discusses various issues and challenges related to information literacy for distance learners.

Keywords : Information literacy, Distance learners, Distance learning, ICT

1. INTRODUCTION

Library and Information Science (LIS) in India is faced with many challenges and opportunities, though there is a mushroom growth of LIS schools in India. There is no professional accreditation, though institutional accreditation through NACC is in place in India. Nomenclature of the courses offered has changed but the course contents are not consistent with the nomenclature and market requirements. Many schools have failed to respond adequately to the ICT-based developments. These schools are seriously suffering from insufficient infrastructure, inadequate faculty, absence of quality research, and lack of document support. While the core is still stuck to classification, cataloguing, indexing, and vocabulary control, the emerging themes such as information literacy, knowledge management, e-learning, ICT application, use of networks in teaching, and teaching about networks have not yet been adequately integrated into the curricula. Therefore, there is an immediate need of curriculum based on the cutting-edge course contents and ICT. The opportunities made available by ICT and the Internet must be used to support e-learning, open and distributed learning (ODL), and globalization of LIS education and research.

2. INFORMATION LITERACY

Information literacy is a set of abilities requiring individuals to "recognize when information is needed and have the ability to locate, evaluate, and use effectively the needed information" (State University of New York, 1997)[1]

Information literacy forms the basis for lifelong learning. It is common to all disciplines, to all learning environments, and to all levels of education. It enables learners to master content and extend their investigation, and to become more self-directed and assume greater control over their own learning.

Information literacy is a new art that extends from knowing how to use computers and access information to critical reflection on the nature of information itself, its technical infrastructure, and its social, cultural and even philosophical context and impact (Shapiro & Hughes, 1996)[2]

Information literacy is increasingly important in the contemporary environment of rapid technological changes and proliferating information resources. Information is available through libraries, community resources, special interest organizations, media and the Internet. Increasingly, information comes to individuals in unfiltered formats, raising questions about its authenticity, validity and reliability. In addition, information is available through multiple media including graphical, aural and textual, and these pose new challenges for an individual in evaluating and understanding it. The uncertain quality and expanding quantity of information pose large challenges for society. A set of skills becomes essential to help the individual to locate, evaluate and use information effectively.

3. INFORMATION LITERACY AND INFORMATION TECHNOLOGY

Information literacy is related to information technology skills. Information technology skills enable an individual to use computers, software applications, databases, and other technologies to achieve a wide variety of academic, work-related and personal goals. Information literate individual necessarily develops some technology skills. Information literacy, while showing significant overlap with information technology skills, is a distinct and broader area of competence. Increasingly, information technology skills are interwoven with and support information literacy. 'Computer literacy' is concerned with rote learning of specific hardware and software applications, while 'fluency with technology' focuses on understanding the underlying concepts of technology. 'Information literacy' focuses on content communication analysis, information search and evaluation, whereas 'information technology fluency' focuses on a deep understanding of technology and increasingly skilled use of it.[3]

Fluency with information technology may require more intellectual abilities than the rote learning of software and hardware associated with computer literacy, but the focus is still on the technology itself. Information literacy, on the other hand, is an intellectual framework for understanding, finding, evaluating and using information – activities which may be accomplished in part by fluency with information technology and in part by sound investigative methods, but most important, through critical discernment and reasoning. Information literacy initiates, sustains and extends lifelong learning through abilities, which may use technologies but are ultimately independent of them.

4. INFORMATION LITERACY AND DISTANCE LEARNING

Distance education was developed to meet the educational needs of a diverse and geographically scattered population. Moore (1990) defines distance education as that which 'consists of all arrangements for providing instruction through print or electronic communication media to persons engaged in planned learning in a place or time different from that of the instructor or instructors.[4]

Developing lifelong learners is central to the mission of higher education institutions. By ensuing that individuals have the intellectual abilities of reasoning and critical thinking, and by helping them construct a framework for learning how to learn, colleges and universities provide the foundation for continued growth throughout their career, as well as in their roles as informed citizens and members of communities. Information literacy is a key component of and contributor to lifelong learning. Information literacy competency extends learning beyond formal classroom settings and provides practice with self-directed investigations as individuals move into internships, first professional positions and increasing responsibilities in all arenas of life. Because information literacy augments students' competency with evaluating, managing and using information, it is now considered by several regional and discipline – based assessment and accreditation agencies as a key outcome for college students.[5]

Recently, discussions of library support have been intertwined with the philosophy that distance education students must also acquire information literacy skills in preparation for lifelong learning. Howard (1983)[6] states that individuals earning a degree via distance education should graduate with the ability to continue learning independently of course work, and that this ability "is dependent upon acquiring skills in library use and and knowledge of information resources." In his study for the Carnegie Foundation for the Advancement of Teaching, Boyer (1987)[7] asserts that bibliographic instruction and the use of library resources are an essential part of the university experience. Correspondingly, Appavoo (1985)[8] affirm that the philosophy of post secondary education is, "in part, to graduate individual with the ability to learn outside the formal framework of courses" and that the challenges for librarians involved in continued independent learning. This philosophy is shared by Kascus and Aquilar (1988)[9] who emphasize the necessity for distance education students to "assume a share of the responsibility for their own learning process" to "become independent self-directed learners and information literates when, according to one survey (Dodds, Lawrence, & Guiton, 1984),[10] they perceive limited library access to be a significant disadvantage?

In another survey (Burge, Snow & Howard, 1989), [11] distance students' responses showed low expectations and inadequate knowledge of library services, yet it also reflected opinion that placed high value on information literacy skills.

5. ISSUES AND CHALLENGES

A wide range of new issues and challenges confront the field of distance learning librarianship, including and not limited to developing results-oriented online information literacy programs for faculty and students, building large digital resources that require a keen understanding of complex licensing and copyright agreements with publishers, constructing the appropriate Web portal architecture of patrons to easily navigate around, recognizing the working of information technology and campus computing departments, and meeting challenges that are typically the result of inadequate resource allocations that stress library management on the both the human and technical sides.

One of the major issues in the distance education realm is that faculty and students need to be better informed about the growing Web presence of libraries and how that presence can be utilized effectively inside their online classes. Basically, the onus falls on library staff to instruct its patrons on how to access and ferret through massive amounts of information now available online.

Part of the challenge relates to the growing use of free information available via search engines like Google, coupled with libraries adding more and more proprietary, full – text electronic information to the campus archives from publishers and information aggregators. The end result is oceans of information that can confuse students rather than help them as they conduct research.

6. CONCLUSION

Developing library and information literacy skills appears to be important for all students whether they are on or off campus, traditional or non-traditional. Remote access to library services and electronic resources has certainly moved distance education students close to equity of "the university experience" However, the challenge of providing them with opportunities to achieve information literacy remains. Because of their isolation, it is imperative that distance education students acquire information literacy skills to "effectively access and evaluate information for problem solving and decision making" (Rader and coons, 1992) and to carry out research assignments associated with university courses.

REFERENCES

1. American Library Association Presidential Committee on information Library. Final Report (Chicago American Library Association 1989)
2. Hughes S.K. & Shapiro J. J (1996) Information literacy as a liberal art: Enlightenment proposals for a new curriculum. Educom Review, 31 (2).
3. National Research Council Commission on Physical Sciences, Mathematics, and Applications Committee on information Technology Literacy, Computer Science and Telecommunication Board, Being Fluent with information Technology, Publication (Washington D.C. National Academy Press, 1989) *http://www.nap.edu/catelog/6482* html.
4. Moore, M.G. (1990) Introducing: Background and overview of contemporary American distance education. In M.G. Moore (Ed.). Contemporary issues in American Distance Education (pp.xii-xxvi) New York: Pergamon Press.
5. Several key accrediting agencies concerned with information literary are. The Middle States Commission on Higher Education (MSCHE) the Western Association of Schools and Colleges (WASC) and the Southern Associating of Colleges and Schools (SACS)
6. Howard, S. (1983, June), Library use education for adult university students. Canadian Library Journal, 40 149-15

7. Boyer, E. L (1987), College: The undergraduate experience in America New York: Harper & Row.

8. Appavoo, P.J. (1985, August) Library and information access in education : The role of technology. Paper presented at the world Conference of the International Council for Distance Education, Melbourne, Australia

9. Kascus, M, & Aguilar W. (1988) providing library support to campus programs, Colleges & Research libraries 49, 29-37.

10. Dodds, A.E, Lawrence, L.A. & Guiton P, de C. (1984) University students' perceptions of influence on external studies, Distance Education, 5, 174-185.

11. Burge, E. J, Snow, J., & Howard, J (1989, September) Interactive libraries; Dimensions of interdependence, Paper presented at the International Council for Distance Education Conference Cambridge, England.

21

An Analysis of Shodhganga : The Indian ETD Project

Surendran Cherukodan
Dr. S. Humayoon Kabir

ABSTRACT

Theses and dissertations are important part of information resources in any university. The access to these resources is generally limited to the university community. Most of the libraries don't allow photocopying, lending or distribution of theses and they are often difficult to obtain in full text through commercial distribution channels. Modern library and information professionals overcome this barrier through building digital theses projects. They are known under the umbrella term Electronic Dissertations and Theses (ETDs). The initiation of an ETD by the Information and Library Network (INFLIBNET) Centre of the University Grants Commission (UGC) was an important step towards building an Indian ETD repository, called Shodhganga. The paper discusses various aspects of Shodhganga project like software platform, structure, process of joining, access policies, metadata scheme, submission procedure etc.

Keywords : ETD Project, Digital Theses Project, Shodhganga, Theses Repository

1. INTRODUCTION

Theses and dissertations are important part of

information resources in any university. The access to these resources is generally limited to the university community. Most of the libraries don't allow photocopying, lending or distribution of theses and they are often difficult to obtain in full text through commercial distribution channels. Modern library and information professionals overcome this barrier through building digital theses projects. They are known under the umbrella term Electronic Dissertations and Theses (ETDs). The Australian Digital Theses Programme (ADT) of the Council of Australian University Libraries, The Electronic Theses and Online Service (EThos) programme of British Library UK, The National ETD Portal of South African Theses and Dissertations by the National Research Foundation, The Theses Canada Project by the Library and Archives, Canada are some of the examples of ETD programmes world wide.

"An ETD is a document that explains the research or scholarship of a researcher/student. It is expressed in a form simultaneously suitable for machine archives and worldwide retrieval. The ETD is similar to its paper predecessor" (*http://etdguide.org/*). Improved visibility and enhanced access are the key motives for having ETDs. They are basically a subset of an institution's local digital repository and it showcases the intellectual achievements of a university by making them available to a worldwide audience. ETDs offer open access (OA) to theses and dissertation to the academic community worldwide.

2. DEFINITION OF ETDS

The Online Dictionary for Library & Information Science (ODLIS) defines ETD as "The Master's theses and Ph.D. dissertations submitted in digital form rather than in print on paper, as opposed to those submitted in hard copy and subsequently converted to machine-readable format.

3. ETD INITIATIVES IN INDIA

There are several universities in India that maintain ETDs. The first ETD in India was started at the Indian Institute of Technology Bombay in 1999. Since then a number of small ETD repositories have been developed throughout India. The Directory of Open Access Repositories (Open DOAR, 2011) lists 22 ETD repositories in India. These include those from institutions such as, the Indian Institute of Science, the Indian Institute of Technology, the National Institute of Oceanography, the Central Marine Fisheries Research Institute, and the Indian Institute of Astrophysics. The demand for a national level system for archiving and accessing the entire Indian Theses in a single platform was initiated by the University of Mysore, with its Vidyanidhi Project (*http://dspace.vidyanidhi.org.in:8080/dspace/*) . It was a bold step towards the bibliographical control as well as knowledge management of research outputs in India. The Table 1.1 shows the major ETD initiatives of India.

3.1. The Shodhganga Project

The ETD initiatives in India were mainly developed at individual institutional level. The 'Vidyanidhi' Project of the University of Mysore was an important initiative in India that aimed an ETD at the national level covering all universities in India to facilitate the creation, archiving and accessing of doctoral theses. 'Vidyanidhi' project was started in the year 2000 at the Department of Library and Information Science, University of Mysore, with the sponsorship of National Information System for Science and Technology, Government of India, Ford Foundation and the Microsoft. The Project's vision was to build and strengthen the research capacities and enhance the quality of doctoral research in India. Vidyanidhi was envisioned to evolve as a national repository and a consortium for e-theses through participation and partnership with universities, academic institutions and other stake holders. Vidyanidhi enhanced access to Indian theses and enlarged the reach and audience for Indian doctoral research works. However, the project could not cover all universities and their theses due to several factors including the absence of provision for the mandatory submission of an electronic copy of every thesis submitted to Indian Universities. Hence, there was a need need for a national agency to cover all universities and their theses under one repository in India. The initiation of an ETD by the Information and Library Network (Inflibnet) Centre of the University Grants Commission (UGC) was an important step towards building an Indian ETD repository. The Shodhganga Project (*http://shodhganga.Inflibnet .ac.in/*) of Inflibnet Centre in 2010 brought a permanent platform for all Indian theses.

As on 11-2-2013, India has 620 universities including 298 State Universities, 130 Deemed to be Universities, 44 Central Universities and 148 Private Universities. (*http://www.ugc.ac.in/*). Building a common platform for showcasing all Indian theses is a great task that needed huge amount of investment and human resource. The University Grants Commission (UGC) of India recognized the need for a national repository of Indian theses. The submission of electronic version of theses was to be made mandatory. UGC assigned the task of creating the repository to Inflibnet in 2009. The Inflibnet Centre is responsible for creating an infrastructure for sharing library and information resources and services among academic and research institutions in India. To fulfill the need for a national level platform for accessing PhD theses in digital form submitted to all universities in India, Inflibnet Centre started Shodhganga in 2010. The word "Shodh" originates from Sanskrit and stands for research and discovery. The "Ganga" is the holiest, largest and longest of all rivers in Indian subcontinent. Shodhganga stands for the reservoir of Indian intellectual output stored in a repository hosted and maintained by the Inflibnet Centre. The current study is aimed at exploring the features and functions of Shodhganga Project. The study shall focus on the methods and strategies adopted by Inflibnet centre in collecting, processing, archiving and providing access to Indian theses.

3.1.1. Shodhganga - An Analysis

A systematic examination of the contents of the Shodhganga Website (*http://shodhganga.Inflibnet.ac.in/*) was done from July 2013 to October 2013. The data provided in the websites were collected for understanding the the objectives and functions of Shodhganga Project, the methods adopted by Shodhganga to deposit digital thesis by Indian Universities, the features of Shodhganga with regard to Software, Hardware, Acceptable Document Format, Search Strategies, Preservation Methods, Access policies and strategies adopted for preventing plagiarism. Finally, to understand the growth of Shodhganga with regard to the number of theses and the state wise contribution of theses, the total 140 universities were listed in an MS-Word table. This table was manually employed to derive conclusions.

"Shodhganga" is the name coined to denote digital repository of Indian Electronic Theses and Dissertations set-up by the Inflibnet Centre. The figure 1 shows the screenshot of Shodhganga website.

The UGC Notification (Minimum Standards & Procedure for Award of M.Phil. / Ph.D Degree, Regulation, 2009) dated 1st June 2009 mandates submission of electronic version of theses and dissertations by the researchers in universities with an aim to facilitate open access to Indian theses and dissertations to the academic community world-wide. This would overcome serious problem of duplication of research and poor quality resulting from the "poor visibility" and the "unseen" factor in research output. As per the Regulation, the responsibility of hosting, maintaining and making the digital repository of Indian ETD is assigned to the Inflibnet Centre.

Fig. 1. Screenshot of Shodhganga website.

3.1.2. Shodhganga-Software Platform

The Shodhganga@Inflibnet is set-up using an open source digital repository software called DSpace (*http://www.dspace.org/#*) developed by MIT (Massachusetts Institute of Technology) in partnership between Hewlett-Packard (HP). The DSpace uses internationally recognized protocols and interoperability standards. DSpace is currently used by more than 1400 institutions across the world. There are more than 100 DSpace systems in India alone. DSpace supports "Open Archives Initiative's Protocol for Metadata Harvesting" (OAI-PMH) and uses a qualified version of the Dublin Core schema for its metadata.

3.1.3. Shodhganga-Structure

Shodhganga replicates academic structure of each University in terms of Departments/ Centres/ Colleges each University has to facilitate ease of navigation. This structure facilitates research scholars from universities to deposit their theses in the respective Department / Centre / College. The option for simple search and advance search are available on the home page along with browsing facility through universities and departments. There is a semantic web-based interface to facilitate subject-based browsing, navigation, search and retrieval of content available in the repository. The Figure 2 shows the structure of Shodhganga.

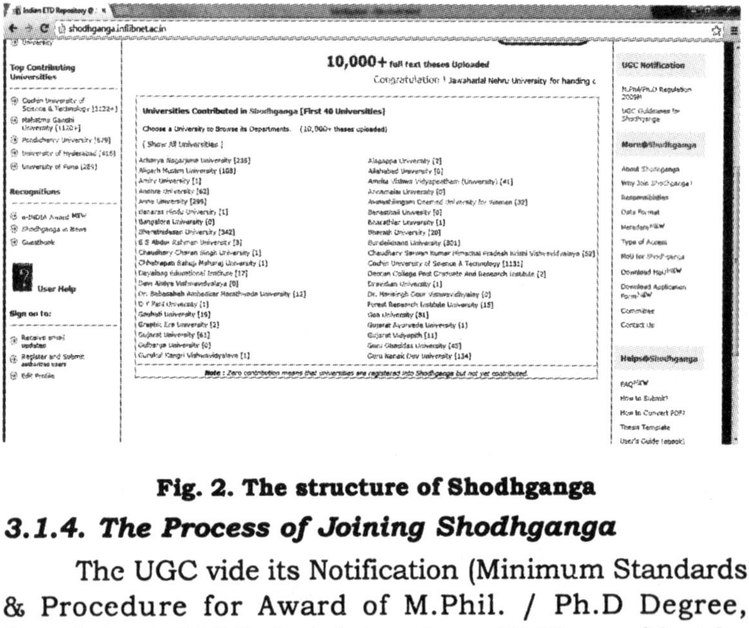

Fig. 2. The structure of Shodhganga

3.1.4. The Process of Joining Shodhganga

The UGC vide its Notification (Minimum Standards & Procedure for Award of M.Phil. / Ph.D Degree, Regulation, 2009) dated 1st June 2009 provides for submission of electronic version of theses and dissertation by the researchers in universities in Shodhganga maintained by the Inflibnet Centre. Universities are required to sign an MoU with the Inflibnet Centre to participate in the Shodhganga project. This MoU spells out the responsibilities of Universities and Inflibnet Centre related to Shodhganga. Based on the agreement, Inflibnet Centre would recommend to UGC for the release of Grants earmarked for the Shodhganga project. Universities that sign MoU with the Inflibnet Centre may get financial assistance from the UGC for digitizing their back-files of theses. As on 23rd October 2013, 144 Universities have sighed MOU with Inflibnet Centre for participating with Shodhganga.

3.1.5. Access Policies of Shodhganga

All theses and dissertations submitted to Shodhganga are available in full-text in open access to the academic community world-wide. However, it is possible to impose restrictions on access as a special case, if so desired, by the university/research scholar. The theses are uploaded not as a single file but multiple files representing the preliminary pages as well as various chapters. This is helpful for fast downloading of the files. The files are in PDF format and users get the contents in downloadable format. PDF is the preferred document format for submission of thesis in the Shodhganga. The use of other open standard document formats such as HTML, XML, Tex, LaTeX is also allowed.

3.1.6. Metadata Scheme in Shodhganga

Metadata is "structured data about data". Metadata is descriptive information about an object or resource whether physical or electronic. Shodhganga uses the qualified Dublin Core set of elements for furnishing metadata. The basic Dublin Core sets consist of 15 elements and the qualified set has about 31 elements inShodhganga.

3.1.7. Submission procedure of Theses to Shodhganga

Inflibnet encourages individual researchers to submit their theses and dissertations either online or off-line (through E-mail or CD / DVD) on voluntary basis till universities adopt and implement UGC Notification, 2009. Workflow for submission of electronic version of theses and dissertations consists of the following six steps:

Step 1. Registration/Login by the Ph.D. student/ his / her research supervisor or an authorized representative of the University.

Step 2. Validation of Account by an e-mail from the Inflibnet Centre.

Step 3. Submission of content / metadata by the registered user. During the process of submission, the submitter is also asked to grant non-exclusive rights to the Inflibnet Centre to host his / her theses in the Inflibnet 's open access digital repository.

Step 4. Verification of submitted metadata and content by the research supervisor or university representative or alternatively by the Inflibnet staff.

Step 5. Publish on ETD repository- Once the metadata and uploaded content are verified for its completeness and correctness in the process mentioned above, theses get published in the ETD repository.

Step 6. Intimation to stakeholders- All stakeholders including researcher, guide and the university will be informed through email which will be triggered automatically by the ETD repository. RSS Feed technology will be used to disseminate and deliver new content added to the ETD repository to the users.

3.1.8. Role of Shodhganga in preventing Plagiarism

Plagiarism is a major concern in the area of research which results in the poor quality of research. Proper software tools are now available to detect and deter plagiarism. The increased visibility of theses and dissertations through open access repositories would further act as a deterrent to plagiarism. UGC may provide financial assistance to the Inflibnet Centre for subscription to software tools that detect plagiarized portion of theses and dissertations. Access to software designed to detect plagiarism will be provided to universities that sign MoU with the Inflibnet Centre for Shodhganga.

3.1.9. Growth of Theses in Shodhganga

The Shodhganga project was started in 2010. As on 15th October 2013, it has completed around four years of functioning. The project is still continuing and the analysis is based on data gathered upto 15th October 2013. The website of Shodhganga claims that 144 universities have signed MOU with Inflibnet Centre for contributing contents. However, as on 1st July 2013, there are 104 Universities (72%) so far listed on the website with a contribution of 6996 theses. The investigators collected the information on the number of theses after a period of three and half months and it was found that the collection has grown to 8400 making an increase of more than 1400 theses. The Shodhganga Project has marked a monthly increase of 400 theses and a yearly growth of 2100 theses.

3.1.9.1. University wise Contribution

The contributions of individual universities show an uneven pattern in Shodhganga. There are only two universities with more than thousand theses each. Ten universities are having more than 200 theses each and nine universities have contributed more than hundred theses each.

3.1.9.2. State wise Contribution

The 104 Universities listed in the Shodhganga website represent various Indian states and Union Territories. There are 25 states including union territories that contribute theses to Shodhganga. The Table shows the state wise contributions to Shodhganga.

The state wise analysis shows that the major share (30%) of these in Shodhganga came from the state of Kerala followed by Andhra Pradesh (12%) and by Tamil Nadu and Maharashtra (10% each). The Union Territory Pondichery, the States of Uttar Pradesh, Punjab, Karnataka, Gujarat, Haryana, Madhya Pradesh and Chattisgarh have a contribution of 8% to 1%.

Table 1. State wise Contribution of Doctoral Thesis to Shodhganga

State	No. of Theses
Kerala	2518
Andhra Pradesh	984
Tamil Nadu	876
Maharashtra	815
Pondicherry (UT)	679
Uttar Pradesh	635
Punjab	452
Karnataka	390
Gujarat	296
Haryana	264
Madhya Pradesh	233
Chhattisgarh	74
Delhi (UT)	37
Jammu & Kashmir	31
Manipur	21
Assam	19
Goa	18
Jharkhand	15
Mizoram	15
Rajasthan	10
West Bengal	8
Tripura	6
Bihar	3
Himachal Pradesh	1
Total	8400

3.1.10. Growth rate of Participating Universities in Shodhganga

The number of Universities that singed MOU with Inflibnet Centre for participating in the Shodhganga project in 2010 was 10 (7%) followed by 2011 with 38 (26%) and by 2012 with 51 (36%) and 2013 with 45 (31%).

4. CONCLUSION

The universities in the country are now able to deposit their theses in electronic form to the Shodhganga website so that the intellectual inputs are made accessible to the academic community worldwide. The open access repository maintained by the Inflibnet Centre is not only meant to act as a deterrent to plagiarism that destroys the research quality but also facilitate the launching of alerting and analytical services deploying data mining and other technology tools. Shodhganga is developing a semantic web-based interface to facilitate subject-based browsing, navigation and retrieval of content available in the repository. The Shodhganga Project has achieved considerable growth during the few years of its inception. The process of scanning backlogs of theses in numerous universities would be a biggest task for the Inflibnet Centre in the future. It can also be noted that only 22 % Universities in India have signed MOU with Inflibnet Centre. Many universities have to come forward to take the challenging job of digitizing and and making open their theses to the wide public.

REFERENCE

1. Copeland, S. (2011). Electronic Theses and Dissertations. In *Digitisation Perspectives* (pp. 103-113). Sense Publishers.
2. Copeland, Susan and Penman, Andrew (2007). The development and promotion of electronic theses and dissertation (ETDs) in the U.K. New Review of Information Networking, May, Vol.10, issue 1, p.19-32.
3. Dawrs, Stuart (2012). Virtually there: Open access and the online growth of Pacific dissertations and theses, Contemporary Pacific, Vol.4, issue 2, p.348-357.
4. Fineman, Y. (2003). Electronic theses and dissertations. *Portal: Libraries and the Academy, 3*(2), 219-227.
5. Fox, E. A., Mcmillan, G., & Srinivasan, V. (2012). Electronic Theses and Dissertations. In *Putting Knowledge to Work and Letting Information Play* (pp. 95-110). SensePublishers.

6. Sheeja, N. K. (2011). The Development of an Indian Electronic Theses and Dissertations Repository: An Overview. *The Journal of Academic Librarianship, 37*(6), 546-547.

7. Urs, Shalini R and Raghavan, K.S.(2001). Vidyanidhi: Indian digital library of electronic theses, *Communications of the ACM*, May, Vol.44, issue 5, pp.88-89.

8. Vijayakumar, J. K., Murthy, T. A. V., & Khan, M. T. M. (2007). Electronic theses and dissertations and academia: A preliminary study from India. *The Journal of Academic Librarianship, 33*(3), 417-421.

9. *http://shodhganga.Inflibnet .ac.in/*

22

Information Support to Decentralised Planning in Kerala

Dr. K. Dinesan
Dr. M. Bavakutty

ABSTRACT

Our society is marching towards an Information Society. The chief driving force of social change is information. In decentralised and participatory planning , the elected representatives play key role in planning and development. They require diverse kinds of information at all levels of planning. This very fact makes it imperative to study the significance of information support to decentralised planning in Kerala. The study emphasises that inspite of the devolution of fund and powers to the grass root level, the information support to decentralised and participatory planning is not properly ensured. The study suggests that the information base of decentralised planning should be made strong by establishing a network of Village Information Centres in the state.

Keywords : Information society, Information support, Decentralised planning, Information base, Village Information Centre.

1. INTRODUCTION

Participatory decentralisation requires more informed representatives and citizens for decision making at the local level because informed participation makes the participation meaningful. Therefore dissemination of information, access to information by the beneficiaries and ensuring people's right to information are very important for participatory development. People's true participation is essential for effective planning. When the planning is at the local levels, people's involvement is necessary at all stages of planning, implementation and supervision. In local level planning all citizens have the right to participate in their governing, preparation of plans, implementation, evaluation and monitoring. This asserts the citizen's right to inform and to be informed. The programmes seem to be participatory and decentralised may not be so in reality as the clever keep the participants ignorant of the facts about the matters in which they have to involve. Sometimes the participants are given distorted version of things, or cleverly keep away the informed and knowledgeable one. Therefore participation in planning, implementation, monitoring and evaluation can be ensured only if efficient information systems for the people exist to disseminate information and protect people's right to information.

1.1. Significance of the Study

The information infrastructure of a society has a direct relationship with its nature of socio-economic progress. The economic system that supports every society is in real sense an information system. Effective and efficient development planning and implementation of plans require easy flow of and exchange of information:

a) Among those responsible for development policy and planning,

b) Among individuals and groups in the community i.e. beneficiaries and participants in development planning, and

c) Between the planners and beneficiaries.

The planner needs information on all present aspects of the society and also on the recent past, which has created the conditions for the development. There are three distinct but inter-related aspects to be noticed in considering information support to grassroots level development. They are the following:

1. There should be provision for and communication of pertinent data and information to support rural people's efforts for their own development in agriculture, literacy, health, housing, employment, natural resources conservation and environment matters.
2. The fund of valuable native knowledge related with food, health and medicine, plants and animals, social and cultural value systems, ethno music and arts etc. are to be recorded, processed, disseminated and utilised on a much wider scale. A good part of such information may not be in written or printed form but transmitted orally.
3. Information required for preparing development plans at the local levels, data on demographic aspects, development sectors, social welfare schemes etc. are to be provided to the planners, plan implementers and supporting agencies.

At the state level, State Planning Board is having a large library and information support system that can be used by the top officers of planning. They have also access to other information system at the State Capital. It has been agreed that planning and development should be decentralised. Powers have been delegated to grassroots level, resources have been devolved to Local Self Government Institutions (LSGIs); but knowledge and skill pertaining to local level planning has not been imparted to the Panchayat functionaries and activists. The facilities to provide quality library and information systems that can support LSGIs have not been thought of seriously. No District Panchayat, Block Panchayat or Grama Panchayat has a good library and information system that can provide information support to local level planning. There should be a very efficient library and information system in each and every Panchayat which can fulfill the information requirements of the people of the region. In this context the investigator conducted a study to examine the present information support to decentralised planning in Kerala.

1.2. Objectives of the Study

The main objective of the present study is to examine the information support to the ongoing local level participatory planning in Kerala. The following specific objectives are identified to achieve the same:

1. To examine whether the knowledge of decentralised planning has been imparted to the grass roots level.
2. To understand the role played by local libraries in providing information support to decentralised planning.
3. To suggest measures for strengthening the information support to decentralised planning.
4. To understand the present status of the information base of decentralised planning in Kerala.

1.3. Methodology

Multi-stage sampling was employed for the selection of the sample. In this method, sample is selected in various stages but only the last unit is studied. The universe of population of the present study consists of 16139 elected members of 999 Grama Panchayats of Kerala. The fourteen districts of Kerala State have been grouped in to three regions namely southern, central and northern. In the first stage, Block Panchayats were selected from each region using the random table. Eleven Block Panchayats from among 46 Block Panchayats of southern region, 16 Block Panchayats from among 64 Block Panchayats of central region and 13 Block Panchayats from among 42 Block Panchayats of northern region were selected. From each Block Panchayats selected, one Grama Panchayat each was selected through random sampling method. Thus, in the second stage, 11 Grama Panchayats one each from 11 Block Panchayats of southern region, 16 Grama Panchayats from 16 Block Panchayats of central region and 13 Grama Panchayats from 13 Block Panchayats of northern region were selected for the study. In the third stage, all the 183 elected members of 11 Grama Panchayats of southern region, 241 elected members of 16 Grama Panchayats of central region and 223 elected members of 13 Grama Panchayats of northern region were selected as the sample of the study. Thus 647 members of forty Grama Panchayats (4 per cent) in forty Block Panchayats of three regions of Kerala State constitute the sample of the study and questionnaires were sent to them. It is found that 435 members (67.2 per cent) from 32 out of 40 Grama Panchayats (80 per cent) responded. It can be seen that 107 elected members (24.60 per cent) are from the southern region, 146 members (33.56 per cent) from the central region and 182 members (41.84 per cent) from the northern region. Participant observation of Grama Sabhas, Development Seminars and such other meetings and conferences was conducted by the investigator to supplement the data obtained through questionnaires. Structured questionnaires were prepared and administered to the members of Grama Panchayats selected. The purpose of the questionnaire was to obtain data from the Panchayat Members regarding their information needs in local level planning, their information use pattern, the information sources, the channels of communications, the barriers in getting information, the requirement of an information system that supports local level planning, the importance of indigenous knowledge in the decentralised planning and the digital literacy of the elected members. The name, address and telephone numbers of the Presidents of the selected Grama Panchayats were collected from the Panchayat Guide 2006. The Panchayat Presidents were contacted over telephone and requested their co-operation. The number of members of the Grama Panchayats was ascertained from the website of the Local Self Government department. The questionnaires to be served to all the members of each Grama Panchayat were mailed to the Presidents with a request. Stamped and self addressed envelops were also enclosed for mailing back the filled questionnaire to the investigator. The data collected were analysed and findings were made using appropriate statistical methods.

2. INFORMATION SUPPORT TO DECENTRALISED PLANNING IN KERALA

The information support and expertise available for centralised planning in Kerala has been very strong. The devolution of powers and plan fund to grassroots level has made the Local Self Governments more powerful. It is examined whether the knowledge and expertise of decentralised planning has been devolved into the local level along with the devolution of powers and money.

2.1. Devolution of Knowledge to Grassroots Level

The opinion of Elected Members of Grama Panchayats about the devolution of knowledge of decentralised planning to grassroots level was obtained and it is summarised in Table 1. When asked whether the knowledge of decentralised planning has to be devolved to grassroots level along with devolution of powers, nearly 93 per cent of the members answered positively. It means that knowledge of decentralised planning has to be devolved to local level along with devolution of powers. It is seen that 89.72 per cent of the members of southern region, 93.15 per cent and 94.51

per cent each of them in the central and northern regions expressed positive responses. The members with positive responses are more from the northern region than the other two regions.

Table 1. Opinion of the Grama Panchayat Members about the devolution of knowledge to grassroots level

Region	Whether the knowledge of decentralised planning has to be devolved to grassroots level along with devolution of powers?					
	Yes		No		Total	
	No.	%	No.	%	No.	%
Southern	96	89.72	11	10.28	107	100
Central	136	93.15	10	6.85	146	100
Northern	172	94.51	10	5.49	182	100
Total	404	92.87	31	7.13	435	100

The study revealed that large majority of Grama Panchayat Members in Kerala needs knowledge of decentralised planning to be devolved to local level along with devolution of powers and more members of the northern region favour this opinion.

2.2. Knowledge of Decentralised Planning Imparted to Local Level

The members were also asked whether the knowledge of decentralised planning has been presently imparted to local level. The summary of responses presented in Table 2 shows that 50.47 per cent of the Panchayat Members of southern region, 45.21 per cent of the members of the central region and 37.91 per cent of them from the northern region show positive responses. As a whole, 43.45 per cent of the respondents are of the opinion that knowledge has been imparted to grassroots level. The negative responses by the majority (56.55 per cent) of the members indicate that knowledge of decentralised planning has not been really imparted to local level. More members of the northern region (62.09 per cent) have this feeling.

Table 2. Opinion of the Grama Panchayat Members about the knowledge imparted to local level

Region	Whether knowledge of decentralised planning has been imparted to local level?					
	Yes		No		Total	
	No.	%	No.	%	No.	%
Southern	54	50.47	53	49.53	107	100
Central	66	45.21	80	54.79	146	100
Northern	69	37.91	113	62.09	182	100
Total	189	43.45	246	56..55	435	100

The analysis showed that knowledge of decentralised planning has not been fully imparted to local level and more members of northern region have this view.

2.3. Role of Local Libraries in Imparting Knowledge of Decentralised Planning

Libraries and Information Centres do provide services to different categories of people in the society to meet their information needs. The Grama Panchayat Members rate the usefulness of services provided by the libraries of their locality as shown in Table 3.

Table 3. Role of local libraries in imparting knowledge of decentralised planning to the Grama Panchayat Members

Response	Southern		Central		Northern		Total	
	No.	%	No.	%	No.	%	No.	%
Very useful	34	31.78	27	18.49	27	14.84	88	20.23
Useful	27	25.23	42	28.77	43	23.63	112	27.75
Not useful	46	42.99	77	52.74	112	61.54	235	54.02
Grand Total	107	100	146	100	182	100	435	100

The libraries of their locality are 'very useful' for providing necessary information in decentralised planning according to 20 per cent of the members and are 'useful' to 27.75 per cent of them. But, majority of the members (54 per cent) consider that the services provided by the libraries are' not useful' in decentralised planning. Those who rated the library services as 'not useful' are more in the northern region (61.54 per cent) than central region (52.74 per cent) and southern region (43 per cent).

It is revealed that the libraries of the locality of the respondents are partially useful in imparting knowledge of decentralised planning to the members. It means that the local libraries are not fully equipped with resources for providing information support to the Grama Panchayat Members in the different phases of local planning and the role of local libraries in imparting knowledge of decentralised planning to the local level is not significant.

2.4. Need for Community Information Centre (CIC) in the Villages of Kerala

At present there is no provision for the dissemination of development information to the members of Grama Panchayats or to the public in the villages of Kerala. Therefore the necessity of establishing Community Information Centres (CICs) in the Grama Panchayats is examined. The responses of the Panchayat Members on this matter are summarised in Table 4. It shows that large majority (94 per cent) of the respondents need CICs to be established in the villages to provide development information. It is seen that 93.40 per cent members of southern region, 97.95 per cent members of central region and 91.21 per cent of them from the northern region support the necessity of CICs.

It is found that large majority of Grama Panchayat Members need Community Information Centres to be established in the villages to provide development

Information and almost all members of the central region support this view.

Table 4. Opinion of Grama Panchayat Members about the need for Community Information Centre

Region	Whether Community Information Centre needed in the villages to provide development information?					
	Yes		No		Total	
	No.	%	No.	%	No.	%
Southern	100	93.40	7	6.60	107	100
Central	143	97.95	3	2.05	146	100
Northern	166	91.21	16	8.79	182	100
Total	409	94.02	26	5.98	435	100

2.4.1 Community Information Centre in the Local Library

Opinion of the respondents in respect of starting of CICs in the local libraries was collected and the summary is given in Table 5.

Table 5. Opinion of the Grama Panchayat Members about establishing Community Information Centre in the local libraries

Region	Whether the Community Information Centre established in the local library?					
	Yes		No		Total	
	No.	%	No.	%	No.	%
Southern	73	68.22	34	31.78	107	100
Central	91	62.33	55	37.67	146	100
Northern	140	76.92	42	23.08	182	100
Total	304	69.89	131	30.11	435	100

It is seen that nearly 70 per cent of the Panchayat Members need the CICs to be started in the local library. More members from northern region (76.92 per cent) expressed this view. However a sizable number of members (30.11 per cent) are not in favour of establishing CICs in the local libraries.

It is found that majority of Grama Panchayat Members favour of starting CICs in local libraries and more of them are from the northern region.

2.5. Information Services to the Public

Information services are to be provided not only to Grama Panchayat Members but also to the general public of the society. Who is responsible for providing such a service? The region wise distribution of the members with their first options for providing information services to the public is given in Table 6. It shows that 65.42 per cent of the members of southern region, 62.33 per cent of the central region and 58.79 per cent of them of northern region support the starting of new CICs as their first option. More than 25 per cent of them favour the libraries to act as Information Centres, 8 per cent believe that information has to be obtained from the government offices and a very few (1.61 per cent) suggested to continue the present system.

Table 6. Distribution of the Grama Panchayat Members according to their choice to provide information services to the public

Response	Southern		Central		Northern		Total	
	No.	%	No.	%	No.	%	No.	%
Establishment of Community Information Centre	70	65.42	91	62.33	107	58.79	268	61.61
Make the Libraries as an Information Centre also	23	21.50	28	19.18	59	32.42	110	25.29
From the Government Offices	8	7.48	19	13.01	9	4.95	38	8.28

Continue present system	4	3.74	2	1.37	1	0.55	7	1.61
Others	1	0.93	2	1.37	2	1.10	5	1.15
No opinion	1	0.93	4	2.74	4	2.20	9	2.07
Grand Total	107	100	146	100	182	100	435	100

It is revealed that there is an urge to establish Community Information Centres in the Grama Panchayats of Kerala as suggested by majority of the members to provide information services to the public. More members from southern region are of this opinion.

2.6. Information Services to the Grama Panchayat Members

Timely access to the required information is possible only through a system capable of collecting, organizing and retrieving information. The members were asked to indicate their first choice among the given options. As can be seen from Table 7 majority of members (56.32 per cent) proposed to 'strengthen the training programme'. It is seen that 39 per cent of them are of the opinion of networking the Panchayat Raj Institutions of Kerala and thus providing online information support. For a few members (2.76 per cent) the present system has to be continued and only some (1.38 per cent) of the members have not indicated any response. More members from the central region (47.26 per cent) prefer the networking of Panchayat Raj Institutions and more members from the northern region (62.64 per cent) favour 'strengthening of training programmes'.

Table 7. Distribution of the Grama Panchayat Members according to their first choice to provide information support

Response	Southern		Central		Northern		Total	
	No.	%	No.	%	No.	%	No.	%
Form a network of Panchayath Raj Institutions	38	35.51	69	47.26	62	34.07	169	38.85
Strengthen the training programme	60	56.07	71	48.63	114	62.64	245	56.32
Continue the present system	6	5.61	2	1.37	4	2.20	12	2.76
Others	2	1.87	-	0.00	1	0.55	3	0.69
No opinion	1	0.93	4	2.74	1	0.55	6	1.38
Grand Total	107	100	146	100	182	100	435	100

It is found that there is a need to strengthen the training programmes for the members of Grama Panchayats in Kerala as indicated by majority of the members and it is also necessary to provide networking of Grama Panchayats.

2.7. Necessity of Information Base

A strong information base is essential for any development programme and an efficient information system is a part of an efficient economic system. The respondents were asked to indicate their opinion about the essentiality of information base and the responses are summarised in Table 8. It shows that nearly 88 per cent of the members of the southern region, 90 per cent of them from the central region and 91 per cent from the northern region indicate positive response. The responses from large majority (90 per cent) of the Panchayat members of Kerala show that a strong information base is essential for local planning and governance. The number of members expressed this opinion increases from south to north.

Table 8. Opinion of the Grama Panchayat about the information base of decentralised planning

Region	Whether a strong information base is essential for local planning and governance?					
	Yes		No		Total	
	No.	%	No.	%	No.	%
Southern	94	87.85	13	12.15	107	100
Central	131	89.73	15	10.27	146	100
Northern	165	90.66	17	9.34	182	100
Total	390	89.66	45	10.34	435	100

The analysis showed that a strong information base is essential in Kerala for local planning and governance as opined by the large majority of Grama Panchayat Members and there is an increase in the number of the members who put across this view from south to north.

2.7.1. Information Base for Decentralised Planning in Kerala

When asked whether the present information base of Kerala is capable of supporting decentralised planning, majority of them responded negatively. The details are shown in Table 9. About 50 per cent of the members from southern and northern regions and 48 per cent from central region expressed positive responses. It means that the information base of Kerala is not capable of supporting decentralised planning.

Table 9. Opinion of the Grama Panchayat Members about the capability of information base in Kerala

Region	Whether the information base Kerala capable of supporting decentralised planning?					
	Yes		No		Total	
	No.	%	No.	%	No	100
Southern	53	49.53	54	50.47	107	100
Central	64	43.84	82	56.16	146	100
Northern	90	49.45	92	50.55	182	100
Total	207	47.59	228	52.41	435	100

It is revealed that the present information base of Kerala is not capable of supporting decentralised planning as indicated by majority of Grama Panchayat Members and more members from the central region are of this view.

2.7.2. Status of Information Base in Kerala

The respondents were asked to express their opinion about the information base of decentralised planning in Kerala and the responses are summarised in Table 10.

Table 10. Distribution of the Grama Panchayat Members according to their opinion about the information base of the decentralized planning in Kerala

Response	Southern		Central		Northern		Total	
	No.	%	No.	%	No.	%	No.	%
Not necessary	2	1.87	2	1.37	2	1.10	6	1.38
Very weak	55	51.40	78	53.42	71	39.01	204	46.90
Strong	34	31.78	50	34.25	98	53.85	182	41.84
Very strong	10	9.35	9	6.16	4	2.20	23	5.29
No Opinion	6	5.61	7	4.79	7	3.85	20	4.60
Grand Total	107	100	146	100	182	100	435	100

The information base of decentralised planning in Kerala is found to be 'very weak' as indicated by considerable number (47 per cent) of respondents. On the other hand 42 per cent of members consider the information base as 'strong'. Strangely 5 per cent indicated that it is 'very strong'. For 1.38 per cent of the members the information base is 'not necessary' and 4.60 per cent have not responded at all as given in Table 10.

It is found that the information base of decentralised planning in Kerala is weak. Majority of the members of central region consider it as very weak, on the other hand majority of the members of northern region consider it as strong.

3. MAJOR FINDINGS OF THE STUDY

The important findings of the study are given below:

1. A large majority (93 per cent) of the Grama Panchayat Members indicated that knowledge of decentralised planning has to be devolved to local level along with devolution of powers and more members of the northern region (95 per cent) favour this opinion.
2. The knowledge of decentralised planning has not been fully imparted to local level as opined by majority (57 per cent) of the Panchayat Members. The skills and expertise of local level planning imparted to the members are not satisfactory due to the presence of communication barriers and inadequacy of capacity building programmes. A regular increase in the number of members with this view is noticed from southern region (50 per cent) to northern region (62 per cent).
3. The libraries of the locality are found to be not useful in imparting knowledge of decentralised planning as indicated by majority (54 per cent) of the members. It means that the local libraries are not fully equipped with resources for providing information support to the Grama Panchayat Members in the different phases of local planning and the role of local libraries in imparting knowledge of decentralised planning to the local level is not significant. A regular increase in the number of members with this opinion is noticed from south (43 per cent) to north (62 per cent).
4. A large majority (94 per cent) of Grama Panchayat Members indicated the need of Community Information Centres in the villages to provide development information to the Panchayat Members as well as the people of the locality. It is found that almost all the members of the central region (98

percent) support this view.

5. Nearly 70 per cent of the Panchayat Members need the CICs to be started in the local library. More members from northern region (77 per cent) expressed this view. However a sizable number of members (30.11 per cent) are not in favour of establishing CICs in the local libraries. It is found that majority of Grama Panchayat Members favour of starting CICs in local libraries and more of them are from the northern region.
6. There is an urge to establish Community Information Centres in the Grama Panchayats of Kerala as suggested by majority (62 per cent) of the members to provide information services to the public. More members from southern region are of this opinion.
7. There is a need to strengthen the training programmes for the members of Grama Panchayats in Kerala as indicated by majority (56 per cent) of the members. However a sizable number of members (39 per cent) indicated the networking of Panchayat Raj Institutions. The members of the northern region are more (63 per cent) with the view of strengthening training programme and more of them from central region prefer networking of Panchayat Raj Institutions.
8. A strong information base is essential in Kerala for local planning and governance as opined by the large majority (90 per cent) of Grama Panchayat Members and there is an increase in the number of the members who put across this view from south (88 per cent) to north (91 per cent).
9. The information base of Kerala is not capable of supporting decentralised planning as indicated by majority (52 per cent) of Grama Panchayat Members and more members from the central region (51 per

cent) are of this view.

10. The information base of decentralised planning in Kerala is really weak. A good number of members (47 per cent) indicated that the information base of decentralised planning is very weak and equal number of them (47 per cent) considers it as strong. Majority (53 per cent) of the members of central region consider it as very weak and majority (54 per cent) of the members of northern region consider the information base as strong.

4. CONCLUSION

The existing library and information systems are likely to be incapable of providing information support to the poor villagers and the disadvantaged in local level planning. Kerala has more than 6000 public libraries that serve mainly the rural public. They played a very significant role in the Total Literacy Campaign of 1990 in Kerala. These libraries that came up through people's initiative existed and they extended library services to remote corners of the state. As these libraries are not equipped with relevant information sources, services, and trained staff they are not in a position provide information support to decentralised planning. Therefore, at least one library in each Grama Panchayat has to be revamped to meet the information requirements of the elected members and the general public.

Now it is possible to extend information services of quality and relevance even to remote rural areas with the application of Information and Communication Technology (ICT). A villager who is in need of any data from any where in the world at any time he/she requires can access the same. Such an information system can be maintained in our rural libraries. It will be made less costly if the information infrastructure is well planned. Therefore, the rural libraries may be uplifted to Community Information Centres (CICs) by providing the necessary information infrastructure facilities. These centres have to become live spheres of social activity which make the decentralised planning and development real with informed participation. The CICs should act as service outlets of state information infrastructure with the application of ICT. The District Informatics Centre now functioning in the District head quarters may be further expanded and linked to CICs. These centres should look after all the information requirement of the community. It should provide services similar to all that library and information services provided by State Planning Board at state capital. Development and information support is not for planners and bureaucrats only but for the general public also. This concept is in conformity with UNESCO's vision of knowledge society where everyone has access to information that is relevant to them and where everyone has the opportunity and skills to use their information in meeting their needs and aspirations.

REFERENCES

1. Adiseshiah, Malcolm S. (1994) Decentralised planning and panchayathi raj, New Dlehi, Concept Publishing.
2. Aiyer, Mani Shanker (2002). Panchayati Raj: The way forward. Economic and Political Weekly, 37(31), pp. 3293-3297.
3. Biswas, Subal C. and Midda, Abdul M. (1999) Role of information technology in managing rural development information in India. IN: Proceedings of twenty second All India Conference of IASLIC on Information Management in the Context of Fast Emerging Information Society. Calcutta, IASLIC.
4. Government of Kerala. (2006) Ten years of Panchayath Raj in Kerala: a rapid assessment study. Thiruvananthapuram, Kerala State Planning Board.
5. Government of Kerala. (2007) Economic Review 2006. Thiruvananthapuram, State Planning B
6. Neelameghan, A. (1997) Information support for socio-

economic development planning: information needs of urban planners. IN: A. Neelameghan, ed. Information support for socio-economic development planning. Bangalore, Sarada Ranganathan Endowment For Library Services, 2..

7. Neelameghan, A. (1998) Information technology and rural development. Information Studies, 4(1), pp. 56 – 57.

8. Oomen, M. A. ed. (2007) A decade of decentralisation in Kerala: Experience and lessons. New Delhi, Har Anand Publications.

9. Palanithurai, G. (2001) Capacity building for local leaders. New Delhi, Concept Publishing Company.

10. Raman Nair, R. ed. (2003) Information Technology for participatory development. New Delhi, Concept Publishing House.

11. Thomas Isaac, T. M. (2000) Local democracy and development: peoples campaign for decentralized planning in Kerala. New Delhi, Left Word Books Thomas Isaac, T. M. and Harilal, K. N. (1997) Planning for empowerment: people'scampaign for decentralized planning in Kerala. Economic and Political Weekly, XXXII (1-2), pp. 53-8.

23

Quality Assurance in LIS Education in India through Accreditation Issues and Challenges

Dr. Manzoor Babu.V

ABSTRACT

Education plays a vital role in the development of any nation. Therefore there is a premium on both quality and quantity (relevance and excellence of academic programs offered) of higher education . Like any other domain, the method to improve quality remains the same, that is finding and recognizing new needs and satisfying them with products and services of international standards. Similarly finding out the drawbacks of the existing system of education by means of analyzing strength and weakness is very essential. Weaknesses of the system should be attended and channelized into new opportunities or to be modified according to revised curriculum. In such a context accreditation of the LIS (Library and Information Science) programs are very essential. The author discusses the quality assurance in LIS education in India through accreditation.

Keywords: Quality assurance, LIS Education, Accreditation

1. INTRODUCTION

Education plays a vital role in the development of any nation. Therefore there is a premium on both quality and quantity (relevance and excellence of academic programs offered) of higher education . Like any other domain, the method to improve quality remains the same, that is finding and recognizing new needs and satisfying them with products and services of international standards. Similarly finding out the drawbacks of the existing system of education by means of analyzing strength and weakness is very essential. Weaknesses of the system should be attended and channelized into new opportunities or to be modified according to revised curriculum. In such a context accreditation of the LIS (Library and Information Science) programs are very essential.

2. ACCREDITATION

Accreditation is a process of quality assurance and improvement; whereby a programme in an institution is critically appraised to verify that the institution or the programme continues to meet and exceed the norms and standards prescribed by the appropriate designated authorities. Accreditation does not seek to replace the system of award of degree and diplomas by the Universities/ Colleges/ Departments; but it provides quality assurance that the academic aims and objectives of the institution are honestly pursued and effectively achieved by the available resources, and that the institution has demonstrated capabilities of ensuring effectiveness of the educational programs over the validity period of accreditation (Usually 5 years).

2.1. Significance of the accreditation

In the present context accreditation of the programmes are essential because:

1. It make the institute / Department aware of the

weakness of the programme offered by it and act on suggestions for improvement.

2. It encourages the institute to move continuously towards the improvement of quality of its programme, and the pursuit of excellence.
3. It facilitates institution for updating themselves in programme curriculum, teaching and learning processes, faculty achievements, students' skills, abilities and knowledge.
4. To excel among stakeholders (peers, students, employers and societies)
5. To facilitate receiving of grants from Government regulatory bodies and institutions/ agencies such as UGC/ AICTE etc.
6. To attain international recognition of accredited degrees awarded.
7. To facilitate the mobility of graduated students and professionals.

2.2. Existing accreditation in LIS education in India.

University Grants Commission is the statutory body that looks over the funds and functions of the Indian universities. It has set up The National Assessment and Accreditation Council (NAAC) for evaluative assessment of the courses and curricula as offered by the Indian universities on the basis of a set of criteria on a regular interval on Institutional &Departmental performance. Different grades are offered as a result that signifies the concerned LIS Department's degree of conformity with the Model Curriculum. But so far no LIS Department has been reported so far (Sarkhel, 2006). The NAAC Accreditation is basically concentrate on infrastructural facilities like class rooms, faculty rooms, laboratory, library and number of staff, student-staff ratio etc. But in the modern times accreditation has become more subjective and it is based on the objectives and outcomes of the courses are being offered. The agencies like NBA

(National Board of Accreditation) evaluates the institutions on the basis of out comes of the programmes being offered by the institute and whether the graduates are fit for the job market in which they are going to work. The basic parameters for the assessment are taken from the Washington Accord and other western systems like ABET (Accreditation Board of Engineering and Technology).

At present there is no accreditation agency in India like the American Library Association (ALA) Committee on Accreditation in USA and Canada, Australian Library and Information Association (ALIA), for Australia, Chartered Institute of Library and Information Professionals (CILIP) for UK etc. to ensure reasonable standards and quality of educational programme being offered in the field of Library and Information Science in India.

The report of the Committee on National Policy on Library and Information System (NAPLIS) stressed the need for a body of accreditation in India. The University Grants Commission, India appointed a Committee "UGC Review Committee on Library Science in Indian Universities" under the Chairmanship of Dr. S.R. Ranganathan in the year 1961 and the report published in 1965. So far departments of LIS in the universities have broadly adopted the schemes of papers recommended by UGC Review Committee on Library Science in Indian Universities, 1965. But its other recommendations regarding staff requirement, physical facilities required and maintenance of department libraries have not been faithfully followed. The Review Committee considered a minimum staff of one reader and two lecturers for the BLIS course. Few universities, who have introduced these courses, have provided the recommended staff standard. The accreditation agency should be responsible for recommending minimum standards in terms of faculty strength, intake criteria, teacher student ratio, evaluation methods, library and laboratory facilities, availability of teaching materials, finance and physical facilities. It should also take care of regular revision of LIS syllabus for uniformity and standardization in the overall LIS education system.

National and International associations have also made sincere efforts by holding conferences and seminars and discussing vital issue of accreditation. Unfortunately, nothing concrete have been done so far. In 1976, IFLA in its annual conference passed a resolution that " to maintain uniformity in the standards in the LIS Education programmes in the country, the Government of India be requested to create a Library Science Council on the pattern of Indian Medical Council" (Baba, 1999, p.570).

In 1994, Nagpur University organized a UGC sponsored national seminar on Accreditation of Library and Information Science Schools in India. This seminar also emphasized the need for establishing an independent National Council to be named as Indian Council for Accreditation of Library and Information Science Education (ICALISE) similar to the American Library Association in USA and Library Association in UK.

The existing scenario of LIS education in India can be summarized as follows:

- Long tradition, but it remains trapped by old theories and principles.
- Grown exponentially
- Not concerned of quality and standardization.
- Diversity of institutions

3. GLOBAL TRENDS

Global trends in the field of Library and Information Science is specifically demanding the accreditation of the courses conducted by Indian schools in Library and Information science. A very good percentage of Indian graduates in Library and Information Science are seeking their employment in Arabian/ Gulf countries. Gulf countries are now insisting on ALA or similar accreditation for appointment of senior librarian or information scientist. Therefore they are preferring American Graduates and well qualified Indian Graduates or PhD holders are working as Library assistants ashamed behind less qualified 'Boss'. Global trends in the field of Library and Information science can be summarized as follows:

- Role of higher and professional eduction is changing
- Traditional role of transmitting knowledge to also providing skilled labour
- Need to contribute to the creation of newer knowledge
- Enhanced demand for higher and professional education.
- As role changes, institutions have to make sure they remain relevant to this new need.
- Challenge to deal with digital technology
- Need for equity and balancing of professional degrees awarded by the Universities.

4. PURPOSE OF SELF ASSESSMENT

Every accreditation presupposes to formulate on the basis of self assessment and evaluation. NAAC accreditation is done on the basis of Self Study Report (SSR) prepared by the institution and NBA accreditation is done on the basis of Self Assessment report (SAR) submitted by the institution. The accrediting agency verifies the self assessment report prepared by the applying institution and on the basis of the verification they recommend for the award of a particular grade to the institution. Self assessment is done to:

1. Identify the organization's strength and weaknesses
2. Issues and problems to be identified and corrected
3. The needs that should be addressed through specific action

4. Existing resources including human resources should be utilized more effectively
5. Organization's outcomes and achievements can be well documented
6. It can generate information useful in planning and decision making
7. Assist in fund arising
8. Provide the stake holders of the institution the information about the organization's performance.

5. ACCREDITATION CRITERIA

National and International agencies are accrediting institutions on the basis of a number of criteria. The criteria set by NBA, NAAC and ALA accreditation for library schools are aimed at same objectives. The major criteria used by them are:

1. Vision/ Mission, Goals, and Objectives

A school/ Institutes's Vision, mission and program educational Objectives (PEOs) are pursued, and its program objectives achieved, through implementation of an ongoing, broad-based, systematic planning process that involves the constituency that a program seeks to serve. Consistent with the values of the parent institution and the culture and mission of the school, program goals and objectives foster quality education. Program Educational Objectives (PEOs) and Program Outcomes (POs) are to be well connected and entire curriculum should be designed accordingly. There should be sufficient planning to ensure that what type of professionals these schools are producing and whether they are loaded with enough skills and practices required for the current job market.

2. Course and Curriculum

The curriculum is based on goals and objectives, and evolves in response to an ongoing systematic planning process. Within this general framework, the curriculum provides, through a variety of educational experiences, for the study of theory, principles, practice, and values necessary for the provision of service in libraries and information agencies and in other contexts. The curriculum is concerned with recordable information and knowledge, and the services and technologies to facilitate their management and use. The curriculum of library and information studies encompasses information and knowledge creation, communication, identification, selection, acquisition, organization and description, storage and retrieval, preservation, analysis, interpretation, evaluation, synthesis, dissemination, and management. The curriculum is continually reviewed and receptive to innovation; its evaluation is used for ongoing appraisal, to make improvements, and to plan for the future. Evaluation of the curriculum includes assessment of students' achievements and their subsequent accomplishments. Evaluation involves those served by the program: students, faculty, employers, alumni, and other constituents. Entire curriculum should be designed is such a way as to ensure the course objectives are met by Course Outcomes (Cos)

3. Faculty

The school has a faculty capable of accomplishing program objectives. Full-time faculty members are qualified for appointment to the graduate faculty within the parent institution and are sufficient in number and in diversity of specialties to carry out the major share of the teaching, research, and service activities required for a program, wherever and however delivered. Part-time faculty, when appointed, balance and complement the teaching competencies of the full-time faculty. Particularly in the teaching of specialties that are not represented in the expertise of the full-time faculty, part-time faculty enrich the quality and diversity of a program.

4. Students

The Institution formulates recruitment, admission, financial aid, placement, and other academic and administrative policies for students that are consistent with the institution's mission and program goals and objectives; the policies reflect the needs and values of the constituencies served by a program. The institution should provide an environment that fosters student participation in the definition and determination of the total learning experience. Students may be provided with opportunities to form student organizations and to participate in the formulation, modification, and implementation of policies affecting academic and student affairs.

5. Knowledge of the discipline

All the accreditation agencies are verifying these aspects on the basis of a variety of methods. It means that whether the students graduated or completed a post graduation course has enough skills and capabilities for for entering into the field and solving the problems in it. It also measures that whether they have capablities for handling modern technological tools used in the field of information processing, handling and dissemination. knowledge and understanding of the librarianship principles and apply these to one's own work, as a member and leader in a team, to manage projects and in multidisciplinary environments. Team working capabilities of students are also assessed under this area.

6. Administration and Finance

The school is an integral yet distinctive academic unit within the institution. Its autonomy is sufficient to assure that the intellectual content of its program, the selection and promotion of its faculty, and the selection of its students are determined by the school within the general guidelines of the institution. The parent institution provides the resources and administrative support needed for the attainment of program objectives. The school's faculty, staff, and students have the same opportunity for representation on the institution's advisory or policy-making bodies as do those of comparable units throughout the institution.

7. Communication

Most of the accreditation agencies are much concerned about the communication skills of the students being graduated from an institution. The students should be able to Communicate effectively on various aspects relating to their joband also able to comprehend and write effective reports and design documentation, make effective presentations, and give and receive clear instructions.

8. Academic Support Units and Innovative practices

Academic support units such as associations of Students and research scholars, facilities for interaction with peers, estra curricular activities and participation and initiation of seminars and conferences are also measured. Innovative practices adopted in teaching and learning and best practices adopted by the isntitution are also add value to the institution's quality.

9. Physical Resources and Facilities

Physical facilities provide a functional learning environment for students and faculty; enhance the opportunities for research, teaching, service, consultation, and communication; and promote efficient and effective administration of the school's program, regardless of the forms or locations of delivery. Instructional and research facilities and services for meeting the needs of students and faculty include access to library and multimedia resources and services, computer and other information technologies, accommodations for independent study, and media production facilities.

6. NEED FOR ILA (INDIAN LIBRARY ASSOCIATION) ACCREDITATION

In India we have a number of institutions providing courses in Library and Information Science such as CLISC (Certificate In Library and Information Science), BLISC (bachelor of Library and Information Science), MLISC (Master of Library and Information Science), PGDLAN (Post Graduate Diploma in Library Automation and Networking), M Phil, PhD and post doctoral research in Library and Information Science. We have enough infrastructural facilities at national level for conducting accreditation. What is lacking is the initiation from the part of the expert level scholars in the field for establishing a national accreditation agency in the field of Library and Information science and ensure its collaboration with International accreditation agencies such as ALA, CILIP etc. CILIP has a reciprocal agreement with the American Library Association (ALA) and the Australian Library and Information Association which means academic qualifications accredited by those bodies are accepted in the UK. Masters degrees accredited by CILIP will be recognized in the USA, Canada, Australia and New Zealand. The Bachelor degrees accredited by CILIP will be recognized in Australia and New Zealand only. Similar agreement in India is a must to ensure the mobility of skilled persons for better employment.

7. CONCLUSION

To achieve academic excellence, it is of utmost importance that standards and norms of education be prescribed and adherence to them be made mandatory. Unfortunately, there is no national accreditation body for LIS education in India. As a result, new LIS schools are opening at a fast pace following different patterns of education and without the basic minimum facilities, resulting in mass production of professionals with sub-standard education and having least or no exposure to practical librarianship. In principle, no new LIS school should be established without the approval of such an accreditation agency. This agency should be responsible for recommending minimum standards in terms of faculty strength, intake criteria, teacher-student ratio, Program educational objectives, course and program outcomes, evaluation methods, library and laboratory facilities, availability of teaching materials, finance and physical facilities etc. It should also take care of regular revision of LIS syllabus for uniformity and standardization in the overall LIS education system which is presently missing. Although UGC, through its LIS Committees has revised and recommended the syllabus for BLIS and MLIS courses, these are not followed by most of the universities as the role of UGC is more recommending in nature rather than accrediting. As a result, each university is designing its own curriculum, follows its own practices, and resulting in wide disparities among programmes.

REFERENCES

1. Association of Indian Universities (2003). Handbook on Library and Information Science, 2003. New Delhi: Association of Indian Universities.
2. ALA accreditation criteria. Available at *http://www.ala.org/* accreditedprograms/ sites/ala.org.accreditedprograms/ files/content/standards/standards_2008.pdf
3. Baba, Abdul Majid (1999). Accrediting agencies for library and information science education. Paper presented at the 45thAll India Library Association Conference, Dec 1999, Hisar, India.
4. Chanda, s and Patkar, V (2007). ICTS: A catalyst for enriching the learning process and library services in India. The International Information & Library Review Volume 39, Issue 1, March 2007, Pages 1-11
5. Dutta ,Bidyarthi and Das, Anup Kumar (2001). Higher Education in Library and Information Science in India. ILA Bulletin, Vol 37, no.1: 25-30.
6. Ghosh, S B and Kanjilal, U. Developing E-Learning Prototype

for Library Management - A Case Study. Available at: *http://www.unige.ch/biblio/ses/IFLA/sat1-Ghosh.pdf*

7. Jain PK and Kaur, Harvinder, and Babbar, Parveen (2007) LIS Education in India: Challenges for Students and Professionals in the Digital Age. In: Building An Information Society For All: Proceedings of the International Conference on Libraries, Information and Society, ICOLIS 2007, 26-27 June 2007, Armada Hotel, Petaling Jaya, Malaysia. ISBN 9789834349103

8. Karisiddappa, CR, Niels Ole Pors and Terry L. Weech (2004). Literacy concepts in the LIS curriculum. In 70th IFLA General Conference and Council, 22-27 August 2004, Buenos Aires, Argentina. Web page: http://www.ifla.org/IV/ifla70/papers/067e-Weech.pdf

9. Kawatra, P. S., & Singh, N. K. (2006). E-learning in LIS education in India. In C. Khoo, D. Singh & A.S. Chaudhury (Eds.), Proceedings of the Asia-Pacific Conference on Library & Information Education & Practice 2006 (A-LIEP 2006), Singapore, 3-6 April 2006 (pp. 605-611). Singapore: School of Communication & Information, Nanyang Technological University.

10. Kumar, P S G (1998). Doctoral studies in Library and Information Science in India : A critical study. Desidoc Bulletin of Information Technology, Vol.18, no.1: 5-8.

11. Lepik, A. The Nordic-Baltic cooperation in doctoral education: the case of NORSLIS. Available at *http://www.ifla.org.sg/IV/ifla71/papers/052e-Lepik.pdf.*

12. Mahapatra, G. (2006). LIS education in India: Emerging paradigms, challenges and propositions in the digital era. Presented at the Asia-Pacific Conference on Library & Information Education & Practice 2006 (A-LIEP 2006), Singapore, 3-6 April 2006.

13. Mangla, P. B.(1998). Library and Information Science Education: Trends and issues, In: Jain, M K, ed. Fifty years of Library and Information Services in India.New Delhi: Shipra:285-293.

14. Patel, Jashu and Krishan Kumar. (2001).Libraries and Librarianship in India. London: Greenwood Press. Satija, M. P. 1998.

15. Sarkhel, J.K. (2006). Quality assurance and accreditation of LIS education in Indian universities: issues and

perspectives. In Khoo, C., Singh, D., Chaudhry, A.S. (Eds),Proceedings of the Asia-Pacific Conference on Library and Information Education and practice 2006 (A-LIEP 2006), Singapore, 3-6 April 2006, School of Communication & Information, Nanyang Technological University, Singapore, Vol. 2006 pp.427-31.

16. Susmitha Chakraborty and Sarkhel (2009) LIS education in India: an appraisal of the parity between the syllabus and the market demands. IFLA world Library and Information congress. Italy 2009.

17. Tammaro, A.M. (2007). Performance indicators in library and information science (LIS) education: towards cross-border quality assurance in Europe. Available at: www.cbpq.qc.ca/congres/congres2007/Actes/Tammaro.pdf.

18. UGC (2001). UGC Model Curriculum: Library & Information Science 2001. New Delhi, University Grants Commission.

19. Whom do we serve? : Doctoral research in Library and Information Science in India. Desidoc Bulletin of Information Technology Vol.18, no.1: 19-24.

24

RSS : Effective Tool for Information Dissemination in Academic Libraries

Vahida Beegam T
Dr. Jalaja V

ABSTRACT

RSS (Really Simple Syndication or Rich Site Summary) is a method for delivering regularly changing and updated web content. RSS feed have allowed traditional library methods to be replaced by faster and accurate ways of transmitting information. This paper discusses about concept of RSS and effective utilization of RSS in Academic Library.

Keywords : Information and Communication Technology, Web 2.0, RSS, RSS Feed, RSS Aggregator.

1. INTRODUCTION

Information and Communication Technology (ICT) has made a profound contribution to modern life and has become an integral part of mankind. The prolific benefit of this new way of communication is the ability of people to experience the world through the comfort of computers. During the last decades there has been a change in all the three major areas of ICT, like computing, communication and content. Rapid advances in ICT have brought revolutionary changes in the concept, organization, functioning and management, information storage and services of library and information systems throughout the world. With the spread of internet, library users can access the library services from anywhere across the world.

Now-a days, web based technologies provide opportunities to libraries to cater to the information need of users without time and geographical limitations. The new web based technology is known as Web 2.0. Web 2.0 is a tool to share and disseminate the information on a specific subject or a topic from one end to another. This associated with website application of *World Wide Web (WWW) that* facilitates participatory information sharing, interoperability, user-centered design and collaboration on the WWW. The application of Web 2.0 on libraries constitutes significant and substantive change in the use of online and personalized services of libraries. Also these services affect library users' information seeking behaviours, communication styles, and expectations. Examples of web tools are social networking sites, RSS feed, blogs, wikis, mashups etc. Blogs are widely used in libraries and blogs are more powerful with the help of tools like RSS feed.

2. RSS (REALLY SIMPLE SYNDICATION OR RICH SITE SUMMARY)

RSS (Rich Site Summary); originally *RDF* Site Summary; often dubbed Really Simple Syndication, uses a family of standard *web feed* formats to publish frequently updated information (*Wikipedia*). It is a very powerful tool that assists internet users in keeping abreast of changes to websites that they have an interest in. Simply RSS is an XML (Extensible Markup Language) format to share web site content. This method of sharing data in RSS reduces the effort required in continually visiting web sites to check for new content. It is a way to easily distribute a list of headlines, update notices, and sometimes content to a wide number of people. It is used by computer programs that organize those headlines and notices for easy reading.

3. RSS FEED

RSS information available from blogs and other frequently updated websites is usually referred as a feed. A feed lists site content that has changed or is new. Feeds are collated for the user by an aggregator. In computing, aggregator termed as a feed aggregator, feed reader or *RSS* reader is *client software* or a *web application* which aggregates *syndicated web content* such as news headlines, blogs, *podcasts*, and *video blogs* in one location for easy viewing (*Wikipedia*). It helps users to consolidate many websites into one page that can show the new or updated information from many sites and also reduce the time and effort needed to regularly check websites for updates, creating a unique information space. Once subscribed to a feed, an aggregator is able to check for new content at user-determined intervals and retrieve the update.

3.1. Types of RSS Feed Reader

RSS readers are programmes designed for gathering information from different sources and display them in a single interface. Most of the readers are available for free download from the internet. There are four types of RSS feed reader:

- Web based feed reader: It offer great convenience of allowing a web feed on the internet. Eg:-Feed reader, Ampheddesk, Feed Demon
- Desktop feed reader: It allows the advantages of a potentially richer user interface and of being able to provide some content even when the computer is not connected to the Internet. Eg:-Bloglines, Oddpost.

- Plug-ins for web browsers and e-mail clients: It is functionally available inside other applications such as e-mail programmes like Microsoft Outlook and Mozilla Thunderbird.
- Browsers with built-in feed readers. Eg:-Opera 7.50.(Zeki Çelikba°,2004)

3.2. Functions of RSS Feed

Without RSS, users will have to check their site daily for new updates. This may be too time-consuming for many users. With an RSS they can check their site faster using an RSS aggregator. Since RSS data is small and fast-loading, it can easily be used with services like cell phones or PDA's. (*w3schools). When* subscribed to a feed, users no longer have to visit many individual sites in order to obtain up-to date information about their content. User got updated information from these subscribed sites because aggregators collect and organize the content of individual sites.

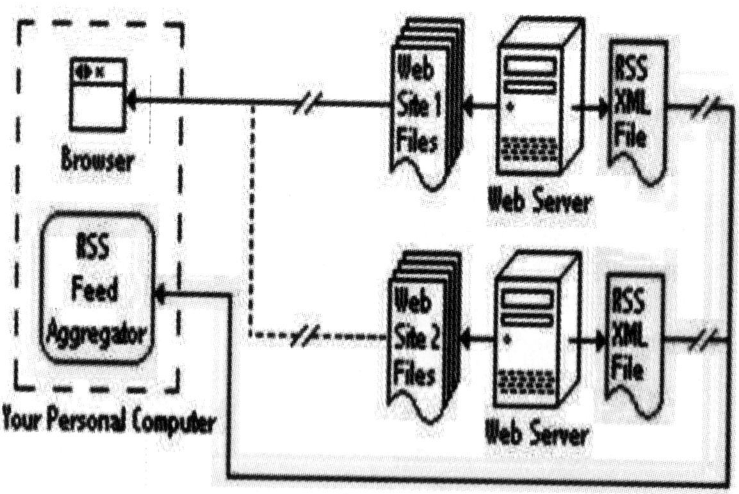

Fig. 1. Functions of RSS Feed (softwaregarden.com/)

This figure shows a web browser being used to read first Web Site one over the Internet and then Web Site two and also shows the RSS feed XML files for both websites being monitored simultaneously by an RSS Feed Aggregator.

5. APPLICATIONS OF RSS IN ACADEMIC LIBRARIES

The primary functions of an academic library are to provide resources and research support for students and faculty of the educational institution. They enable and facilitate the exchange and growth of information, knowledge and culture among their users. Now-a-days library resources are increasingly produced in electronic formats. Advent of Internet changed the communication between librarian and users. Web 2.0 has the potential to promote participatory networking where librarians and users can communicate, collaborate, and generate content (Chau & Goh, 2010). Many academic libraries have been using Web 2.0 applications to promote their services and activities. The capabilities of Web 2.0 enable users to engage the library in two-way communication and knowledge exchanges. Web 2.0 applications include blogs, wikis, social networking sites, social tagging, instant messaging, RSS, file sharing sites, social bookmarking and online virtual games.

RSS is one of the most important applications of Web 2.0 in the dissemination of information in the academic libraries. One of the most interesting advantages of the implementation of RSS feed is the interaction between the libraries and the users. RSS feed on library websites keeps the library users up-to-date with new content on the library. It can provide updates on library collection, new services, new contents in subscription databases and also provides content page information about journals and announcement of events organized by the library, etc. These feeds can be used to deliver web content to targeted user groups. This feed help to get information directly on to users' computer without looking on to other sites.

Examples of academic libraries offering RSS feeds are:

- Stony Brook University
- SUNY at Albay
- SUNY at Fredonia
- Syracuse University

RSS can be applied for some of the services in libraries like current awareness services, table of contents, selective dissemination of information, bibliographic services and bulletin board services. Some RSS utilizations in libraries are discussed below.

5.1. RSS Marketing Ideas

RSS feeds can be used to publish any announcement from the library web blog on activities, exhibitions, promotions and new library resources, especially databases. Web blogs provide more interactive solutions to these kinds of services. Librarians could introduce new resources with a short blog note and users could share their experiences, creating an interchange of questions and answers about the resources. Libraries establish consortia to achieve better value in making large purchases. (Tahereh Karami, 2006)

5.2. RSS Table of Contents for Journals

It is type of current awareness services. Content of new journals issues can be provided through RSS feed. It speeds up the process and reduced library staff labour, improving the efficiency. Google reader is a good example of RSS reader. Google provide flexible and user friendly interface for librarians to forward the content of journal article to the required user by e-mail. There is no separate e-mail account for forwarding these journal contents. Example: "Science Direct Publication accident Analysis and Prevention" through Google reader and option to forward the journal article by e-mail.(Imran Mansuri,2010)

5.3. RSS Book Lists

It is the most practical potential usage of RSS feeds. Now-a-days more and more libraries have begun to provide RSS feeds of new books catalogued as they arrive in the libraries. This feed can be used for announcement of the availability of new books, most wanted books, most reserved books and other resources. (Karami & Oloumi, 2006)

5.4. Social Book Marking

Social book marking services like del.icio.us and digiio.com can create RSS feeds. This feed allows users to store, organize, search and manage favorite web pages, with the option of sharing them with other people.

6. ADVANTAGES AND DISADVANTAGES OF RSS FEED

Following are the advantages of RSS Feed:

- All news at one place
- News when you want it
- Get only the news you want
- Freedom from e-mail overload
- Easy republishing

Following are the disadvantages of RSS Feed:

- Many sites do not offer RSS feeds. Therefore users have to visit these sites regularly.
- Due to time limit some feeds expire.
- Graphics and photos do not appear in RSS feed.
- RSS feed dos not display the actual URL or name of the website; it can get confusing on what website the data has come from.
- RSS feeds create higher traffic and demands on the server. Most of the readers still prefer the whole update over a brief summary of the entry, thus they still access the site.

7. CONCLUSION

The exponential growth of communication technology led to the introduction of web 2.0 tools and its application in library and information field which may revolutionalise the present library activities and services in the long run. RSS feed is one of the important tool of web 2.0, it is creating new opportunities for libraries. It is an effective tool for the dissemination of information in this era, because RSS feed allows users to receive any new content added by a websites and simplify the search of the blogs and websites for the user/reader. The library news and events can be published in library blogs and websites and store in RSS feeds. This will help the user to minimize the time effort on searching the updated events and news of the library.

REFERENCES

1. Chua, Alton Yeow Kuan, & Goh, Dion Hoe-Lian. (2010, July). A study of Web 2.0 applications in library websites. *Library & Information Science Research, 32*(3), 203-211. Retrieved November, 5, 2013 from *http://paarl.wikispaces.com/file/view/FINAL%20Full%20paper_Wawta.pdf/398645794/FINAL%20Full%20paper_Wawta.pdf*
2. Çelikba°, Zeki. (2004). What is RSS and how can it serve libraries?. Retrieved November, 5, 2013 from eprints.rclis.org/5617/1/RSS_and_libraries_EN3.pd.
3. Functions of RSS Feed. (2013). Retrieved November, 13, 2013 from *http://rss.softwaregarden.com/aboutrss.html.*
4. Icons of RSS Feed. (2013). Retrieved November, 13, 2013 from *http://www.culpeperchamber.com/chamber/images/rss-icon-collection.gif&imgrefurl.*
5. Karami, Tahereh & Oloumi, Tahereh. (2006). Libraries and weblogs: The Role of new phenomenon blogs in library services, research and learning. Retrieved November, 5, 2013 from *http://eprints.rclis.org/10824.*
6. Mansuri, Imran. (2010). E-resources in Library and Information Centers. Retrieved November, 5, 2013 from http:// eprints.rclis.org/15319/1/final.pd

7. RSS. (2013). Retrieved November, 5, 2013 from *http://en.wikipedia.org/wiki/RSS.*
8. RSS aggregator. (2013). Retrieved November, 5, 2013 from *http://en.wikipedia.org/wiki/RSS_aggregator.*
9. RSS aggregator. (2013). Retrieved November, 5, 2013 from *http://www.w3schools.com/rss/rss_intro.asp.*

25

Effects of Information Literacy Training Program

B. Asadullah

ABSTRACT

This research article attempts to examine the effectiveness of information literacy training program among the randomly selected students of Arts & Science College, Ambur in Vellore district of Tamil Nadu. 146 students were asked to fill in simple questionnaires two times one before going to the information literacy skill training program and another one after the training program. The collected data were examined statically, which shows that these sort of information literacy skill test are found to be effective in increasing the information skill level of students. The findings of this study are helpful for educational administration of the concerned body for policy formulation regarding creating knowledge assets by giving information literary training program to the students.

Keywords : Information literacy, Computer literacy, Information literacy skill training program

1. INTRODUCTION

Higher Education is a field where every student has to be trained well to cope up the fast developments due to the scientific and technological advancement taking place from time to time.

The growth of digital information demands the more focus on lifelong learning because without knowledge updating, gleaning new information and adopting new technological changes, one cannot remain competent in the field whether it is a single man, or an industry, due to this demand for highly skilled workers have highlighted the need for information-related competencies. Thus, higher education students need to be equipped with strong information literacy skills to succeed in their academic and future professional endeavours.

American Library Association defines an Information literate person as one who is able to recognize when information is needed, and to locate, evaluate and use the needed information effectively. UNESCO includes information literacy skills as part of the wide-ranging information and communication technology literacy skills.

A student who possesses information and communication technology (ICT) literacy skills should be able to recognize information needs and use ICT features and applications to access, retrieve, store, manage, integrate, evaluate, create and communicate information effectively. In addition, he or she should also understand the ethical and legal use of information.

1.1. Information Literacy Education

Information literacy education was initiated historically by academic librarians who used several approaches to develop information literacy among students like user education program, orientation program on library or library tool usage etc. This sort of training provides an ample opportunity to student the skills for information gleaning in their study period and later on same will help him/her in their career. Researchers such as Webber and Johnston advocate the teaching of information literacy as an independent discipline. These courses are often conducted by library professionals.

1.2. Information Skills Assessment

Summative assessments are performed for a variety of reasons such as to judge a learner's ability and readiness to proceed, graduate and for selection purposes. Formative assessments are used to give feedbacks on performance to improve learning. Diagnostic assessments identify students' existing skills and learning difficulties. This information can guide course coordinators and academic advisors in designing an appropriate intervention programme. Laurillard, stress the importance of assessment in an academic curriculum because students learn what assessment assesses.

1.3. Information Skills Test

An important step in information literacy development is to obtain data on students' abilities. These data will indicate areas of improvement and the most appropriate training and services required.

The test consists of 15 multiple-choice questions related to information research process, which consists of five major steps, namely: Defining which information is required; Identifying the main concepts in the research; Developing a search strategy; Performing the search; and Using the search results. Each of these steps requires information literacy skills to make the information search successful.

Based on the Information Literacy Competency Standards for Higher Education published by the Association of College and Research Libraries and the International Federation of Library Associations guidelines on information literacy, the information research skills are grouped into five major themes. The five themes used in the test are:

1. Concept Identification
2. Search Strategy
3. Document Types

4. Search Tools
5. Use of Results

2. METHODOLOGY

The random sample for the study consisted of second and third year Arts & Science students of Mazharul Uloom College. These students were chosen for the belief that they must have already acquired the necessary information skills after undergoing at least three semesters of study. During the first week of study at the college, these students were given initiation program as part of Information Literacy Program; among them some students have also voluntarily attended ICT skills courses during their study programme to enhance their information skills.

Students were informed that the test was on voluntary basis. 180 questionnaires were distributed, of which 145 were returned, after collecting these valid filled in questionnaires these particular students were given information literacy skill program to train them how to glean information from the library and from electronic resources, after completion of these training program same previous questionnaires were again given to these selected students and asked them to fill up in the library itself.

3. RESULTS AND DISCUSSION

All these data collected before and after the information literacy skill program the percentage of students who correctly answered every question in each information literacy theme was analyzed descriptively using IBM SPSS.

3.1. Concept Identification

Figure 1 shows the percentage of students who correctly answered the questions which is related to concept identification in graphical presentation. It is clearly understandable that information literacy skill training to the students yields good result on identifying the correct concept which will help in getting right information in a short span of time period. The information literacy skill training program students increases their ability of retrieving of scholarly information.

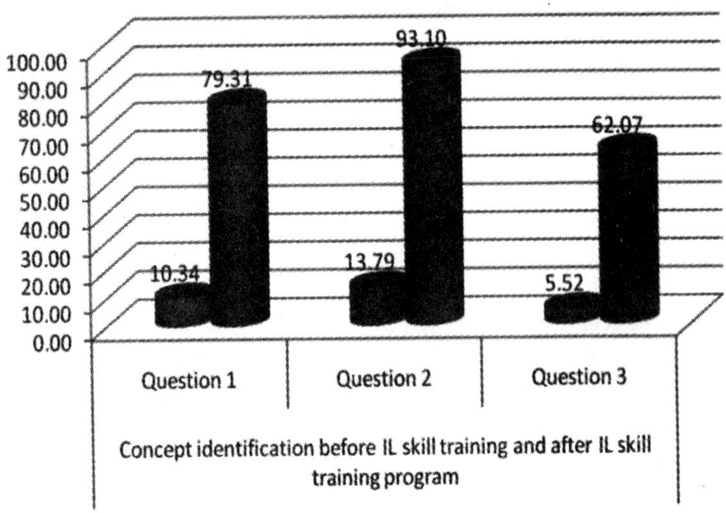

Fig. 1

3.2. Search Strategy

For the question "Where did you obtain your scholarly information using ... Google or E-Journals", before training 16.55% of respondents says Google provides them the required information, when training is given to these group then 100% of respondent recognize that E-Journal only provides them scholarly information.

3.3. Document Types

Only 20.69% of the respondents know when to use Encyclopaedia, Journal, Book, and Internet before training, whereas 91.72% of the respondents know the usefulness of them effectively. About respondents 28.28% do not recognize that a journal is the best document type to obtain the latest information on a subject and their criteria. After the IL skill training program 95.86% of respondents really identifies that E-Journal is the easy way to locate the information.

3.4. Search Tools

About 29.66% of respondents knows when to use a search engine for gleaning information, but 24.14% of respondents are only knows the usage of database. After getting IL skill training 79.31% of respondents are able to effectively use the database for getting the required information.

3.5. Use of Results

A very low respondent (4.83%) know what plagiarism is and how to avoid plagiarism before training, whereas after IL skill training program 86.21% of respondents clearly understand the issue. This lack of knowledge in information usage hinders efficient utilization because the respondents will not be able to gauge the relevance of information and subsequently unable to select the best way to search for information and use the required scholarly information.

4. SCIENTIFIC FINDINGS

By summing up the cumulative percentage of all results obtained through data collection shows that after training the students on information skill training program, students awareness has increased in many fold the skill of gleaning scholarly information from right medium. Same information has been shown in the graphics format in the Figure 2.

To prove above claim scientifically we had applied the statistical tool of paired t' test. So let set the Null Hypothesis (Ho) as "The information skill training has no effect in increasing information skill level of students". By using the statistical tool of t test on the above collected data, we get the output as on Table 1 and Table 2

Fig. 2

Table 1. Paired Samples Statistics

		Mean	N	Std. Deviation	Std. Error Mean
Pair 1	Before IL skill training	18.5300	15	9.48438	2.44886
	After IL skill training	89.3780	15	10.03642	2.59139

The above output in Table-1 shows the mean level of information skill in the individuals before training with supplementary test as 18.53 with a standard deviation of 9.48 and 89.37 with a standard deviation of 10 after training with information skills.

Above output in Table-2 gives the t-value of -25.726 for 14 degree of freedom (df) is highly significant as significant value for two tailed test is 0.000. Therefore we reject the null hypothesis. Hence information skill test has been found effective in increasing the information literacy skill level of students.

Table 2. Paired Samples Test

	Paired Differences					t	df	Sig. (2-tailed)
				95% Confidence Interval of the Difference				
	Mean	Std. Deviation	Std. Error Mean	Lower	Upper			
Pair 1 Before IL skill training - After IL skill training	-70.84800	10.66613	2.75398	-76.75470	-64.94130	-25.726	14	.000

5. CONCLUSION

This study identifies the information literacy skills that of Arts & Science College students need to improve on. These include identifying the most efficient search strategy, evaluating electronic resources, as well as using information ethically. Students' usage of electronic scholarly resources in their course assignments is very minimal. This study has several important implications. Firstly, the poor test results before information skill training, should initiate a probe into the causes so as to identify appropriate actions. It may be a consequence of the lack of awareness among students on the importance of developing information skills. Students should be encouraged to use more scholarly resources in both print and electronic format which will help in their career. Constant assessment and constructive efforts through information skill training should lead to a more integrated curriculum and collaboration between academicians and information literacy specialists like library professionals to produce a well-designed programme and ultimately information literate students.

REFERENCES

1. American Library Association, 1989. Presidential Committee on Information Literacy. Final Report. Chicago: American Library Association.
2. American Library Association, Association of College and Research Libraries. 2004. Information literacy competency standards for higher education. Chicago: ALA.
3. Rajathi, A., Chandran P, SPSS for you, 2010, MJP Publishers, Chennai.
4. Laurillard, D. 2002. Rethinking university teaching: A conversational framework for the effective use of learning technologies, 2nd ed., London: Routledge_Falmer.
5. UNESCO. 2008. Towards information literacy indicator, Paris: UNESCO.

6. Webber, S., and B. Johnston. 2000. Conceptions of information literacy: new perspectives and implications, Journal of Information Science, 26(6):381–397.

7. Wilkinson & Bhandarkar, Methodology & Techniques of Social Research, 1991, Himalaya Publishing House, Mumbai.

26

Effectiveness of E-Governance: A Study of Akshaya Centres

Gilsha K.
Jipsi Chacko

ABSTRACT

Information plays an important role in today's society. The progress of modern society depends a great deal upon the provision of the right kind of information in the right form at the right time. As the information whether it may be abstract or concrete is valuable, it must be to proper use. E-governance, i.e. providing services through electronic technology is an effort by the government to bridge the information gap that exists in the society. Those services are mainly made available to the public through Akshaya centres. The entitled study focuses on the people's knowledge, use and satisfaction levels of E-governance services available to them. The study found out that majority of the people is aware about the services and most of them use this service for availing certificates.

Keywords : Information, E-governance, Akshaya centres

1. INTRODUCTION

The progress of modern society depends a great deal upon the provision of the right kind of information in the right form at the right time. The need for information in every sphere of intellectual activity has increased day by day. The world today saw a dramatic increase in the amount of information that is freely available resulting in the characterization of the situation as an information explosion. Today, Akshaya is acting as an important instrument in rural empowerment and economic development. The project is a catalyst in creating massive economic growth and creation of direct and indirect employment in the State by focusing on the various facts of E-learning, E-transaction, E-governance etc. Thus, the project is having a long-standing impact on the social, economic and political scenario of the State.

1.1. Information

Information is one of the basic vital resources that are need and utilized for the nations' well being. The world has now moved from the industrial revolution into information revolution which depends a great deal upon the provision of the right kind of information in the right form at the right time. Information is recorded or gained by the man through experience, observations and experiments. It is therefore necessary that the information generated at any point be procured, organized and disseminated expeditiously to its users for its optimum use.

1.2. Need for information

Information needs of a user vary according to the category he belongs to and assignment on which he is working. It is well known that users make use of different communication media in accessing their information. The information system has the task of organizing the mass of documentary information/ knowledge available for everyone to use- wherever it may be recorded and located and/or whenever it is needed.

1.3. User studies

User studies are concerned with studying

information processing activities of the users. A study which is focused on users to understand directly or indirectly their information needs, use behaviour and use pattern is usually called user study. For the assessment of quality and quantity of the services by various systems and their utility; user studies have become the main ingredients of the system.[2]

1.4. E-governance

The word "electronic" in the term E-governance implies technology driven governance. E-governance is the application of Information and Communication Technology (ICT) for delivering government services, exchange of information communication transactions, integration of various stand-alone systems and services between Government-to-Citizens (G2C), Government-to-Business (G2B) and Government-to-Government (G2G) as well as back office processes and interactions within the entire Government frame work. Through the E-governance, the Government services will be made available to the citizens in a convenient, efficient and transparent manner. Generally, four basic models are available-Government to Customer (Citizen), Government to Employees, Government to Government and Government to Business. E-governance can transform citizen service, provide access to information to empower citizens, enable their participation in government and enhance citizen economic and social opportunities, so that they can make better lives, for themselves and for the next generation.[3]

1.5. Akshaya centre

Akshaya started with the noble intention of making at least one member in each of the 64 lakh families E-literate. The pilot project started in Malappuram, and was inaugurated by His Excellency Dr. A.P.J. Abdul Kalam, former President of India on 18th November 2002. Cent percent E-literacy was achieved in eight districts in Phase

1 and the vision and scope of the project is beyond comparison.

Akshaya, an innovative project implemented in the State of Kerala aimed at bridging the digital divide, addresses the issues of ICT access, basic skill sets and availability of relevant content. Quality ICT dissemination and service delivery facilities ('Akshaya Centres') are set up within a maximum of 2 KM for any household and networked leveraging entrepreneurship. Though originated as an initiative to address the backwardness of Malappuram district, Akshaya was conceived as a landmark ICT project by the Kerala State Information Technology Mission to bring the benefits of this technology to the entire population of the State. The modus for this was establishment of grass roots level ICT centres at the Panchayath/Municipal ward level. Today, Akshaya is acting as an instrument in rural empowerment and economic development. The project is a catalyst in creating massive economic growth and creation of direct and indirect employment in the State by focusing on the various facts of E-learning, E-transaction, E- governance etc. Thus, the project is having a long-standing impact on the social, economic and political scenario of the State.[4]

1.5.1. Key missions of Akshaya centres

The key mission of Akshaya centres includes mainly five services. They are E-literacy, Educational programs, Entegramam, Citizen Services, SPARK (Service and Payroll Administrative Repository of Kerala).

1.5.2. Importance of Akshaya centres

Akshaya was conceived as a landmark ICT project by the Kerala State Information Technology Mission (KSITM) to bridge the digital divide and to bring the benefits of ICT to the entire population of the State. Now Akshaya is emerged as one of the finest common service centre networks in the nation. The Akshaya E-centres encourage social inclusion of hitherto hereby marginalized communities and under-privileged sections of the rural society. The project opens up immense opportunities for women participation at various levels as entrepreneurs, master trainers, social animators and finally as trainees etc.

It has been common for villagers to travel long distances to district/taluk headquarters in order to obtain copies of public records, submit applications, meet officials, or to seek information regarding their day-to-day needs or to enquire prevailing prices in commodity markets etc. These barriers can be overcome by the Akshaya centres placed at various localities.

1.6. Dharmadam Gramapanchayath

Dharmadam is a village in Kannur district of Kerala, India. Dharmadam is a census town in Thalassery taluk. Dharmadam village Panchayath was established in 1950. The Panchayath is located at a distance of four kilometers on the North-west of Thalassery Town, just adjacent to the Thalassery taluk. It has four desams (villages) namely, Melur, Andalur, Palayad and Dharmadam.

As of 2001 India census Dharmadam had a population of 29,169. Males constitute 47 per cent of the population and females 53 per cent. Dharmadam has an average literacy rate of 87 per cent, higher than the national average of 59.5 per cent: male literacy is 88 per cent and, female literacy is 86 per cent.

There is an Industrial Estate in the village with about 39 small scale industries, apart from a number of other small industrial units such as the ice factory, printing press, matchbox company, die making, milk products and production, textile industry etc., located in different parts of village. The village has five public libraries and nine reading rooms and is known for having the educational institutions starting from the level of Lower Kindergarten (LKG) to the level of University PG and research departments.

1.7. Akshaya centres in Dharmadam Gramapanchayath

There are three Akshaya centres in Dharmadam Gramapanchayath. They are situated at Chirakuni, Palayad and Meethalapeedika. The Akshaya centre in Chirakuni started in the year 2005. The number of staffs is three and the working time is from 9 am to 6 pm. Chirakuni Akshaya centre has a sub-centre started in 2010 near Kannur University, Thalassery campus.

1.8. Services of Akshaya centres in Dharmadam Gramapanchayath

In Dharmadam Gramapanchayath, Akshaya centres provide mainly ten services. They are discussed as follows:

1.8.1. E-District

E-District project conceived under the National E-governance plan, aims at electronic delivery of public services enabling citizens to avail the services through Akshaya. Under E-district programme about 20 revenue certificates are given to the public through Akshaya centres. They are

- Residential certificate
- Nativity certificate
- Solvency certificate
- Valuation certificate
- Domicile certificate
- Income certificate
- Community certificate
- Possession and non-attachment certificate
- Intercaste marriage certificate
- Life certificate
- One and the same certificate
- Conventional certificate
- Dependency certificate

- Non-marriage certificate
- Relation certificate
- Possession certificate
- Widow widower certificate
- Family membership certificate
- Destitute certificate
- Caste certificate

1.8.2. Online application of Ration Card

Department of Civil Supply has launched the facility to submit online application for ration card through Akshaya. The project was introduced in Trivandrum North. This is enacted all over Kerala from August 2010 onwards.

1.8.3. CHIAK Registration (Comprehensive Health Insurance Agency of Kerala)

Government introduced their social health insurance programme with Akshaya and almost cent per cent of BPL families have been now brought under the CHIAK programme in the state.

1.8.4. NRK (Non-Resident Keralites) Welfare Fund

Akshaya has been designated as the agency for collection of yearly subscription amount from the members of Kerala Non-Resident Keralites Welfare Fund Board (KNRKWFB).

1.8.5. E-payment

Akshaya had rolled out many E-services through E-centres. E-payment means collecting payment from public.

- E-payment KSEB
- E-payment BSNL landline
- E-payment BSNL mobile
- E-payment water

1.8.6. E-grants

SC/ST Welfare department has launched online filing of application form to provide stipend for post metric SC/ST students of Kerala. Registration will be done through Akshaya E-centres.

1.8.7. UIDAI (Adhaar)

It is a 12 digit individual identification number issued by the Unique Identification Authority of India (UIDAI) on behalf of the Government of India. This number will serve as a proof for identifying address anywhere in India, any individual irrespective of age and gender who is a resident in India. It provides access to services like banking, mobile phone connections etc.

1.8.8. AABY registration (Aam Admi Bima Yojana)

The Life Insurance Corporation of India in association with the comprehensive health insurance agency of Kerala has launched AABBY in the state. It provides insurance to the head of the family or an earning member of rural landless households between the age of 18 to 59 against natural and accidental death and partial permanent disability. Eligible citizen will be registered through Akshaya centres.

1.8.9. Educational programmes

Akshaya E-centres are emerging as platform for ITC related education to people for capacity building. E-learning programmes like Intel learning, medical transcription, E-vidya, other computer courses etc.

1.8.10. E-manal

NIC has developed a special online system for this project and Akshaya Centres have been issued ID and password for login. Details of the applicant are entered in this online system and a token which is generated from the site is issued to the applicant. A date and counter to collect manal pass is mentioned in this token and applicant approaches the counter with this token in an allotted day for collecting manal pass.

1.9. Extension activities

In Dharmadam Gramapanchayath, Akshaya centres provides a number of extension activities like conducting different computer courses, carrying out Panchayath project works, photocopy facilities, cafe system, Sabarimala online booking, DTP works, colour printing, CD writing etc.

1.10. Objectives of the study

The following are the objectives the study:

1. To identify the various services under E-governance providing through Akshaya centres in Dharmadam Gramapanchayath.
2. To understand the awareness of people about the services provided by Akshaya centres in Dharmadam Gramapanchayath.
3. To know the most used services of Akshaya centres by the people of Dharmadam Gramapanchayath.
4. To find out the barriers to access the services of Akshaya centres.

1.11. Need and significance of the study

Information services in rural communities must be recognized and empowered. The diverse nature of rural communities indicates that their information needs are many and multidimensional. Akshaya centre play major role in the society for achieving target objectives. Akshaya centre acts as the second hand to the Government service. In this study investigator assess the satisfaction level of users towards the Akshaya services.

1.12. Methodology

Methodology is a way to systematically solve the research problem. It is the procedures that the researcher has to follow in collecting, organizing, analysing and presenting the data. The present study is an attempt to understand the services of Akshaya centres and the satisfaction level of the people in Dharmadam Gramapanchayath. The investigator visited the households in Dharmadam Gramapanjayath and chooses 90 households from 18 wards. The investigator asked questions personally in each household.

2. DATA ANALYSIS AND INTERPRETATIONS

The purpose of the data analysis and interpretation phase is to transform the data collected through structured questionnaire into credible evidence about the development of the intervention and its performance. The objective of the study can be attained only by the analysis of the collected data using appropriate statistical techniques. The analysis done is given below under the following headings.

2.1. Awareness

The details of the awareness of the people in Dharmadam Gramapanchayath about E-governance is given in the Table 2.1.

Table 2.1. Awareness about E-governance

Responses	Number	Per cent
Yes	88	98
No	2	2
Total	90	100

The Table 2.1 shows that 88 per cent of people in Dharmadam Gramapanchayath are aware of the E-governance services through Akshaya centres. Whereas, 2 per cent are not aware of those services. Majority of the people are aware of the E-governance provided through Akshaya centres.

2.2. Effectiveness

The services provided by a system must be effective enough to reach the user group. The details regarding the effectiveness of the E-governance through Akshaya centres among the users is given in the Table 2.2.

From the total population, about 95 per cent of the people are of the view that the services provided are effective, whereas 5 per cent of the people found the service ineffective.

Table 2.2. Effectiveness of the services

Effectiveness	Number	Per cent
Effective	85	95
Ineffective	5	5
Total	90	100

Majority of the people found the E-governance service through Akshaya centres effective.

2.3. Awareness of services

The users must be aware about the services provided so as to make use of it efficiently. The details of the awareness of people about the services provided by Akshaya centres in Dharmadam Gramapanchayath is given in Table 2.3.

From the Table 2.3, it's clear that all of the people are aware of Aadhaar registration and 94 per cent of the people are aware of health insurance service. Various types of bills can be paid at the centres and 70 per cent of the population are aware of that service. About 80 per cent are aware of E-manal service whereas, 73 per cent are aware of certificate services offered by them. Nearly, 78 per cent is not aware of the NRI services offered. Out of the total population, 43 per cent of people are aware of E-grants services and about 20 per cent of people are aware of the AABY services.

Table 2.3. Awareness of Akshaya centre services

Services	Response					
	Aware		Not aware		Total	
	Number	%	Number	%	Number	%
Bill Payment	63	70	27	30	90	100
E-manal	72	80	18	20	90	100
New Ration Card Application	38	42	52	58	90	100
Certificates	66	73	24	27	90	100
Adhaar Registration	90	100	00	00	90	100
Health Insurance	85	94	5	6	90	100
NRI	20	22	70	78	90	100
E-Grants	39	43	61	57	90	100
AABY Registration	18	20	72	80	90	100

It is found that all of peoplc in Dharmadam Panchayath are well aware of Aadhar service. Howevet, few people are not aware about health insurance, E–manal, registration service and certificates services from Akshaya centres. And least number of people are aware of NRI and AABY registration services.

2.4. Sources of information

The details of the sources of information about Akshaya centre services in Dharmadam Gramapanchayath are given in the Table 2.4.

Table 2.4. Sources of information about Akshaya centre

Sources	Responses	
	Number	Per cent
Panchayath	31	34
Akshaya centre	28	31
Medias	11	3
Neighbours	20	22
Total	90	100

The above table shows that out of the total population around 34 per cent people in Dharmadam Panchayath are getting information about Akshaya centre services from Panchayath, 31 per cent from the Akshaya centre, 3 per cent getting information from media and 22 per cent through neighbours.

It is revealed that majority of people are getting information about Akshaya centre from Panchayath. And only a few people use media as a source for getting information about the services.

2.5. Utilization of extension services

The details of the utilization of extension services of Akshaya centres in Dharmadam Gramapanchayath are given in the Table 2.5. The table shows that 50 per cent of people are utilizing the computer courses provided under extension services by Akshaya centre. When compared to utilization of computer courses only few people utilizes online bookings, CD writing and Photostat services.

Table 2.5. Utilization of extension services of Akshaya centres

Services	Utilization of extension services provided by Akshaya centre					
	Utilized		Not utilized		Total	
	Number	%	Number	%	Number	%
Computer courses	45	50	45	50	90	100
Online booking	25	28	65	72	90	100
CD writing	5	6	85	94	90	100
Photostat	15	17	75	83	90	100

It is found that half of the population are utilizing the computer course services provided by Akshaya centre. Rest of the people are utilizing online booking, CD writing and photostat service.

2.6. Utilization of services

The detail of the use of various kinds of Akshaya centre services in Dharmadam Gramapanchayath is given in the Table 2.6.

From the table, it's clear that all the respondents in Dharmadam Gramapanchayath utilise Aadhaar registration service available at the Akshaya centre. Around 54 per cent of people are utilising the services for the payment of various bills and 59 per cent are utilising E-manal service.

Out of the whole population, 34 per cent of people are utilising the service for registration of new ration card. Certificate services are utilized by 80 per cent of peoples, whereas, 94 per cent of the people are utilising health insurance registration service. Only 16 per cent are utilising NRI services and E-grants services are used by 37 per cent. About 83 per cent of people are not utilising AABY registration service.

Table 2.6. Utilization of E-governance services of Akshaya centres

Services	Utilized		Not Utilized		Total	
	Number	%	Number	%	Number	%
Bill payment	49	54	41	46	90	100
E-manal	53	59	37	41	90	100
New Ration Card Application	31	34	59	66	90	100
Certificates	72	80	18	20	90	100
Adhaar Registration	90	100	00	00	90	100
Health Insurance	85	94	5	6	90	100
NRI	14	16	76	84	90	100
E-grants	33	37	57	63	90	100
AABY Registration	15	17	75	83	90	100

It is found that almost all people in Dharmadam Gramapanchayath are utilizing Adhaar service. But, only a few people use NRI and AABY registration services offered by Akshaya centres.

2.7. Computer courses undergone through Akshaya centres

The details of the computer courses undergone through Akshaya centres in Dharmadam Gramapanchayath is given in the Table 2.7.

The Table 2.7 indicates that 26 per cent of the people utilized Akshaya centre services for studying MS Office. Nearly 20 per cent have studied Basics, 14 per cent have studied DTP and 12 per cent have studied Photoshop from Akshaya centres.

Table 2.7. Computer courses undergone through Akshaya centres

Courses	Studied		Not studied		Total	
	Number	%	Number	%	Number	%
Basics	18	20	72	80	90	100
DTP	13	14	77	86	90	100
MS Office	23	26	67	74	90	100
Photoshop	11	12	79	88	90	100

It can be concluded that majority of the people have utilized the E-governance service for studying MS Office and some of them studied computer courses like basics, DTP and Photoshop.

2.8. Payment of bills through Akshaya centres

The details of the payment of bills through Akshaya canters in Dharmadam Gramapanchayath is given in the Table 2.8. The table shows that 52 per cent of people make use of Akshaya centres for payment of telephone bills. Around 38 per cent of people pays current bill through Akshaya centres, whereas, water bills are not paid through Akshaya centre of Dharmadam Panchayath.

Table 2.8. Payment of bills through Akshaya centres

Bill payment facility	Using Number	Using %	Not using Number	Not using %	Total Number	Total %
Current bill	35	38	55	62	90	100
Telephone bill	47	52	43	48	90	100
Water bill	–	–	–	–	–	–

It is revealed that nearly half of the people in Dharmadam Panchayath are using Akshaya centre facility for remitting telephone bills.

2.9. Category of certificates availing

The details of the payment of bills through Akshaya centre in Dharmadam Gramapanchayath is given in the Table 2.9.

Table 2.9. Category of certificates availing through Akshaya centre

Category	Responses Number	Responses Per cent
Education	44	49
Job	28	31
Pension	18	20
Total	90	100

Table 2.9 shows that 49 per cent of people are availing certificates from Akshaya centre for educational purpose. Only 31 per cent of people are availing certificates for their job and 20 per cent for pension purpose.

It is found that majority of the people avails certificates from Akshaya centres for their education purpose.

2.10. Purpose of visit

The details of the purpose of visit of the Akshaya centres in Dharmadam Gramapanchayath is given in the Table 2.10.

The table shows the purpose of peoples to visit Akshaya centres. About 48 per cent of people visits Akshaya centre for registration purpose. Whereas, 22 per cent visit Akshaya centre for education purpose and 15 per cent visits Akshaya centre for trade purpose. Only 10 per cent visit Akshaya centre for construction works service.

Table 2.10. Purpose for visiting Akshaya centre

Purpose	Responses	
	Number	Per cent
Education	22	24
Trade	15	17
Registration	43	48
Construction works	10	11
Total	90	100

Majority of the people visits Akshaya centre for registration purposes.

2.11. User's opinion about the Akshaya centre

The details of the user's opinion about Akshaya centres in Dharmadam Gramapanchayath is given in the Table 2.11.

Table 2.11. User's opinion about the Akshaya centre

Opinion	Responses	
	Number	Per cent
Very good	24	27
Good	55	61
Average	11	12
Total	90	100

Table 2.11 shows that 61 per cent of the people's opinion about Akshaya centre are very good, 21 per cent's opinioned as only good. According to 12 per cent of the people, performance of Akshaya centres in providing E-governance services is only average.

Majority of the population have good opinion about Akshaya centres.

2.12. User satisfaction with the services

The details of the user's satisfaction with the services provided by Akshaya centres in Dharmadam Gramapanchayath is given in the Table 2.12.

Table 2.12. User's satisfaction with the services

User's satisfaction	Responses	
	Number	Per cent
Fully satisfied	30	34
Satisfied	58	64
Dissatisfied	2	2
Total	90	100

The above table shows that 34 per cent of the users are fully satisfied with the services provided by the Akshaya centre. When 64 per cent of the people are satisfied with the services, only 2 per cent of the people are dissatisfied with those services of Akshaya centre.

It is found that majority of the people are satisfied with the services provided by the Akshaya centre.

2.13. Barriers faced by the people in using Akshaya centre services

The details of the barriers faced by the people in using Akshaya centre services is given in the Table 2.13.

Table 2.13. Barriers faced by the people in using Akshaya centre services

Barriers	Responses	
	Number	Per cent
Distance	48	54
Limited number of Akshaya centres	30	33
Insufficiency of staff	12	13
Total	90	100

The above table shows the responses of peoples towards the barriers they face in accessing services from Akshaya centre. About 54 per cent of people are facing distance as the main barrier for accessing services. Nearly, 33 per cent of people feel that the number of Akshaya centres is limited in Dharmadam Panchayath. Only 13 per cent of the people are facing the problem of insufficiency of staff s in Akshaya centres.

Analysis shows that majority of the people are facing distance as the main barrier for accessing the services offered by Akshaya centres. A few of them have the problem of limited number of Akshaya centres in their locality and insufficiency of staffs.

2.14. Suggestions for improving the services

The details of the suggestions for improving the services in Akshaya centres is given in the Table 2.14.

Table 2.14. Suggestions for improving the services

Suggestions	Responses	
	Number	Per cent
Appoinment of qualified staff	21	23
Increase the number of Akshaya centres	37	41
Increase the number of staffs	32	36
Total	90	100

The above table shows that 41 per cent of people suggested about increasing the number of Akshaya centres in Dharmadam Panchayath. Nearly, 23 per cent suggested for appointing qualified staff in the centres and about 36 per cent of the people suggested increase in the number of staffs.

Majority of the people suggested to increase the number of Akshaya centres in Dharmadam Panchayath.

3. MAJOR FINDINGS

The major findings of the study are given below;

1. Majority of the people are aware of the E-governance provided through Akshaya centre.
2. Most of the people have utilized E-governance through Akshaya centres.
3. All of the respondents are aware of Aadhar registration service.
4. A large majority of the people are aware about health insurance service through Akshaya centre.
5. Most of people aware about E-manal service.
6. Most of them are aware of getting certificates from Akshaya centres.
7. Majority of people are getting sources of information from Panchayath.
8. All of the people in Dharmadam Gramapanchayath have utilised Adhaar service.
9. A large majority of the people are utilising E-manal service.
10. Most of the people utilized the health insurance registration service.
11. Most of the people are utilized certificates services from Akshaya centres.
12. Majority of the people utilized the extension service for studying MS Office.
13. Most of the people pay telephone bill through Akshaya centre.
14. Majority of the people avail certificates from Akshaya centre for their education purpose.
15. Majority of the people visit Akshaya centre for the purpose of registration services.
16. Majority of the people opinion about Akshaya centres are good.
17. Majority of the people are satisfied with the services provided by the Akshaya centre.

18. Analysis shows that majority of the people are facing distance as the barrier for availing services from Akshaya centre.
19. Majority of the people suggested the increase in the number of Akshaya centres for availing better services.

4. SUGGESTIONS FOR IMPROVING THE FACILITIES AND SERVICES OF THE AKSHAYA CENTRES

With the help of analysis concluded, the investigator rises to put forward the following suggestions for improving the services and facilities provided by the Akshaya centres. The suggestions are following;

1. Appoint qualified staffs.
2. Increases the number of Akshaya centres in the area.
3. To increase the number of staffs.

5. CONCLUSION

The investigators have tried to study the services provided by Akshaya centre for the people of Dharmadam Panchayath. Services offered include Government services like Adhaar, E-manal, health insurance and other services. From the study its found that there are many faults regarding the running of Akshaya centre. For rectifying all those problems suggestions from people and faculty members are to be considered. Thus the services can be improved and it can be made available to the users effectively.

REFERENCES

1. Abraham J. and Ramesh Babu (2000). Usage of Information and Communication Technology (ICT), Information seeking and Use pattern of the Industrial Information System with Reference to Small Scale Industries. IN: Future Concepts of Library and Information Services. New Delhi, Ess Ess Publications, 218-222.

2. Prasad, H N (2012). IN: Information Needs and Users, Delhi, BR Publishing Corporation, 47-55.

3. http://en.wikipedia.org/wiki/E-Governance (Accessed on 10/11/2013)

4. *http://www.akshaya.kerala.gov.in* (Accessed on 22/11/2013)

5. *http://www.akshaya.kerala.gov.in/index.php/achievements* (Accessed on 06/11/2013)

6. *http://www.akshaya.kerala.gov.in/index.php/values-and-purpose* (Accessed on 09/11/2013)

7. *http://www.dharmadam.gov.in* (Accessed on 16/11/2013)

27

Health Information System and Services in Dharmadam Grama Panchayat – A Situational Study

Sreelatha K.
Sangeetha K. K.

ABSTRACT

The purpose of this paper is to assess the health information system and services in Dharmadom Grama Panhayath. The objectives of the study were to know the extent of awareness about the services provided, sources through which they are getting services, their problems and satisfaction level regarding the health information among the people of Dharmadom. Out of the 18 wards of the Panchayath , 5 households were taken as sample from each ward and the data were collected from these 90 households. For that purpose, survey method has been adopted by the investigator which comprises of administering questionnaires and interviewing the members of the households. Questionnaires comprising of 18 questions has been distributed among the households for collection of data. For data analysis percentage technique has been adopted. The major findings of the study were, majority of the respondents are aware of the health information and services provided by the health institutions, the respondents are satisfied with the services and they are not utilising the information and services to the maximum.

Keywords : Health information, Information services, Health information system.

1. INTRODUCTION

Information is an important resource and is essential for the progress of an individual and that of a nation. Access to right kind of information or possession of correct and relevant information resolves various problems faced by individuals. Information plays significant role in removing the hurdles for development. The importance of information increases as publications increase at the right time deprives the poor people their right to development.

1.1. Information System (IS)

An information system (IS) can be viewed as a system that accepts data resources as input and processes them into information products as output. It may be defined as an organized flow of information to users. IS, in the words of O'Brien, is a set of people, procedures and resources that collects transfers and disseminates information in an organization. Encyclopaedia of Computer Science defines IS as a collection of people, procedures and equipment designed, built, operated and maintained to collect, record, process, store, retrieve and display information.

1.2. Role of Information System

The present society is generally termed as information society. A major challenge for the information society is to manage its information resources to benefit all members of the society. This means, for example, using information systems to find more efficient ways of using the world's limited supplies of material, energy and other resources. For these resources, information systems play in a vital role in our society, dependent as it is on the effective use and management of information resources.

1.3. Health Information

The term health information has been defined in different ways. In many countries, the term is interpreted to mean health statistical, epidemiological and other health oriented data used in the planning and management of health services by the decision makers and administrators. It has also been interpreted to mean health science literature covering health information at various levels. Some authorities safely consider health information as a health literature. Health information is information about people's health and what they, the government and others are doing about it. It describes the incidence, prevalence and causes of major diseases as well as the availability and effective of curative activities.

In primary health care, it particularly concerns preventive health activities and the community to improve environmental conditions. According to WHO, health information is information that contributes to knowledge and understanding that, in turn, provides part of the basis for making decisions in developing and managing services to improve health and health care .It also recognizes the three components of health information as (a) management and operational information; (b) health statistics and (c) health literature.

1.3.1. Health Information System

Health Information Systems (HIS) is interpreted in most countries as consisting of health statistical, epidemiological and other health-related information useful for health planning and management. It is generally recognized as necessary, fundamental and an integral element for the development of health services. According to WHO, a national health information system is to constitute to assemble, analyze, interpret and transmit to the right users....This definition comprises any kind of information that is requested for, or generated by a country's health care services. WHO's Conference on Health Information System, held in Copenhagen in 1973 defined HIS as: A mechanism for the collection, processing, analysis, and transmission of information required for organizing and operating health services and also for research and training. In a fully co-ordinate HIS all the relevant data are collected, complied, stored, retrieved, and analyzed and published. A HIS should be effective in organizing storage, documentation services and communication of information (both in verbal and non- verbal i.e., print form) to the users and at the same time should be adaptable enough to meet any other health information needed by the users of varied groups at present and in the future.

1.3.2. Importance of Health Information System

Societal or national development depends, to a large extent, on the productive contribution of every person in his/her assigned or chosen field of activity. But the productivity of an individual depends very much on the state of his/her health as well as that of every other individual in the community. If the state of the public health is not sound, the social, economic and political system of the society also will be suffered. So HFA (Health for All) is a must.

To quote the Prime Minister of India whatever development we want to do in the country depends upon the capacity of the people to do their work efficiently and to on increasing productive capacity in any field of work that can take up. And if this is to be done, health becomes a very primary consideration. The provision of HFA is a challenge to the planners, policy makers, professionals, paraprofessionals, as well as individuals and families in every walk of me. Mahler, Director General of WHO said If health does not start with the individual, the home, the family, the working place and the school, we shall never get to the goal of HFA. If the challenge of HFA is to be dealt with, the public also should be fully and repeatedly informed about the healthy lifestyle. However, importance of health information and its dissemination and transmission not only to the people but also to the members of the health profession, not only to the people but also to members of health profession, has administrators, professionals, Para-professionals so that they in their turn can educate the people. According to Dr.Niroshi Nakajima, Director General of WHO: reliable health information is demanded not only by health professionals, politicians and business people who need it to meet the various responsibilities of their job, but by individuals and families in every walk of life.

1.4. Dharmadam Panchayath

Dharmadam is a village in Kannur district of Kerala, India. Dharmadam Village Panchayath was established in 1950. The Panchayath is located at a distance of four kilometers on the North-west of Thalassery Town, just adjacent to the Thalassery. The National Highway No.47 passes through this Panchayath. It is an Island, encircled on three sides, by the Anjarakandy River, flowing from the North, and taking diversions towards the East and the West and descending into the Arabian Sea that lies on the South and South West. It has four desams (villages) namely, Melur, Andalur, Palayad and Dharmadam.

As of 2001 India census Dharmadam had a population of 29,169. Males constitute 47% of the population and females 53%. Dharmadam has an average literacy rate of 87%, higher than the national average of 59.5%: male literacy is 88% and, female literacy is 86%. In Dharmadam, 9% of the population is under 6 years of age. There is an Industrial Estate in the village with about 39 Small scale Industries, apart from a number of other small industrial units such as the ice factory, printing press, Matchbox Company, die making, milk products and production, textile industry etc. ,located in different parts of village. The village has five public libraries and nine reading rooms and is known for having the educational institutions starting from the level of Lower Kindergarten (LKG) to the level of University PG and research departments.

1.5. Health Institutions in Dharmadom Panchayath

Health institutions in Dharmadom Panchayath comprises of Primary Health Centre ,Dharmadom Family Welfare Centre, Andaloor and Homeo dispensary, Dharmadom.

1.5.1. Primary Health Centre (PHC), Dharmadom

PHCs are the most basic units of health information system in India. These are state-owned rural health care centres. The PHC, Dharmadom is the main source of health information and services is the PHC. The PHC, Dharmadom has four Family Welfare Centres working under it. Out of these only Family Welfare Centre, Andaloor have its own building, the other three are virtual. They work as per the instructions of PHC.

The main services of Primary Health Centre, Dharmadom are:

Health care services

1. Comprehensive Health care.
2. Specialty clinics.
3. Rapid Action Epidemic Control Cell- Homoeopathy (RAECH).
4. National Campaign for healthy mother and happy child.

Comprehensive health Care

Providing facilities for preventive, curative, palliative treatment for all the diseased conditions.

Speciality Clinics

- Allergic respiratory ailments,
- Diabetes,

- Rheumatic,
- Pediatrics,
- Thyroid,
- Cancer,
- Rectal diseases,
- Geriatric etc.
- Rapid Action Epidemic Control Cell- Homoeopathy(RAECH)

School Health Programme

Through the programme JYOTHIRGAMAYA, PHC is able to identify and rectify the intellectual and mental aberrations of the students in the Govt. schools.

1.6.2. Family Welfare Centre, Andaloor

Objectives : Implementing Family planning programmes , providing awareness about diseases and conducting immunization programmes.

Activities : This centre is allotted 4 1D 2 wards of Dharmadam Panchayat comprising of 1730 houses. Two health workers are there in the centre. Monthly once they have to visit these houses. So each day they visit 44 houses (22 x 2). Fourth Saturday of every month there is an immunization program.

1.6.3. Homeo Dispensary, Dharmadom

The main objective of the dispensary is public welfare. The dispensary is housed in its own building and the staff comprises of a doctor, pharmacist and a casual sweeper. The average number of patients visiting the dispensary is from 50 to 70 in number. The outpatient registration charge is Rs.2/- per patient. Medicines for the dispensary is supplied by the Department of Homeopathy.

1.7. Objectives of the study

- To know about the extent of awareness of the people of Dharmadam Grama Panchayat about the health information and services.

- To identify the sources of health information used by the villages.
- To study the services provided by the health institution in Dharmadam Grama Panchayat.
- To identify the most preferred system of medicine used by the people.
- To assess the satisfaction of the people in getting the health information and services.
- To understand the problems faced by the people in getting health information and services.

1.8. Methodology

Methodology is the means to explain the relationship between the theories or statement and the methods of reaching conclusion about the nature of the study. In other words it is the summary of procedure or techniques adopted in an investigation or research.

To study the health information system and services, the initial step was a search in to the primary sources and documents of health centre (ayurveda, allopathy, homeopathy) its origin objective and administrative mechanism. This has been gathered from the original documents, namely it's by- laws, manuals and other documents published from time to time. This was followed by a review of the various studies conducted on health sector. There are 1 primary health centre and its 4 sub – centres and one homeopathy dispensary in Dharmadam Panchayath. Investigator visited these health institutions to know about its activities. This helped to revise the hypotheses and objectives and methodology. The investigator used questionnaires as the tool for the collection of the data. The health institution services were identified and questions were asked based on those services.

2. DATA ANALYSIS AND INTERPRETATION

Analysis of data means studying the collected data. It involves breaking down the complex factors into simple parts and putting these parts together to make the interpretation easier. Data analysis and interpretation form the basis of the research report.

The purpose of the analysis is to build up a sort of intellectual model where the relationship involved are carefully brought out, so that some meaningful inferences can conclusively drawn. The data collected by means of questionnaires and personal interviews are tabulated and presented as under:

2.1. Awareness of Health service

The investigator attempted to study the awareness of people in Dharmadam Grama Panchayath regarding the health services, health information, immunization program, personal hygiene, environmental hygiene, pre-monsoon diseases, life style diseases, and pain and palliative care. The role health information in day to day life is gaining importance. The recent developments in the field of health sector, like new schemes, programmes etc., should reach the public to attain the desired result. Here comes the importance of this study. The details of awareness of people in Dharmadam Grama Panchayath about the health services ae shown in Table 2.1.

Table 2.1. Awareness of people in Dharmadam Grama Panchayath about the health services.

Response	Awareness of health services	
	Number	Per cent
Aware	85	94
Not aware	5	6
Total	90	100

It is found that 94 per cent of the populations are aware of the health services and 6 per cent are not aware of the health services. Majority of the people of the Panchayat are aware of the health services.

2.2. Awareness of Health information

The data on awareness of people in Dharmadam Grama Panchayath about the health information ae shown in Table 2.2.

Table 2.2. Awareness of people in Dharmadam Grama Panchayath about the health information.

Responses	Whether aware about health information?	
	Number	Per cent
Yes	80	89
No	10	11
Total	90	100

It is found that 89 per cent of the population are aware of the health information and 11 per cent are not aware of the health information. As such majority of the people are aware of the health information.

2.3. Awareness of immunization program

Table 2.3 portrays the awareness of people in Dharmadam Grama Panchayath about the immunization program.

Table 2.3. Awareness of immunization program

Response	Awareness of immunization program	
	Number	Per cent
Aware	82	91
Not Aware	8	9
Total	9	100

It is found that 91 per cent of the population are aware of the immunization program and 9 per cent are not aware of the immunization program. Majority of the people are aware of the immunization program.

2.4. Awareness of personal and environmental hygiene

The awareness of people in Dharmadam Grama Panchayath about the personal and environmental hygiene is given in the table 2.4, below:

Table 2.4. Awareness of personal and environmental hygiene

Responses	Whether aware about personal and environmental hygeine?	
	Number	Per cent
Yes	85	94
No	5	6
Total	90	100

As per the table, it is found that 94 per cent of the populations are aware of the personal hygiene and 6 per cent are not aware of the personal and environmental hygiene. Majority of the people are aware of the personal and environmental hygiene.

2.5. Awareness of Pre-monsoon diseases

The responses of people in Dharmadam Grama Panchayath about the awareness of the pre-monsoon diseases are shown in Table 2.5 below:

Table 2.5. Awareness of Pre-monsoon diseases

Response	Whether aware about Pre-monsoon diseases?	
	Number	Per cent
Yes	70	78
No	20	22
Total	90	100

It is found that 78 per cent of the populations are aware of the Pre-monsoon diseases and 22 per cent are not aware of the pre-monsoon diseases. Majority of the people are aware of the pre-monsoon disease.

2.6. Awareness of life style diseases

The Table 2.6 shows the awareness of people in Dharmadam Grama Panchayath about the life style diseases.

Table 2.6. Awareness of life style diseases

Response	Whether aware about life style diseases?	
	Number	Per cent
Aware	80	89
Not Aware	10	11
Total	90	100

It is seen that 89 per cent of the population are aware of the life style diseases and 11 per cent are not aware of the life style diseases. Majority of the people are aware of the life style disease.

2.7. Sources of Health information

The investigator attempted to study the sources from where of people in Dharmadam Grama Panchayath are getting the health information. The role of health information in day to day life is gaining importance. The recent developments in the field of health sector, like new schemes, programmes etc., should reach the public to attain the desired result.

The data on Sources of Health information is presented in Table 2.7.

Table 2.7. Sources of Health information

Sources	Responses	
	Number	Per cent
Health institutions	30	33
Health workers	40	44
Newspapers	10	11
Panchayath	10	11
Total	90	100

As per the responses 33 per cent get health information from health institutions, 44 per cent from the health workers and 11 per cent each are getting information from newspapers and panchayath. Majority of people are getting information from health workers and some of the people getting source of information from health institution. Rest of the people are getting information from news papers and panchayath.

2.8. Sources of Information about immunization

One of the main functions of the health institutions in Dharmadom Grama Panchayath is conducting immunization programmes at regular intervals. Table 2.8 shows the sources through which the people are getting information.

Table 2.8. Sources of Information about immunization

Sources	Responses	
	Number	Per cent
Newspaper	20	22
Asha workers	50	56
Notices	15	17
Anganvadi	5	6
Total	90	100

It is seen that out of 90 people, 22 per cent are getting information from newspaper, 56 per cent people getting information from Asha worker, for 17 per cent of the people, the source of information is notices and for 6 per cent source of information is Aanganavadi. Majority of the respondents opined that their source of immunization about immunization is Aasha workers.

2.9. System of Medicine preferred by the people

Table 2.9 summarises the preferences of the in choosing the system of medicine for treatment.

Table 2.9. System of Medicine preferred by the people

Systems	Responses	
	Number	Per cent
Ayurveda	20	22
Allopathy	60	67
Homeopathy	10	11
Others	-	-
Total	90	100

It is found that 22 per cent of the respondents prefers Ayurveda system of treatment, 67 per cent of prefers Aallopathy and 11 per cent of the respondents prefers homeopathy. Majority of the people preferred Allopathy and a few people preferred ayurveda and homeopathy.

2.10. Satisfaction of the service and facilities of health institutions and health workers

The investigators attempted to study the satisfaction level of people in Dharmadam Grama Panchayath regarding the service and facility of health institutions and health workers. Table 2.10 shows the satisfaction level of the people in Dharmadam Grama Panchayath regarding the facilities provided in the health institutions in the panchayath.

Table 2.10. Satisfaction of the service and facilities of health institutions and health workers

Responses	Whether satisfied with the facilities provided in the health institutions?	
	Number	Per cent
Yes	68	76
No	22	24
Total	90	100

Is found that 76 per cent of the population are satisfied with health service facility and 22 per cent are not satisfied with health service facility. Majority of the people are satisfied with the health service facility.

2.11. Satisfaction of the services of health workers

The table 2.11 shows the satisfaction level of people in Dharmadam Grama Panchayath regarding the services of health workers

Table 2.11. Satisfaction of the services of health workers

Responses	Whether satisfied with the services of health workers?	
	Number	Per cent
Yes	70	78
No	20	22
Total	90	100

It is found that 78 per cent of the population are satisfied with health workers' service and 24 per cent are not satisfied with health workers' services. Most of the people are satisfied with health workers' service.

2.12. Satisfaction level in respect of Health information

The satisfaction level of people in Dharmadam Grama Panchayath in respect of health information is shown in Table 2.12, below

Table 2.12. Satisfaction level in respect of health information

Responses	Whether satisfied with the health information?	
	Number	Per cent
Yes	69	77
No	21	23
Total	90	100

On analyzing the above data it is found that 77 per

cent of the population are satisfied with health information and 24 per cent are not satisfied with health information provided by the health institutions of Dharmadom Grama Panchayath. Most of the people are satisfied with health information.

2.13. Barriers in communication of health information

Data collected on barriers in communication of health information is shown in Table 2.13

Table 2.13. Barriers in communication of health information

Barriers	Number	Per cent
Lack of health workers	35	39
Unawareness of people	25	28
Negligence from the part of health institutions	30	33
Total	90	100

From the table we can understand that, lack of health workers is the main barrier in getting health information. (39 per cent), 28 percent of people are unaware and 33 per cent negligence from the part of health institutions in getting the required health information. Analysis shows that majority of the people are having the barrier of lack of health workers. Negligence from the part of health institutions also makes them difficulty in getting health information. Few of them are having the problem of unawareness in getting health information.

3. FINDINGS AND SUGGESTIONS

- the analysis revealed that the health institution has a very important role in society as indicated by all respondents.
- Allopathy is the most preferred system of medicine by the respondents.

- Majority of the people are aware of the health information and services.
- Most of the people are getting information from health workers.
- Majority of the people are satisfied with facilities health institutions.
- Most of the people are satisfied with health workers services.
- Majority of the people are satisfied with health information.
- Lack of health workers is the major barrier for the communication of health information.

SUGGESTIONS

- The number of ASHA workers and health nurses has to be increased.
- Many of the services like immunization, pain and palliative care, family welfare etc should be improved.
- Immediate attention should be given to widen the physical facilities of the health institution.

4. CONCLUSION

The investigator has tried to study the information and services of health institution by the people of Dharmadam Panchayath with the overall services provided, health service facility, immunization, pain and palliative care, awareness of diseases etc. Here there are many faults regarding the running of health institution. For rectifying all those things suggestions from people and faculty members are to be considered. Thus the services can be improved.

REFERENCES

1. Ahuja, Ram(2001).Research Methods,Jaipur: Rawat Publications

2. Ansura Kazlauskiene and Ramute Gaueite (2011) Informing the society about pre-school and pre primary education: Education Policy Implementation in Lithuania; Social and Natural Science Journal: vol.4 28-32.pp.

3. Devarajan.G. and Kurien Pulikuthiel,Joseph (2011). Information Access, Tools, Services, and Systems. New Delhi: Ess Ess Publication

4. http://www.dharmadam .co.in

5. Nujoud Al-Muomen, Anne Morris, Sally Maynard, (2012) "Modelling information-seeking behaviour of graduate students at Kuwait University",Journal of Documentation, V. 68 No.4, pp.430 – 459

6. Oxford Advanced Learner's Dictionary of Current English (2005).New York: Oxford University Press,1557

7. Robert Fox, (2011) "Information fluid dynamics", OCLC Systems & Services, V. 27 No.2, pp.87 – 94

8. Webster's encyclopaedic unabridged dictionary of the English language (1996). New York: Gramercy Books, 1320

28

Web Based Information Sources in LIS

Sumana K. P.
Muhammed Najeeb V.

ABSTRACT

Web has a great role in providing access to diversified information sources in varied disciplines. Library and information professionals have active role to customize and optimize access to these resources. This include Web sites, E-mail based information services, Online indexes and abstracts, Full text documents, Usenet news, Online Directories, Online chatting, Virtual/ online conferencing, E-Journals and E-books, List serve, Online-learning and online-courses, Subject Gateways and Portals, FAQs, Virtual Help Desks, Mailing Lists ,Online-Book shops and many more. This paper introduces such web resources in Library and Information Science domain.

Keywords: Web resources, online resources, Information sources in Library and Information Science

1. INTRODUCTION

In this newer scenario, the library professionals are left with very little choice except to reignite themselves with newer skills and leading edge knowledge to confront the changing technologies and users. They are required to make themselves highly competent and well equipped to face new the new challenges in the emerging information world to survive and thrive in the digital ecosystem. Web has a great role in providing access to diversified information sources in varied disciplines. Library and information professionals have active role to customize and optimize access to these resources.

2. WEB2.0 AND LIBRARY 2.0

Web 2.0 mainly emphasizes in user generated content, data and content sharing and collaborative effort, together with use of various kinds of social software, new ways of interacting with Web-based applications, and use of the Web as a platform for generating, re-purposing and consuming content. E.g. wikis, Blogs, Mash-ups, Peer-to-peer networking, Podcast, RSS Web services. Library 2.0 is borrowed from Web 2.0 and Business 2.0 in Libraries will result in a meaningful and substantive change in libraries, its collection, services and methods of delivery of services.

3. WEB BASED INFORMATION SOURCES

With the advancement of technology the libraries are moving towards digital resources, which are found to be less expensive and more helpful for easy access. These are helpful especially to distant learners who have limited time to access the libraries from outside. Valuable collection of texts, images and sounds from many scholarly communications now exists only in electronic form and may be accessible from the Internet. The internet resources are also called as web resources.

4. VARIOUS TYPES OF WEB BASED INFORMATION SOURCES

This include Web sites, E-mail based information services, Online indexes and abstracts, Full text documents, Usenet news, Online Directories, Online chatting, Virtual/ online conferencing, E-Journals and

E-books, List serve, Online-learning and online-courses, Subject Gateways and Portals, FAQs, Virtual Help Desks, Mailing Lists ,Online-Book shops and many more.

5. LIBRARY AND INFORMATION SCIENCE WEB RESOURCES

Library and Information Science is an interdisciplinary field that applies the practices, perspectives, and tools of management, information technology, education, and other areas to libraries; the collection, organization, preservation, and dissemination of information resources; and the political economy of information.

6. OBJECTIVES OF THE STUDY

The main objectives of the study are:

1. To compile a list of World Wide Web resources in Library and Information science.
2. To identify the kind of web resources which contain/ publish information in LIS field.
3. To determine whether LIS related information is available on all the different kinds of web resources.
4. To enhance the awareness of LIS students regarding the web resources in LIS.

7. SIGNIFICANCE OF THE STUDY

The ever-increasing number of people using web resources coupled with recent explosion of information communication technology may have considerable implications for their teaching, learning and research. The present study is an attempt to find out the web-based information resources in library and Information science as a tool for information gathering by people who were interested in Library and Information science field. Investigator think that the list of World Wide Web sites may be found useful by practicing Library and Information professionals around the world.

8. SCOPE AND LIMITATIONS OF THE STUDY

The study is concentrated only the web-based information sources in LIS field. Although Library websites and weblogs contain information regarding LIS, they are not considering for the study. The present study enlists the types of web resources include websites, mailing lists and listservs, open directories, databases, gateways and portals in LIS field.

Since there are infinite relevant web resources of all kinds, the paper included only the most significant to the purpose of the study. Since the author was working under time constraints, including all links is not practical or possible. So the listing given is not comprehensive.

9. DATA COLLECTION PROCEDURE

Investigator gathered information on the relevant World Wide Web resources by making use of Internet search engines (Google, AltaVista, and Yahoo). Author used as key words "web-based resources in LIS", "web resources in LIS" and "Internet sources in LIS". Investigator also performed searches of the database include Libdex, dmoz, DOAJ, Open J-gate, OJASE Contents, and the World Wide Web for information on additional relevant sources by using the following key words: Websites in LIS, E-resources in LIS, Indexes and Abstracts in LIS, Databases in LIS and Directories in LIS. In addition, author reviewed the information provided in the initially identified sources to find additional World Wide Web links that contained data relevant to LIS.

10.1 Websites

In this era of global village, there is a need for the Library and other Information Centers to go towards the people instead of waiting for them. Now Libraries and Information Centers are being transferred to the internet for fast access and retrieval of information. Websites can act as a media of publicizing the new trends and issues in LIS field. Following are the websites which contain information related in LIS. LIS useful links are listed as below. Library websites were not listed in the table.

Table 1. List of Websites in LIS

Sl No.	Websites	URL
1.	ALA	http://www.ala.org/
2.	Digital Librarian	*http://www.digital-librarian.com/librariana.html*
3.	ExLibris	http://www.exlibris.co.il/
4.	Internet Library for Librarians	*http://www.itcompany.com/inforetriever/*
5.	Internet Public Library	*http://www.ipl.org/div/subject/browse/ref00.00.00*
6.	LC web guides	*http://www.loc.gov/rr/program/bib/libsci/guides.html*
7.	Libdex	http://www.libdex.com/
8.	Librarian's Yellow Pages	http://www.librariansyellowpages.com/
9.	Library and Information Science Virtual Library	http://www.library.illinois.edu/lis/
10.	Library Science reference sources	*http://www.lib.usf.edu/ref/bibs/libscience.html*
11.	Library spot	http://www.libraryspot.com/
12.	LibraryLaw.com	http://www.librarylaw.com/
13.	ODLIS	*http://www.abc-clio.com/ODLIS/odlis_A.aspx*
14.	Planning and building libraries	http://www.slais.ubc.ca/resources/architecture/index.htm
15.	Reference links	*http://www.libraryspot.com*
16.	School of Library and Information Science home	*http://www.uky.edu/CommInfoStudies/SLIS/*
17.	The British Columbia Digital Library	http://www.bcdlib.tc.ca/tools-manuals.html
18.	The Researching Librarian	http://www.researchinglibrarian.com/
19.	The Web of Science for access to ISI citation databases	http://www.burioni.it/news/novita/isi.htm

20. Today's Librarian .com	*http://www.todayslibrarian.com/*
21. Your Library is Dying	*http://www.splicetoday.com/digital/your-library-is-dying*

Investigator visited the above listed websites and it was found that those websites will help the LIS people to bring progresses in their career and general knowledge. These websites contain information regarding current trends, opportunities, issues, happenings etc.

10.2. Mailing list and Listservs

A program that allows people to send email to one address, which resends that message to all of the other subscribers to the list. A list server (mailing list server) is a program that handles subscription requests for a mailing list and distributes new messages, newsletters, or other postings from the list's members to the entire list of subscribers as they occur or are scheduled. (A list server should not be confused with a mail server, which handles incoming and outgoing e-mail for Internet users.) Mailing list is list of e-mail addresses identified by a single name, such as mail-list@sandybay.com . When an e-mail message is sent to the mailing list name, it is automatically forwarded to all the addresses in the list.

A mailing list is a collection of names and addresses used by an individual or an organization to send material to multiple recipients. The term is often extended to include the people subscribed to such a list, so the group of subscribers is referred to as "the mailing list", or simply "the list". Discussion facilities provided by the Internet attract a lot of people to the net. Listservs and mailing lists are the popular terms and both mean the same. We can use both for discussion. It can also be used as a resource for getting answers to our questions. Some of the relevant Mailing list and Listservs are listed as below:

Table 2: List of Mailing list and Listservs in LIS

S N	International Librarianship Discussion Groups/Listservs	URL
1.	ACQNET (acquisitions)	*http://www.acqweb.org/acqnet.html*
2.	AUTOCAT (cataloging)	*https://listserv.syr.edu/scripts/wa.exe?A0=AUTOCAT*
3.	CoOL- Conservation Online	http://cool.conservation-us.org/
4.	DIGLIB (for librarians, information scientists, and other information professionals to share information about the many issues and technologies pertaining to the creation of "digital libraries.")	*http://www.ifla.org/II/lists/diglib.htm*
5.	IASL-LINK (International Association of School Librarianship; for members only)	*http://www.iasl-online.org/about/handbook/iasl-link.html*
6.	LIBLICENSE-L (licensing digital information)	*http://www.library.yale.edu/~llicense/mailing-list.shtml*
7.	LIBREF-L (general library reference)	*http://listserv.kent.edu/archives/libref-l.html*
8.	MEDLIB-L (for medical librarians)	*http://www.mlanet.org/discussion/medlibl.html*
9.	NGC4Lib (Next Generation Catalogs For Libraries)	*http://dewey.library.nd.edu/mailing-lists/ngc4lib/*
10.	SERIALST (serials processing)	*http://www.uvm.edu/~bmaclenn/serialst.html*
11.	Web4Lib (issues relating to the creation, management, and support of library-based World-Wide Web servers, services, and applications)	*http://lists.webjunction.org/web4lib/*
12.	LIS-Forum (an e-mail based discussion forum for Library and Information professionals in India)	*http://ncsi.iisc.ernet.in/mailman/listinfo/lis-forum*

10.3. Open Directories

It is constructed and maintained by a vast, global community of volunteer editors. As the Internet grows, so do the number of net-citizens. These citizens can each organize a small portion of the web and present it back to the rest of the population, culling out the bad and useless and keeping only the best content.

Its editorial standards body of net-citizens provide the collective brain behind resource discovery on the Web. The Open Directory powers the core directory services for the Web's largest and most popular search engines and portals, including Netscape Search, AOL Search, Google, Lycos, HotBot, DirectHit, and hundreds of others. The Open Directory Project is the largest, most comprehensive human-edited directory of the Web. It is constructed and maintained by a vast, global community of volunteer editors.

Table 3: List of Open directory websites containing LIS resources

Sl no.	Directories	URL
1	Digital Imaging and Media Technology Initiative Linklist	http://images.library.uiuc.edu/resources/links.htm
2	Directory of European libraries	*http://www.theeuropeanlibrary.org/tel4/discover/contributors*
3	Directory of online libraries	*http://www.lib-web.org/*
4	DOAJ	*http://www.doaj.org/*
5	*Floyd Ingram's Den - Library Resources*	*http://www.coatopa.com/fi-lib.html*
6	Internet Public Library	*http://www.ipl.org/div/subject/browse/ref00.00.00*
7	Libdex	*http://www.libdex.com*
8	LIS in yahoo directory	*http://dir.yahoo.com/Reference/Libraries/Library_and_Information_Science/?skw=Yahoo+directory+of+%2 2Library+and+Information+science%22*
9	OCLC world cat registry	*http://worldcat.org/registry/Institutions*
10	*School Libraries*: A directory of websites created by school	*http://schoollibrarywebsites.wikispaces.com/*

	librarians around the world.	
11	*Search for Public Libraries* in US	*http://nces.ed.gov/surveys/libraries/librarysearch/*
12	*The National Libraries of Europe*	*http://www.theeuropeanlibrary.org/portal/libraries/map_en.html*
13	*Weblogs*: Exhaustive list of blogs for librarians by librarians.	*http://www.libdex.com/weblogs.html*
14	OCLC *WorldCat Registry*	*http://worldcat.org/registry/institutions*

10.4. Subject Gateways and Portals

Subject gateways or portals are similar to subject directories but each one is subject-specific rather than offering a range of topics. Resources included in gateways cover a wide spectrum, from electronic journals and books to academic and government reports, as well as referring users to relevant web sites. Gateways are collections of databases and informational sites, arranged by subject. They are assembled, reviewed and recommended by specialists, usually, librarians/information specialists. These gateway collections support research and reference needs by identifying and pointing to recommended, academically oriented pages on the web. A list of subject gateways and portals in the area of library and information studies are as follows:

Table 4. List of Gateways and Portals containing LIS

Sl no.	Gateways and Portals	URL
1	Érudit	http://www.erudit.org/these/
2	*Internet Library For Librarians*	*http://www.itcompany.com/inforetriever/*
3	*Library iPortal*: A portal for librarians by the Lahore University of Management Sciences.	*http://libraryportal.lums.edu.pk/*
4	*LISGateway.com*	*http://www.lisgateway.com/*
5	Proquest digital dissertations	*http://http://www.lib.umi.com/disertations/intrial/gateway*

6	Theses Canada Portal	*http://www.collectionscanada.gc.ca/thesescanada/*
7	UNESCO Libraries Portal	*http://www.unesco-ci.org/cgi-bin/portals/libraries/page.cgi?d=1*
8	Library of Congress WWW/ Z39.50 Gateway	http://www.loc.gov/z3950/

10.5. Online Databases

Database is an organized collection of information, of a particular subject or multi-disciplinary subject areas. The information of an e-database can be searched and retrieved electronically. It usually updated on a daily, weekly, monthly or quarterly basis. Full-text databases contain the whole content of an article such as citation information, text, illustrations, diagrams and tables. Bibliographic databases only contain citation information of an article, such as author name, journal title, publication date and page numbers. A list of databases in the area of Library and Information Science is given in Table 5.

Table 5 : List of Databases in LIS

Sl no.	Database	URL
1.	Book Review Digest Plus	http://ebscohost.com/
2.	*Books in Print (Global)*	*http://www.booksinprint.com*
3.	Digital library resources and projects	http://www.infolibrarian.com/dlib.htm
4.	EBSCO	*http://ebscohost.com/*
5.	Elsevier Social Sciences - Library and Information Sciences	http://www.elseviersocialsciences.com/libraryscience
6.	Emerald Insight	*http://www.emeraldinsight.com/browse.htm?content=journals_books&by=subject&subject=83*
7.	ERIC	*http://www.eric.ed.gov/*
8.	Information Science & Technology Abstracts	*http://www.ebscohost.com/corporate-research/information-science-technology-abstracts*
9.	International Library and Information journals and	*http://www.britishcouncil.org/info@uk/links5.htm*

	websites	
10.	JSTOR	http://www.jstor.org/
11.	Library and Information Science Abstracts (LISA)	*http://www.csa.com/factsheets/lisa-set-c.php*
12.	Libdex	http://www.libdex.com/journals.html
13.	Library Market Place	*http://www.literarymarketplace.com/lmp/us/index_us.asp*
14.	Library, Information Science & Technology Abstracts (LISTA)	*http://www.ebscohost.com*
15.	Open J Gate	*http://openj-gate.org/*
16.	*Project Muse*	*http://muse.jhu.edu/browse/library_science_and_publishing*
17.	*Proquest Library* Science	*http://www.proquest.com/en-US/catalogs/databases/detail/libraryscience.shtml*
18.	RLUK (Research Libraries UK)	http://www.rluk.ac.uk/database
19.	Taylor and Francis	*http://www.tandfonline.com/action/showPublications? display=byAlphabet*

10.6. E-journals

Electronic publishing is getting a tremendous impetus from the publishing industries as well as Library and Information centres. (LIS's). Electronic journal may be defined broadly as any journal, magazine, e-zine, webzine, newsletter or type of electronic serial publication which is available over the internet and can be accessed using different technologies such as World Wide Web, Gopher, ftp, e-mail or list serve. In some cases, print equivalents exist; other has charging mechanisms of different types. Hundreds of electronic journals are available in the different fields of study on the internet for the benefit of information users. Electronic journal is nothing but a journal available in electronic format using internet technology. Though it has the same charactaristics as the printed journals, but the difference is that, the electronic journal is available electronically.

227 e-journals have been listed from databases including DOAJ, Open J-gate, OJASE and SCImago

Journal and Country Rank. These journals include peer reviewed, full text articles and abstracts. From the analysis it is found that the e-journals listed are being published from more than 35 countries in various languages like Arabic, Bulgarian, Chinese, Danish, French, English etc. E-journals include various subject headings like librarianship, digital library, documentation, information literacy etc. Archives are found in majority of e-journals, some starting from publishing year and some are started from recent years.

11. CONCLUSION

Recent developments in information format and retrieval have had a define impact on the LIS community, who have been required to change their methodology in accessing information. Web-based information resources have rapidly established themselves as a viable media in all fields. Because of their rapid publication capabilities they are often the best source of information on current research and developments in all fields. There is a great future for web resources among LIS community.

REFERENCES

1. Jetty, Sreedevi, et al. (2010). Web-based information sources with references to Forensic science. IN: Emerging Technologies and Changing Dimensions of Libraries and Information Services. Ed. Sanjay Katariya and et al. New Delhi, KBD publications, 715-718.
2. Mahajan, Preeti and Chakravarthy, Rupak (2009). Open access information products for LIS researchers. IN: Library and Information Science in Digital Age. Ed. Singh, Jagatar et al. Ess Ess publications, New Delhi, 372 – 381.
3. *http://www.doaj.org/* (Accessed on 02/8/2013)
4. *http://oajse.com/subjects/library_and_information_science.html*(Accessed on 08/08/2013)
5. http://openj-gate.org/ (Accessed on 12/08/2013)
6. *http://en.wikipedia.org/wiki/Mailing_lists* (Accessed on 28/2/2011)

7. Sujatha, H.R. and Mahesh, Mudhol (2006). Electronic information resources on fisheries: a study. *Annals of Library and Information Studies.* 53(6), 96-102.

8. Vishala, B.K. and Bhandi, M.K. (2006). Availability of library and information science electronic journals through UGC-INFONET project. *Annals of Library and Information Science.* 53(6), 65-69.